Indictments from the Convicted

Rants, Articles, Interviews and Essays

K. M. Patten

Indictments from the Convicted: Rants, Articles, Interviews and Essays

STAIRWAY PRESS—APACHE JUNCTION

Cover Design by Guy D. Corp, www.GrafixCorp.com

STAIRWAY⹀PRESS

www.StairwayPress.com
1000 West Apache Trail—Suite 126
Apache Junction, AZ 85120 USA

INTRODUCTION

AS A TOTALITY, the pieces that follow represent not one thing, but several. First, they are a promise to myself and to my family. Halfway through my prison stint I finally realized what I wanted to be in life, and promptly stated in one of my many letters home: a journalist; specifically, with a polemical prospective. I realized there were only two ways to invoke real, everlasting change: strong arguments, coupled with practical secession. Buildings come and go, but as Christ said, they matter little compared to what they represent. As long as the mindset that erected those structures still exists, so shall they be rebuilt.

Congruously, everyone born into this world should have the natural right to distance themselves from whatever institution their compass points away from. Therefore, this book is a guarantee that I'll never again commit such a stupid crime, and to continue—to the best of the ability—what I set out to do nearly a decade ago.

Secondly, this is a mendicant's resume. Obviously, if a writer does it for activism, he needs an outlet. (If for therapy, standing on any old crate in a closet will do.) A beggar requires a benefactor. Since I'm dedicated to the former (and have only occasionally been the latter), this book is also a plea to the marketplace of ideas. A sort of, *Will you consider publishing me? Question.* Sometimes you can't *beg* publishers to tell you to fuck off.

That immediately takes me to the third purpose of this work: a demonstration of the development of my writing. I've come to discover, while obsessive "thinking" might be an innate proclivity, an annoying habit hard to be rid of, the act of grammatical composition is a skill that should—in theory—see some sort of plateau. It isn't the hardest part, I mean to say. *Research*: this is the truly strenuous component. Reading requires funds and demands concentration. Putting together inquiry, research, and analysis, and composing a coherent paragraph, is what I believe constitutes writing as an "art form." As scattered as these pieces are, I hope a bit of art is seen in the pages. Nevertheless, like many writers, I look back at some of these past pieces and cringe at their syntax—the run-on sentences, the repetition of words, the terribly-placed commas. Therefore, I edited these pieces. Most are not as they were originally composed. Even then, if some of them appear like amateurish ranting—that's because they are. Please forgive.

Projects. Desired reportage. Fanciful philosophizing. With these, many ideas come to mind. Prevention? Aside from the difficulty in finding publishers who are willing to give me the time of day, it seems I'm trapped within a new set of bars. For the last two years, the Golden State's child protection "services" have deemed me as "unfit" for parentage, and I must prove myself to the State ever since. It's a gauntlet that's been slow and boring and emotionally trying. *I'm drained.* Now, destinations practically call out to me from the maps that hang on the walls. It's a feeling reminiscent of all that time ago; one that is hauntingly liberating.

I long to secede from this abominable Los Angeles Valley.

But a nagging conscience forbids abandoning my one and only son. So I stay. And I continue to jump through flaming hoops and maintain my balance across barbed tightropes, waiting for the day that I am untethered with a hopeful attainment of full custody. Providing that day comes, and soon, I offer this, the indictments from a convicted man. Convicted not only in the eyes of the State, but also convicted in some very serious moral concerns.

Lastly, this book is a manifesto. Every theoretician, martyr, and quack should have a set of ramblings that announce a consistent ideal. Complexity often disallows one concrete principle, leaving a junky relativism that prescribes or proscribes as consequences shift.

But, there is at least one more principle in my mind. On the horizon, I see no answer to human liberation. I am not a purveyor of optimism. To answer Disraeli's question about whether we descend from of angels or apes, I recognize the obviousness of our ancestry. In a way, setting the bar low gives me hope. If we were of angels, we would have little improvement to strive for, and would loiter through our lives wondering why God had forgotten us. Instead, I take a Nietzschen or Godwinian approach to the matter, and believe that it is the responsibility of every thinking person to push evolution along. If this is done through theorizing or criticizing or even condemning—so be it.

After all, as an anarchist, it is a requirement to expose the operations of every institution with power—whether statist, corporatist, religious, or familial. Because, as importantly, I think, *I must hold*, that our species' liberation sees it's attainability by treating our offspring like the human beings they are, and not like the balls of clay mandated by ancient edicts.

With these convictions stated, let me grab my pen, and offer up a few of my indictments....

—K. M. Patten

Contents

Indictments from the Convicted

A Brief Study of Freedom in an Unchanging Day

BEFORE WE ARE even conceived there are forces dictating the energy of our soul without our control, putting a handicap on the weight of our Freedom. Nobody had a choice about whether they actually wanted to exist in this world. No one had a selection of physical, mental, and emotionally characteristics. Race, sex, family, religious heritage—each have a substantial effect on the individual.

For example, if you are a female, then statistically you are a better target for rapists. If your family is of Islamic beliefs, you are obligated to be a Muslim for life, and punished in certain nations by being put to death for any attempt at conversion. Anyone living today could just as easily been born into Hitler's Germany or Stalin's Russia, with absolutely no choice.

At this point it must be acknowledged that the "individual" cannot really be considered an individual. In actuality, we're just organisms. It is the uncontrollable choices of Life (in its most broad definition) that makes up our person. A much better term to describe this organism is "slave." The reason for this is because we are merely property to another organism, or at the very least the prisoner of someone else. More often than not, we are the legal merchandise of another, usually with debts owed to our parents, country, or corporations.

Once that has been established, we are pushed into a position to meet and accept a given society's expectations, while also controlled by that land's ruling government.

For example, it is not natural for children to be forced into a chair and spend their time reading and learning about subjects they have no interest in. If there was ever a shred of distinctive personality within that organism, the powers-that-be would make it their duty to expunge it from their consciousness. With nobody to build their roads or police the masses or fight their wars or pay their taxes, the System would collapse. So they set up an order of rules and restrictions that ensure that the slaves are in almost complete obedience—all the while making rules look and feel righteous. Given a little comfort and security and the majority will give their lives to their master.

It is my opinion this is because the human Mind craves someone to make decisions for them. It is easier to have somebody else make a resolution for them instead of having to go to war with themselves and come up with their own reasonable and objective opinion. Most are trained from birth to follow "the standard." Eventually it becomes too much of a burden to think for themselves. They believe that they will become outcasts and discriminated against for thinking for themselves...they live in a mental and emotional prison. To fill the empty hole in their Mind, they make a valiant effort to identify with a seemingly valid supremacy. Country, religion, cults, gangs, marriage: all have their place in the lonely human psyche. Most of which are blatantly fictitious.

Last, but most certainly not least, is the fact that creatures in this world are in constant competition with other creatures. It happens every second of every day of every year and in every era of our world. We feel the irresistible urge to show that we are in control. We must exhibit superiority in every way possible. We actually get satisfaction in the anguish we cause to another, with rarely a reasonable justification. This is no doubt caused by an inferiority complex. It is like a cancer, constantly fed by control and obedience. It is eternal. Control and suffering will go on forever. It will never end. "Freedom," thus, does not exist.

The only sensible way to escape servitude is to cut off as many ties to your ruling existence as possible, perhaps with the exception of family: as I brought life into this world, I must be held responsible for it.

For thousands of years people, lived in harmony with a basic natural order. Mother Earth and small tribes relied on each other. In the 21st Century people, accept the ignorance holding them in confinement.

There is one certain way to end this horrible life. One day, billions of years from now, the Universe might collapse on itself.

And with that, suffering and control might finally be finished.

The God Deception

ASK YOURSELF A question: if you were born in a different part of the world, with different surroundings, mightn't you have a different religious belief?

Would it be wrong to have that belief?

"God." A three-letter, one-syllable word that mankind has used for thousands of years to describe the highest, most powerful entity in or outside of our universe. When we look into a telescope or witness the miracle of birth, can we possibly sum up these wonders with a single word?

Thus, can we possibly know the entire secrets of the universe in one book? Religion therefore becomes a mere symbolic interpretation for the Unknown. It consists of metaphors, cultural history, and a lot of mythology.

Immediately we give the Creator a sexual preference. By using "he" we indicate that "God" has a penis. The paradox of this assessment is that Yahweh commanded the Jews to cut off the foreskin of their children. Does this mean that "God" was circumcised? Was the Creator, in fact, mutilated?

Next, "God" is shown leisurely walking through the Garden of Eden with his first creation, Adam. If we study this myth, we find that "Adam" is an anagram meaning "many." If we are to believe that "God" was just casually walking through a garden, then it would be equally possible for Zeus to have been throwing lightning bolts off of Mouth Olympus.

Further, are we supposed to believe that the kind, loving Creator—taught about in our churches—is the same Being depicted in the Old Testament as a bloodthirsty monster, who, out of all the inhabitants of earth, chose the Jewish tribe as His vessel, and, in turn, ordered the death of hundreds of thousands? The one who ordered Moses to conquer and take sex slaves right after the Ten Commandment were given to them!

What about all the other hundreds of legends about a catastrophic flood found in every corner of the earth? Is it impossible to believe other populations had the idea and ability to build a boat? And, if Noah and his family were the only humans who survived, how is it that they evolved into different races of man within a relatively short period of 6-8 thousand years?

And yet, time after time, religious zealots constantly try their hardest to defend these blatant inconsistencies. Due to a herd-like mentality or complete close-mindedness, rarely do they entertain the validity of an alternate philosophy. This writer truly believes that the reason for this stubbornness is because the average person is scared. They demand something to look forward to after death. In doing so they convince themselves that *this book* has all the answers, and that it's in Black & White—Right & Wrong; knowing in the back of their mind that the Bible and other religious beliefs have failed to answer any hard questions.

Information about dinosaurs and extraterrestrials and past civilizations and even the cure for cancer are not to be found anywhere in the "perfect" book. Constantly I hear, "But it doesn't say it does," or, "It doesn't say it doesn't." All I can say to that is: omission is the worst form of mistruth, as Orwell observed, and the book leaves a lot of important questions unanswered.

On top of all this, these same people are deliberate hypocrites. They must have their beliefs to flaunt a moral superiority. How many times does someone preach about Jesus Christ's love and then turn around and perform the most wicked of crimes, completely disregarding the Golden Rule? "Forgive me for my sins" becomes an oft-repeated phrase but has absolutely no validity. The mentality is: "I can do anything I want as long as Jesus is there"—without ever truly trying to better themselves.

The ignorant masses do not even realize that the "Savior" myth has been used many times before Jesus, as in the personas of Horus and Krishna. So, why is it hard to believe that certain governmental powers orchestrated the creation of the whole Jesus legend by combining Judaic belief with Pagan belief, ala the Sabbath becoming a Sunday and the traditional holidays of Christmas and Easter, then adding Christ's influential attributes to fabricate the most ingenious form of political and profitable organizing in the history of mankind? Why is it that Christ couldn't have healed the sick and taught wonderful things while still having erections and begging for bread? If the Lord was supposed to have experienced everything that man had, how is it possible without an antagonizing wife and children to feed?

Is it not remotely feasible that within two thousand years the Gospels were rewritten and retranslated so many times that today they are no longer the original text? In reality, I could take this very rant, go out to the desert, dig a big hole, and, 1,000 years from now, the discoverers of this work would claim it as absolute truth. Furthermore, they might add or take away from it as they please.

Now, I admit—we don't even have the slightest idea of God. But I've often heard a quote from one time or another.

> *We are, in truth, all that existed, and ever will exist, I am you, you are me, I am everything, and everything is me. We are not only part of that infinite energy, we are that energy.*

Even our thoughts and our emotions could be considered as such. The existence of all this energy and matter certainly gives the impression of a Creator—the Watchmaker if you will. But this

Creator could not possibly be secular—it is impossible to say God can only be found in *this* religion or *that* culture or *this* kind of prayer, while everything else is condemned to damnation for all eternity. It makes no sense that the god of the Abrahamic religions spoke only to half-stupefied peasants in the desolate Middle East.

Would the Creator who gave me free will damn me for using it when questioning that which makes no sense? Especially when trying to understand the corruption of man, or the fate of our souls (or "energy" inside of us)? If my conclusion is different, will I suffer forever in a fiery realm even if I was a good-natured, loving, giving person who was only raised with a different set of beliefs?

The "freewill" gifted to us is limited. As humans we use much less than one percent of our functioning brains. If we could use more freewill, might we have a more complete understanding—which, by Hebrew definition, is the true meaning of "faith?" This is of course impossible with our limited knowledge—which was "blessed" upon us by our all-powerful Creator.

I am not suggesting the Torah and the prophesies in it—or a man named Jesus—are illegitimate. But the fact that anything is possible in this Universe, along with the truths about our subjects at hand, leads me to doubt and to strive for a more accurate account. Because, for me, it is intellectually dishonest to say I'm sure of all the teachings found in our major religions.

In this modern day, technology has the capability to determine the age of certain texts and writings through chemical analysis and carbon dating. With this, we can at least come close to defining the age and source location of a given artifact. But there is no test we can use to prove that it was written by "God."

Again, we come back to faith, but using the same logic: how can one so full of doubt have complete understanding? Can we not say that this is God's Will? Perhaps the Creator wanted those to doubt as to show alternatives to the conventional belief system.

We can use this same logic to a more extreme degree. If one were to feel compelled to commit an act—violent or peaceful—

and had felt so strongly about their own justification for this undertaking that they were convicted to perform it, can we not also say that that is God's Will?

Is this the same as when the Israelites were told to slaughter all those tribes?

There is no argument in the simplistic answer of "no—that is not God's will." Anyway, the Biblical God had dealings with Satan. Book of Job anyone? Also, as the Zealots proclaim, God knows everything. Well then, monsters like Hitler and Stalin were not only created by God, but were also allowed to commit their evil crimes. It's the same as letting your dog play in a park full of little kids—knowing it's a vicious animal with rabies who likes to attack children. You have all the power to stop the beast, and you know that the dog can't tell the difference between kibbles and kids; so you have to ask yourself: what is the right, moral thing to do?

One more particular concern in regard to religion and the belief in God is that it promotes a certain distain for everyone who does not share in it. Extreme examples of this come from personalities like Patterson and Falwell and the Islamic martyrs of September 11th, people who themselves denounce the so-called evils of freewill and demand radical changes in our society and our right to individual freedom. They would happily implement curfews, censorship and mandatory prayers into the schools, or suppress the study of evolution and the cosmos because it doesn't fit their values. Or even worse—cowardly blow up innocent families for the expansion of totalitarian religious regimes.

Few can be said to be devout followers of the Bible, which says both "eye for an eye" and "turn thy cheek." And it has all sorts of passages about killing your own children and selling your daughter into slavery. Who then can follow such absurd laws? And if we don't follow them, can we be deemed a true believer? Would the pastors who preach Christ sell their Mercedes and help the poor? Very doubtful, indeed. So who then is a real believer?

The closest could probably be credited with the Islamic Nations—and I personally don't want that sort of government anywhere near the Western hemisphere. There's no need to drive down the street and see a woman beheaded because she forgot to cover her face; or homosexuals stoned to death because of the way they were born. The list of deplorable atrocities is endless. But the good part is that over here we have a separation of Church and State, and thus won't have any sick shit like that anytime soon. Hopefully.

Religion can be said to produce more wars, more false hopes, and more hypocrites than any other force on earth. There is nothing wrong with individual convictions, but conditioning and forcing of another without proper investigation—both into the religion itself and the consequence of the one succumbing to it— is extremely harmful. If for nothing else, for restricting critical thinking.

Everyday a new child is subjected to the religious mutilation of circumcision. Just mentioned are the barbaric practices in the Middle East. Are these evil methods part of "God's plan?" If so, then that is not my God, and not my Creator.

Who could ever possibly determine who is right and what is wrong? Perhaps it would be better to let the next child find their own way—guided by their own conscience before merciless force against one's will becomes the end of us all.

Generation of Change: My Election Day 2008 Experience

FOR ME, IT could have been Groundhog Day. In prison, it all seems like the same old shit: feet hitting the floor in the morning, eating, reading, walking, and then working-out—with too many endless sighs in between, the tired kind that exaggerate your frustration.

However, I know in the back of my head, beyond the frustration and the apathy, that it is an important time in the world. As irritating as this place is, it's given me an opportunity to reflect upon Life and all its Positives and Negatives, which, as we've come to accept, are merely random occurrences.

I sit in here, and by the simple task of reading the newspaper and catching bits of CNN, I watch society attempt to overcome the hardships—sort of the way a kid rides in the backseat of a car and sees the everyday public go about their business, knowing that one day they'll be out there too, navigating the hurdles.

But for right now I'm sitting in here, longing to participate in America's current happening: which is Election 2008.

The Grand Arena of Politics gives me a new sense of reality. One so important, yet so goddamn technical at times. As handicapped as I am in here without the Internet or magazine subscriptions, I find a way to learn, and always feel triumphant when I have the advantage in a heavy conversation.

But my pride shouldn't run so deep. My developing mastery of political issues is irrelevant to most people in the facility. While I delve into the so-called "conspiracy theories," these guys are content discussing prison life, which, obviously, encompasses the entire criminal culture; drugs, gangs, prison war stories—all those activities that give them a reason to come back.

Yes, Mr. Gangster Tough Guy—the California Department of Corrections is happy doing business with you. Continue lying to yourself as you grow old and your family slowly forgets about you...I'm sure your kids will have a lot of fun with your wife's Sancho.

That was off subject, and I couldn't resist, but now it's time to return to what is important...current events. As Joseph Campbell observed, solitary thought combined with deep reflection make a person arrive at great revelations. I'm having deep thoughts about all those "random occurrences," defined more specifically here as History, which every so often gives us an event so monumental, so massive in what it is, that they are not soon to reach oblivion.

The morning of September 11th, 2001 is one this generation will certainly never forget—something that will go down in records, books, and archives.

Forever.

That word is a rarity in my vocabulary, as I realize everything ends *eventually.* But practically, in humanistic terms, those two planes flying into the World Trade Center is something that even thousands of years from now, as the Age of Capricorn reaches the cosmos, when these years become mere numbers to be mentioned in a time long forgotten, our future generations will still speak of Nine-One-One as a day of infamy.

Some will note the heroism; others, more cynical—or maybe even more realistic—will examine all the consequences of that day and wonder if mankind had regressed back to its primal, savage nature. After all, the most powerful nation in the world was supposed to be dedicated to justice, not vengeance.

Seven years later, as "culprits" remain uncaught, and the people see an endless war, a collapsing economy, and a slavery to foreign fuel—all those detrimental factors indicating a civilization on the brink of destruction—they see the face of one man: Mr. George Herbert Walker Bush.

It's important to note that Bush will probably, from now on, be mentioned in the same breath as such monsters as Hitler and Stalin. These pretenses are what led to Barack Obama's landslide victory. The people reflected upon all these things, and immediately correlated a political party to a failed policy. Obama couldn't lose, because to the people—that unruly mob—he embodied something *different*.

How does a no-name forty-seven-year-old Senator from Illinois, handicapped by the color of his skin in a country only accustomed to Anglo-Saxon presidents, manage to raise more money in a campaign than any other presidential candidate in history and go on to become elected into the highest office? Necessary questions, but I think I know why.

First, that's small talk. Those are trivial facts you hear about all over the place. However, the facts only mentioned in the media outlets—but held strongly in the average public conversation (and conservative talk radio)—is that of Mr. Obama's "radical associations."

For starters, he attended a church whose pastor shouted anti-American statements. "U.S. of KKKA." "The chickens have come home to roost," meaning that the nations victimized by the U.S. have come to pay back their oppressor. These hate-filled sentiments are confirmed by Wright himself. When interviewed, he justified them:

> You can't commit terrorism on others and not expect it to
> happen to you.

It was even rumored that Wright's church offered publications made by Hamas, the terrorist organization currently embattled against Israel.

Obama's other "radical association" is one Mr. William Ayers—the unrepentant domestic terrorist from the 60s' and a former member of a communist group that bombed the Pentagon, among other national buildings.

For years, Barack Obama enjoyed close relationships with these gentlemen. One could imagine the conversations amongst them. Sitting around long after the church congregation has gone, wistfully talking about how the rich should be taxed and the wealth divided among the poor.

These things are known. Someone with a reflective mind could get an idea of how Obama feels about such important issues. There's no way the United States population so ardently supported him if the majority didn't agree—or at least relate in some small way.

It remains correct that throughout the years, long past when Vietnam forced people to question the motives and actions of the American government, simmering now in the Age of Information, a new depiction has been developing among the masses. Barack Obama is the incarnation of these revelations. He represents all these unanswered questions. This is why the whole world sees him not as a black man, or a socialist, but as a man symbolizing what governmental policy has forced us to desire. *Change.*

He could have been running around with a copy of *The Communist Manifesto* shouting anti-Zionist epithets, and he would still have been adored by the people.

This election was a no-brainer. All his campaign had to do was promise "change," and say it loud enough and long enough until the prospect was engraved in our heads. Quote a little of John McCain's voting record, and the rest is History. Having Sarah Palin as the Republican's running mate didn't hurt Barack's chances either.

In the passing days after the historic win I've been thinking. Obama? *Obama?* I recall my newfound academic guru, Noam Chomsky, and think about the past, oh, six presidents we've had. "They've all got dirt under the rug," a political grad student in Chuckawalla once told me. And indeed they do. While their actions wouldn't normally justify that cliché, due to the prevalent belief that "America can do no wrong," at the very least the actions of our past Presidents are those which would earn condemnation for other national leaders.

But as already stated: the times are changing. While there are still many swept in patriotism and praise, our former leaders fear that the facts about their actions are becoming known and the old perceptions are wearing thin...America *can* do wrong.

National pieties aside, Nixon still ordered eighteen months of relentless bombing of Cambodia—furthering the Vietnam War and U.S. hegemony in Asia; Reagan supported death squads in Latin America for the same reasons; Clinton had some thirty people murdered in Arkansas, without a single prosecution (only Bob Barr cared about the blowjob); and Bush Junior....well, needless to say, the Iraq War was an embarrassing blunder. Morally, it's condemned, especially from men proclaiming Christian ethics. But because of the American Agenda, it's evitable. It is, for all intents and purposes, conquest. While during the campaigns we see just average Joes and Janes, you and me, wandering around Anytown, U.S.A., shaking hands, kissing babies, we know, as an alternative reading tells us, once these politicians get put into office, they commit atrocities.

They're obligated to fulfill a position. Only it's not one "of the people," but of elite influence. Whether business interests or the larger purpose of global domination, all presidents must comply with it.

Now, most of our former presidents fill that role nicely. But when I look at Barack Obama, and after learning of his upbringing, reading his book, and even seeing his kids—I just don't get it. It has me baffled. The mold has been broken.

Regardless, the Agenda must progress. To say he'll rein in our hegemony is utterly unrealistic. American Corporations still demand dominance in the world market, requiring the suppression of citizens around the globe; Israel still needs our funding, no matter how many war crimes they commit; and until an alternative fuel comes out, we'll remain the number one consumer of the world's oil.

No matter what.

We should be anxious to see what happens next. What policies will Mr. Obama and his squeaky clean administration implement first to further accelerate the all-powerful American Empire?

I'll be devastated when I learn of another travesty ala Operation Iraqi Freedom. But I know it's unavoidable. It will happen. It's just a matter of time.

These are the reasons why it's easier for me to believe that Obama, like every president before him, was pre-selected for his mission; put in power via huge contributions and voracious campaign mantras so that he can garner massive public support and "win" the vote. Oozing charisma, pronouncing a paradigm shift in politics, he appeals to this new generation. The Elites knew he couldn't lose.

Flatteringly, these guys want my thoughts on all these matters. And I told them basically the same thing: Obama is a figurehead. He's a puppet adhering to his political party, elite businessmen, and other outside influences. He doesn't speak for me, or you, but for those to whom he made promises.

Maybe this is the reincarnation of the rebellious 60's—a time when a new face was put in the White House and the public dissidence was unwavering. People waited for the horizon to bring us something different.

Be warned though: for we might be surprised if we hear shots ringing out from the distance and watch Barack Obama fall lifelessly to the floor, but it won't come from racist, redneck good-old boys. It'll come from a state-issued, high velocity sniper rifle—the kind you don't buy at Wal-Mart.

Assassination will not happen as long as Obama follows orders and "fills" his position correctly. As horrible as it is, remember: these are truisms as known throughout time.

Authority, tyranny, and corruption—they all work together and there's little we can do except sit back and enjoy the show.

The Pendulum Swings

THERE IS A fine line between those who are praised and those who are condemned. Circumstances and rationalizations play a vital part in deciding who will be "heroes" and who will go down in history as bloodthirsty monsters.

Usually when this happens, the morals that were supposed to be held so close to our hearts will be forgotten in favor of a general (societal) consensus. For example, if we believe the act of murdering an innocent person is a crime that should be condemned, how is it possible that we—as a herd-like society— praise those who perform the act under a different banner? Society holds a permanent frown on those who blatantly kill innocent people. But this rule should apply across the board; no person who does it, or participates in it, should receive any leniency.

Now, if we were to look at recorded history, and all its events of murder, torture, rape and pillage, we find cases in which the person (or persons) responsible for these heinous crimes will, in fact, be glorified for this behavior. Take Ronald Reagan, for instance. During his presidency in the 1980s, the United States supposedly "flourished" under his administration. It was an unprecedented era of "national pride" and prosperity. For this vague reason alone, Mr. Reagan will always be revered as an American hero by the masses.

However, if we apply our standard moral creed to the "Gipper," then he will certainly have to be condemned in the same fashion. This is because Mr. Reagan (along with many others in his cabinet) provided billions of dollars of military weaponry to right-wing dictators in Latin America, who systematically slaughtered thousands of people. We must ask ourselves: Why does a former president deserve our forgiveness? Was it because the threat of Communism was so great as to justify the support of these murderers? "Yes," it is said collectedly. He then becomes exempt from universal morals.

In fairness, a slogan explaining the subjective reasoning gets thrown around from time to time: "One man's terrorist is another man's freedom fighter." The major difference? Opinion. For there is a long list of lone bombers and rouge organizations that could be compelled to fight for a supposed "freedom." Ted Kaczynski, Timothy McVeigh, or any of the numberless Muslim jihadists.

Only a small fraction of people in America would agree with anything these murderers stand for. The masses will simply know what they did, or who they killed, and immediately make the final judgment—disregarding any valid arguments or evidence to the contrary. This principle of hypocrisy is evoked when others do it under a different pretense. "Kill one person, you're a murderer, kill a million, you're a hero"—an old adage. Alexander, Caesar, Napoleon, Stalin, Reagan—every one of them has reached a majority's high respect, no matter how many dead bodies are left in their wake.

This bias—this unconditional justification—happens when there is a logo of patriotic pride. But sometimes it is the result of something even more influential: a cultural trend. As with the toxin that is rap music, nearly all criminal behavior reaches a level of idolization: the worship of a lawless outcast, the admiration for the "Super Anti-Hero" who is exiled from society and has no respect for the rules. Drugs, murder, prostitution—all a (seemingly) decent way to live, or at least admire excessively. More than a few of the ghastly habits that are used in these songs are a breach of what we purportedly hold dear to our hearts.

The logic is this: the music is okay to listen to, but if someone we love or care about starts shooting people, or sells their bodies, it would receive equal attention and condemnation. Contradictions are astounding. The simple point is that the rap industry will always be remembered and revered as an important component of 1990s culture, while drugs and murder will always be looked down upon.

Morals and ethics act like a proverbial pendulum, swinging back and forth to fit the circumstances. When someone picks up a hooker on a street corner, prostitution is okay; when that person's sister occupies that same street corner, prostitution is *not okay*.

When the president intentionally kills innocent people in the name of "National Defense," school textbooks proudly proclaim the brave work. When a disturbed bomber grows tired of the government's random injustices and blows up a federal building, he is the scum of the earth.

Of course, it must be acknowledged that a person's morals cannot be limited to a simple statement or an emotion stemming from personal experiences. They must be reasoned—argued—until they are engraved in our character, solidified in our actions and grounded in an absolute conviction.

Anarchy Isn't a Social Trend

ANARCHY ISN'T A social style, or, at least it shouldn't be. Anarchy's essential ideology, like all political ideologies, should be driven by conviction. Ideally, one gives it a fair bit of thought. And hopefully it is a solitary revolution, meaning that outside influence should not play too big a part in its initial execution.

It's simple enough to read a book or watch T.V. and become instantly, but momentarily, angered by what is seen or unseen. However, it is hoped that the feeling is not arbitrary; that indeed a real personal grievance is developed from within. If not, one leaves themselves open to constant changes in the individual mindset: always fluctuating with different tides of influence. And what good is it to be a robot—programmed day in and day out to adapt and accept standards and conventionalities.

This was the nature of Punk Rock. Kicking a trash can could be constituted as "punk," while following that action could be constituted as "trendy," as said by Billie Joe Armstrong. So with the Punk-genre one was expected to be consistently individualistic. Not just another sheep following a flock.

But that is an irrelevancy, and an obviously immature example. I use it simply as an illustration to demonstrate how a "style" can be defined one way and distorted an instant later.

Anarchy, or more closely characterized by most dictionaries as a lack of government, is intended to be a vague representation of that—not the cultural style so disgracefully showed these days.

It might be fair to assume a majority of those displaying powerful symbols of Anarchy have little basis if forced to defend their political or ideological inclination.

Even during the sixties, the anarchist movement adhered to a socialistic agenda (a contradiction in my opinion). But at the very least, the early years flourished with protesters and activists who wholeheartedly believed something was wrong with their government, particularly its foreign policy. It was only in the later years when such generations began over-indulging in drugs and music. Not necessarily a "bad" thing, or even an immoral one— just a sharp difference from following mainstream governmental unrest.

I always understood anarchy as a concept in which we scrutinize every institution that affects our lives. We watch them, disseminate them, and make sure they demonstrate more positive than negative. And if the concepts of Anarchy prove illegitimate, then steps should be taken to dismantle them or to drastically reform them. No institution should be left out...State or Private.

These steps are show up in various forms of protest, or, in times of serious direness, armed revolution. But for every crowd in uprising, there must be an individual who can be taken aside and be ready to answer the question of why he or she is there. If not, then all we have are scenarios—not unlike Nuremburg— where citizens become afflicted with the overwhelming sensationalism of the situation.

However, very often—for fear of being persecuted by the crowd—we relinquish our ability to think and reason. Here we have another example of the "sheeple." I refer to this phenomenon as the "Robot Syndrome."

It's just another way in which people following in line with the ones yelling the loudest. These things must not happen if true and viable changes are to occur in our society.

Conventional Hypocrite

Once you leave the womb, conservatives don't care about you until you reach military age. Then you're just what they're looking for. Conservatives want live babies so they can raise them to be dead soldiers.
—George Carlin

You have heard that it hath been said, 'You shall love you neighbor, and hate your enemy.' But I say unto you, love your enemies, bless them that curse you, do good to them that hate you, and pray for them which despitefully use you, and persecute you.
—Mt 5:43

IN A REASONABLE world, a nation has a right to defend itself. This means that on our hate-filled planet, War is a regrettable necessity.

Contention exists for various reasons.

However, that is not a justification for every conflict a nation engages in. Why is it then, when one speaks to the average American conservative—the so-called "Christian"—they are willing to reject empathy in favor of relentless approval of their country's adventurism oversees? They are willing to ignore all situations of death—with women and children included in the body count—and attempt to legitimatize any given war.

26

We should ask ourselves if Jesus would condone all these wars.

As stated, defending a nation and its borders are understood, but if one is adhering to the teachings of Jesus Christ, then how can one group of persons be so oblivious to everything that he taught? If Jesus said "love thy enemy" then why does the average conservative insist on killing not only him, but his family and neighbors as well? It would be difficult to find a conservative willing to disagree with any of the wars that the United States has instigated and exacerbated over the years. Vietnam, Grenada, Panama, Iraq: these wars are immune from condemnation in the mind of a conservative.

> You have heard that it was said, 'Eye for eye, and tooth for tooth.' But I tell you, Do not resist an evil person. If someone strikes you on the right cheek, turn to him the other also. And if someone wants to sue you and take your tunic, let him have your cloak as well.
> —Matthew 5:38-40

If one thinks this as an impractical method to apply to our complicated world, there would still be none so unprepared and unqualified to fulfill this passage than...yes, that's right...the standard American conservative. Even in today's newspapers, as the Bush torture memos are dripping out and it's becoming well known what his evil administration engaged in, we must ask ourselves yet again: If Jesus Christ was inside of a room with an untried detainee in Guantanamo Bay, being waterboarded—would he condone it?

For these politicians who think they have "God" on their side—how can they endorse such an absurd image? George Carlin certainly sums up the logic in this argument: Why is the Right so vehemently opposed to abortion (I'm not in favor of it myself) when on the opposite end of the spectrum they are willing to send young men and women off to fight in foreign wars? Where is the pro-life in these actions? How can they be so contradictory to their own purported positions?!

> *The young man said to Him, 'All these commands I have kept; what am I still lacking?' Jesus said to him, 'If you wish to be complete, go and sell your possessions and give to the poor, and you shall have treasure in heaven; and come, follow Me.'*
> —Mt 19:20

Can someone possibly imagine all those "Christian" Republicans sitting on their fortunes way up in their high offices suddenly donating large swaths of their money to the poor and impoverished? Is this unrealistic for any one of us? Maybe, and especially to these proclaimed followers of Christ.

It is my understanding of the New Testament that a true follower of Christ is as distant, as possibly can be, from the implementation of state policies. John 17:16: "They are not of the world, even as I am not of it." Perhaps these are the false teachers of the Word that Jesus warned against. People like Jerry Falwell, or even our most devoted evangelical President, Mr. Bush, who use the passages at their own leisure and twist the meanings of it to fit their agenda.

How can one possible apply one of Jesus's most quoted phrases—"he who is without sin, cast the first stone"—when we have hundreds of untried Muslims in secret prisons all over the place? Who is to be the judge, jury, and executioner? Their "God," or themselves? Do they seek an American Theocracy based on their warped version of Jesus's teachings with public schools requiring mandatory prayers, or legislation forbidding all homosexual acts—destroying our shared ideas of Liberty? This mindset is evil and it must be met with hostility.

Their argument is usually something along the lines of this

being a "nation built on Christian values."

This is an outrageous falsity. Our Founding Fathers were primarily deists with an unspecific belief in a Supreme Being, but not one who intervened in the affairs of the State. On top of that, our Constitution is written without a singular mention of the word "Christianity," leaving us with a secular government.

A true Christian is supposed to be one dedicated to helping people without using violence. Where is the political diplomacy with these conservatives who bomb now and ask questions later? Alas, it'll be a long time before any one of these conservatives becomes the next Gandhi.

One last thought: It has been jokingly mentioned that "Jesus was a Liberal and Yahweh was a Conservative." Reading the discrepancies between the Old Testament and the New Testament, it is not hard to see why this is said. The unchanging Alpha and Omega had several changes in character within a relatively short period of time.

But that's a whole other discussion, and I hope it doesn't give our leaders any ideas.

Cancerfornia: A Letter to the Golden State

THERE IS A cancer growing inside the State of California. It is crushing the social stability of our counties and destroying the lives of thousands. The mass media has lied to you, saying it is in your best interest. But do not be deceived by this creature, for it is our own prison system—The California Department of Corrections and Rehabilitation.

Since 1970 the prison population in the Golden State has grown from 22,000 inmates to anywhere between 160-170,000 inmates (depending on what report you read) in 2009. And it will continue to do so. The simple reason being: there is absolutely no deterrent for criminals to stop committing crimes. When you get to the bottom of it, it is very simple logic: criminals will produce more criminals. This is exactly what is taking place behind the prison walls. And the officials and politicians who are supposed to watch over this monster are in reality endorsing this behavior. Sworn officers who are paid by your tax dollars actually advocate the escalation of criminal activities, for their own so-called "job security."

How do I know this? Because I have just finished serving three years behind those walls. I have watched very intently on what is happening. That time has given me the opportunity to see things that would probably make the average, tax-paying person sick—

for nothing else but the blatant insanity of it all. Anyone doing any sort of research on this matter could clearly see the fraudulent creed of "Rehabilitation." With roughly seven out of ten inmates returning immediately back into jail, a sensible person would probably realize that there is something dangerously wrong. But perhaps it would take the experience of somebody who was inside to explain what is really going on. So regrettably I inform you of this: there is a breeding ground in our State Penitentiaries, with people making a lot of money in the form of luxurious benefits and huge paychecks.

The first thing that is imperative to understand is the general mentality of the prison population. The public has a widespread illusion that because it is prison, it must be a place no one would want to go. This is a mistake. The truth is that behind those gates there is an entire community of very comfortable inmates. Indeed, they are quite happy being the statistics that you read about in all the reports.

As would be expected, the majority of the prison congregation comes from street gangs: Surenos, Bloods, Crips, Skinheads, Wah Ching—to name the major ones. There are plenty of subdivisions within these alluded-to ethnicities, but mostly they fall into five or six categories. In other words, the gangs are almost always divided up by race, with perhaps the exception of the "others"—who are usually Pacific Islanders and other undesignated nationalities.

The Caucasian inmates fall between two primary groups: The Peckerwoods ('Woods) and the Skinheads. The former consist of just about every white man that walks onto the yard while the Skinheads have established more of a hierarchy, constantly stabbing other races—and each other—to move up the ranks. These hypocritical, Hitler-saluting scumbags have a mixture of racist ideologies, blending Nazism and the infamous "88 Precepts" to formulate their supposedly "superior way of life."

Hispanic inmates move in a similar fashion, betraying each

other to move up the ladder of command. With over 500 Hispanic gangs in the Los Angeles area alone, they are *the* major players in the prison game and "run" most of the yards. Not to mention that many of them likely work for the murderous drug cartels in Mexico, running the drugs and doing the dirty work. Their main enemies are the Norteno's from the northern part of the State.

The African Americans are a bit different—less organized and far fewer politics. The majority of them are either Crips or Bloods, again with dozens or hundreds of different sects and turfs. When they're not feuding with each other, they usually fight with the Southerners, which is also a very prominent rivalry on the streets. Asians and Indians are the minority in prison, and they round out my list of categorized prisoners.

Now, read your newspapers. Turn on your T.V. The next time you see a person being arrested for one of the countless crimes committed in the State, remember that that offender first goes through the county jail. In Los Angeles County alone, that process can take up to three days, transferring from one cramped cell to the next. It is not uncommon to see people passed out on the urine soaked floor, or prisoners putting graffiti on the walls. My most vivid recollections of the county jail could easily be likened to a medieval dungeon.

However this is but the tip of the iceberg. When one eventually does get settled into either a dorm or a cell, the real problem will suddenly come to full understanding, the one that set the entire Justice System astray from its original purpose of rehabilitating criminals.

As stated, the gangs are divided up mostly by race, so depending upon the color of your skin, you will be instructed on how "things" will be working in the dorm (or whatever housing unit you are assigned to). This will be done via the "shot-caller." He will explain in detail about the mandatory politics which were established long before you got there. For example: if you are white then there will be no eating, drinking, or showering with any black man. Sharing and conversations should be kept at a minimum.

These pathetic rules, made only by another inmate, will be strictly enforced by the remainder of the "car." If anyone violates these rules it shall be considered a treasonous act and it will be dealt with by rigid discipline, almost always by a group of men pummeling you in the back corner of the room.

Many of these synthetic regulations apply to the other races; there are few exceptions. And perhaps this might sound almost natural at first. After all, it would seem quite normal to stay with your "people" in an environment filled with vicious gangs. But it doesn't stop with the racist unity. These rules have a much deeper effect. They penetrate into every county jail, every prison, and every yard in the entire State. (The exception is the Sensitive Needs Yards, to which I'll return.)

Try now to imagine the socially ostracized inmates, longing to be accepted into a group of similar delinquents, wanting to "fit-in" and "be part of things." The perfect opportunity presents itself. Instead of rejecting the oxymoron (that is—breaking rules, then following them), these individuals now try desperately to be part of a seemingly decent way of life...prison life. They look at the older "homies" as their mentors, and expectedly, the older homies comply—more than happy to have a new fertile mind to corrupt, and do their dirty work.

It is not long after that when the ignorant young inmate is stabbing or assaulting other people on the yard, on orders of the shot-caller. When these "torpedoes" carry out their mission, they are given a tattoo as a sort of praise for their obedience, along with a new release date.

Even more disturbing is, while many are happy to please their new masters, there are many who are never given the choice. Many times the shot-caller instructs the new arrivals to faithfully carry out any demands he might make. Whether a stabbing of another inmate, or simply a brutal assault, the order is given and the shot-caller expects execution. Disobedience, perpetually, requires rigid discipline.

Understand that every time something like this happens, it affects the order of things. No longer is there even the slightest hint of reform. It is criminality compounded with criminality. Once the inmate paroles this newly enforced mentality goes back to the streets, and thus the reason seventy percent (perhaps more) come right back.

This does not happen by itself, indeed there is a master designer at work, pulling the strings. The California Correctional Peace Officers Associations (C.C.P.O.A.) is a union comprised of roughly 57,000 workers. 32,000 of them are sworn officers of duty who plead an Oath, similar to most law enforcement agencies—something to the effect of purporting to uphold the Constitution and be beneficial to the people of the state.

They are one of the strongest unions in the state, which has also garnered a ten billion dollar budget for their operations in 2008-2009, compared to half that amount five years ago. With this enormous increase in money to work with, the average taxpayer might expect the crime rate to eventually drop, or at least stagnate. As just explained, this can't happen as long as inmates are forcing other inmates to commit more criminal activities.

Believe me: this happens with full encouragement of the C.C.P.O.A. It's the old rule of "divide and conquer." Separate the prisoners, label them according to their race or gang, and then segregate them into allocated cells. From there, one can constantly be told to "follow the program," which essentially means do what you're told—by either an officer or another inmate. The wardens and all the other "higher-ups" are aware that as long as the inmates are busy fighting each other, they won't be giving them much trouble. So they enforce the racial hatred to keep the population preoccupied.

I have personally seen wardens' laugh in an almost hysterical tone, while their officers tell me they wish everybody was out committing more crimes—simply to fill their $100,000 paycheck, complete with full benefits for the rest of their lives. In 1980 the average salary of an officer was $14,000 a year, now its $54,000, and usually much higher.

This tyranny is added to the extreme lack of any educational or vocational programs. There might occasionally be an "AA" meeting and sometimes motivational speakers speak at one of the chapels, but overall there is no beneficial programs inside the prisons. Those in place now are simply to appease required state standards. Nothing more.

Once again, any hard-working person who pays their dues would expect more money directed towards schooling and vocational job training, instead of the luxurious benefits of the corrupted officers. How does a state, whose creed is supposed to be "For the People, By the People," allow a tax-dollar supported institution like the C.D.C.R. to make non-negotiable contracts without any oversight?

When all these complications are put together they formulate a very backwards, if not downright evil System—one in which criminals have no chance of becoming the reformed, productive members that society expects. It is nothing less than modern slavery.

Everyday an officer breaks his or her oath of Justice, and actively supports this perversion. That is why the incarceration rate grows every year. And the C.C.P.O.A. constantly demands more and more money. All the while the people see no progress. To put it figuratively: why would they slay the monster when they get paid so much for fighting it?

How can you be so deceived? Because the mainstream media is rarely allowed behind those walls. And even then, they never show an accurate picture. Most people would be appalled at what is happening: fifty naked men cramming their way into one showerhead, or rat feces inside the food. So that all you know is the distorted facts produced by the incompetent media.

If it isn't the press that lies to you, then it's the bogus ads run by the C.D.C.R. itself, complaining about the abuses they're subjected to, expressing their grievances to the public as to invoke sympathy and justify budget increases. The truth is that most of these clips are taken from Level 4 yards, where violent altercations occur more often than in other yards. Assaults on staff do not happen as often as one is led to believe and, subsequently, it is often their own fault for refusing to enable any sort of inmate rehabilitation, or even giving them the chance to do it themselves. Pure propaganda.

The only one who makes any sort of statement regarding these conditions is our own "Governator," Arnold Schwarzenegger. And then even he tells the people that a reform on the 3-Strikes Law would be a detriment to our well-being. In 2004, proposition 66 would have required the third strike to be violent and/or serious. But a week prior to voting, Schwarzenegger launched an intense campaign that made sure this would not happen, saying that 26,000 rapists and child molesters would be set free. This was an outright lie, seeing that at the time only 8,000 people were sentenced to life in prison under the 3-Strikes. The legislation almost passed with 47.3% of California's population voting yes, and 52.7% voting no. Now the courts continue to give out 25-life sentences for extremely minor infractions, thanks to the Governor's rhetoric about "not allowing violent predators out on the streets." Perhaps Mr. Schwarzenegger is trying to live up to his heroic persona depicted onscreen, but I believe he should have stayed in Hollywood and not come to Sacramento, because the fact is: he is ignoring the issue.

There is another perception that is still very prevalent among the masses. That is: the glorification of prison life. If it isn't the rap "artists" who glamorize criminal behavior and make it look so stylish, then its "true-life" reality series like Lock-Up and Gang Land. People seem to be so captivated by the decay of society. And it will only be a problem when a recently-released convict breaks into their house and violates their Freedom. Nobody will ever take the situation seriously, not as long as the public sees prison as a form of entertainment.

Even then, what could be done about it? What would be the first step towards resolving this growing problem?

Right now a large number of prison yards are converting over to "SNY," or Special Needs Yards. Originally these yards were designed to house sex offenders who are typically the target of "mainline" abuse. However, throughout the course of the last several years these yards have been opening up to a larger variety of inmates: homosexuals, snitches, guys who owe debt. But a lot more of them are those who have grown tired of the prison politics, and wish to do their own time.

This is a good thing! It shows willingness on behalf of the inmates to do their own time, and get away from the gang-lifestyle. However, while this might be a necessary first step in alleviating the problem, it is not an overnight solution. But certainly we must pressure our government to accelerate the process.

My proposal is this, however extreme it might be: first, all the prison politicians must be locked down for at least 23 and half hours out of the day. No longer must they be given the option to give orders and manipulate the rest of the prison population, for that is the sole element that is completely undermining the purpose of this state's correctional facilities.

When that happens, the prison yards will then be converted into "Program Yards" in which inmates will finally be allowed to do their own sentence, without the hindrances of other influences. Anyone trying to call shots and give orders will be locked up indefinitely until otherwise stated.

The second action that must be taken is the elimination of the

C.C.P.O.A. As unlikely as it might seem, their Union is helping to destroy the State. What must happen is this: the People of California must make a temporary amendment to the Constitution as to make it possible to hire an outside security agency. Only temporarily! During this time the state will implement new laws that will allow greater oversight for our state workers and their budgets. No more egregious benefits and non-negotiable contracts. With the money saved from the termination of the current State baby-sitters and thus, their outrageous budget, more money can be used towards educational programs.

This critical issue is of the greatest concern. If it is not resolved swiftly then it will eventually end in disaster. For any taxpayer who is interested in Freedom and Justice, this letter is for you. Call your Senators, call your Representatives. Propose new ideas and incentives and begin getting the word out. Negligence will only result in ruination. Something must be done!

Postscript

It might seem irrelevant to the message I'm conveying, but I also suggest Americans exercise his or her Second Amendment right and never hesitate to decorate your wall with the brains of a low-life scumbag—like a Skinhead or a Sureno—if they break your window and come into your house.

Also, although there is plenty of argument against drug legalization, one must objectively discern the horrible underground economy that methamphetamine, heroin, and, to a much lesser extent, marijuana have generated in the streets. Legalization and controlled environments would eliminate the lucrative businesses of the drug cartels.

Bad to Compensate for the Good

WELL THEN, THE best weekend I've had since my release is now over. And while it was rather fantastic (marvelously fantastic, actually), it did not pass without that naturally occurring phenomenon known only as "bad"—more commonly called by its Latin term, *"Goddamnit-Son-of-a-Bitch!"*—appearing shortly thereafter all the good had come to an end.

My weekend started off as a somewhat celebration of Memorial Day and my Fritzy's 21st birthday. It ended with minor regrets…revelations really, that further solidify my belief that everything that Good happens inevitably gets mixed up with a little Bad.

First, I grant myself a long needed sigh—almost like a that-hit-the-spot sort of feeling. After such a long, lonely time…I got laid. That's right: butt naked on the bathroom floor, within the first hour of meeting her. My Fritzy—a cute little Latino girl—came over this past Friday and, well, as said. So let me rehash.

I'll bypass the initial sex, since I've already been ribald enough, and tell you what followed shortly thereafter. That Friday night we went to see the new Terminator movie: *Salvation*. I wept after I saw it, like a little baby. Why couldn't Schwarzenegger have stayed in movies instead of becoming Governor? He attempted a half-ass cameo in the film in the form of a computer generated image on a "T-800 model," but I say that if he wasn't busy getting all his measures voted down in California, he could have done the shot himself and, with good probability, gained a little bit of his popularity back. Alas, poor Arnold is still trying to help the Golden State out of its dire financial status by putting us all on economic life support, but it's not working out so well. If he really wanted to help, he would release a few thousand first-time non-violent offenders and cut the salaries of C.C.P.O.A. officers and corrupt cops alike—along with a few teachers as well, why not?

The image of Arnold's computer-enhanced face haunted me all the way until Fritz gave me the most awesome blowjob I've ever had. Then her face was stuck in my head. Or...err...I mean....anyways. That was Friday.

Saturday, we went to a club in Old Town Monrovia, The 4th Dimension—a nice place that seemed to be rather quiet for a Memorial Day weekend. But it was all groovy. My brother had invited us over and had a convenient friend that worked there—the manager, which meant that my Fritzy could sit at the bar and drink in the few hours before her 21st.

Now, as everyone who knows anything about me knows: I like to drink...excessively. And since my release I've been drinking mostly beer. But the truth is: when I want to get fucked up, beer isn't usually my first choice. It's too filling, and it takes far too long to get a good buzz going. Pitcher after pitcher after endless pitcher, and all you do is walk away with a stomach ache, and not the right head change you were looking for.

This night I started off with a personal favorite: Jack Daniels and 7-Up; four within an hour's time. Fritz was drinking a strawberry margarita and my brother and his friend were drinking a pitcher. I surpassed myself this particular night. Drinking was the name of the game, and I was Babe Ruth (who also didn't mind himself an occasional drink).

We found our way over to another little place that is actually underneath the bowling alley my brother works at. This place had dragons and Samurai-looking ornaments everywhere. When I realized that all the people working there were Asian, I figured that, no doubt, the Triads and Wu-Tang were probably regular customers. None on this night, but then, Memorial Day isn't for everyone.

Everybody was staying groovy, even my brother as he almost threw up after a flaming shot of Bacardi 151. The drink was good, the flames were beautiful and danced with a wonderful rhythm as I dropped the shot in a glass of beer and consumed the bastard with one gulp. "Wasted" is spelled W-A-S-T-E-D. And that was the word to describe me tonight.

So after drinks, pool, and some bowling, we went back home (who drove again?), and topped the night off with a light-hearted argument in my kitchen over how to get Fritzy's BMW home, which was still parked over at the parking lot behind the 4-D. But Mom said everyone to bed, and we all complied.

The next morning I woke up with a splitting-ass headache, and when I turned and lifted the covers' up, I noticed that my Fritzy was stark-naked. What a shocker, which wasn't completely unpleasant, but I wondered if she had gotten like that by herself, or if I had demanded it of her before I passed out.

She awoke and explained to me a few things that had happened during the night—how I showed her pictures of my crime and started bawling my eyes out, because, as clinical depression happens, I couldn't contain myself and repress the loneliness I felt for those three incarcerated years. I told her I loved her. Told her all these things—some true, some half-true, and some which made me wish I had a staple gun so I could have stabled my mouth shut. For a brief moment I wanted to kick her out of my house so that I could find a way to drown my regrets, probably with more alcohol. Fortunately this feeling faded when my mom and my brother were forgiving and said it wasn't that big a deal.

So Fritz and my mom and I went over to the parking lot, and upon getting there saw that the passenger door was left slightly open. Suddenly all my embarrassment vanished, because it was her who forgot to close it all the way. And she was the most sober. Ha! It was left there all night, and luckily nothing was taken, and more luckily the battery wasn't dead.

Then I got behind the wheel of the car and drove onward. Stupid move, I know, seeing as I don't have a license and would immediately go back to prison. But shit—the Beamer was just so nice, and I really wanted to go for a drive.

The rest of the weekend was spent having sex, BBQing, and then going to L.A. to visit her gay friend—all perfect ingredients for a wonderful weekend. But, as it always turns out, she got sentimental, even crying at one point when I tried to explain the changes I'd made in my life. One of them being that I'm not a little kid anymore, and thus, don't fall into foolish notions of "love," those hopelessly ridiculous random acts of committing yourself simply because you might fall in love. Somehow I was able to convince her to leave things the way they were, at least for the time being. She agreed, and proceeded to give me more head. The best ever.

It was around this time that I remembered the holiday, Memorial Day. Certainly I'll never forget this weekend—one very memorable for me. But the National Holiday seems to be quite different. It's supposed to be where we—as red-blooded Americans—honor our veterans and to pay tribute to those who have fallen in war.

But let us take a look at this for a moment. To pay tribute to those who have fallen in War. If we really wanted to analyze it, wouldn't that mean we'd have to discern the wars that they had fallen in, rather than simple take it for granted that they were doing something completely noble and righteous? Was Vietnam justified? Panama? Iraq I? Iraq II? What if we had reversed this unequivocal belief that our troops are heroes and realized that the conflicts that they fell in weren't at all for the safety of America, but rather for the benefits of the Elite—more specifically known as the mega-corporations and politicians who make money off of that stock. Would that not change the perspective at least a little?

After all, how many American soldiers were concerned about Saddam Hussein's atrocities before Bush Jr. declared war? Even going further back—were they worried when Bush Senior (along with his puppet Reagan) were supplying biological warfare to the tyrant in the 80's? Did anybody complain then? Or was it simply a matter of "trust your Government?"

Same with Vietnam: was anybody worried that the Communists were taking over? The answer, then and not now (because no veteran would ever admit that the war they fought in was a mistake) is almost always "no"—they didn't care until Uncle Sam, in whatever body occupying the Oval Office, was telling them that the battle was necessary.

Nowadays, I just chalk it up to manipulation and convince myself that most people are so easily brainwashed that it's easy for them to become pawns. That settles my mental demon right there.

Interesting how I'm always having these thoughts at the damnedest moments. I treated my Fritzy like the big-titted girl she knows I missed. But I'm playful. And by the end of her stay, she was quickly falling under my persuasion...just like the little blonde teen girl on that porno clip I showed her, who horrified her friend's boyfriend.

And, as it happens, at the end of the "good," the "bad" follows right behind. We went for a walk in the park when I realized that I forgot to attend my orientation for school. Fuck, there goes my summer semester. They say it's a hard course anyways, plus there's always fall.

It was just like that time I applied for K-Mart, in which I had to drug test for the company before I could start work. My uncle had paid fifty dollars for a "system cleaner" which would temporarily make my body "clean" from the vile toxins I was consuming at the time, marijuana being the concern. I spent the whole morning at his apartment with this damn solution: two pills and a vile of some sort of liquid. I drank the magic juice, along with the nearly two gallons of water as instructed on the back of the box, and just as I was making my way outside of his door to head on down to the place, I ran back inside of his bathroom and threw up what was an ungodly amount of clear-ish looking puke. But, I tested clean as a whistle. The following week I was to attend the initial orientation, and once again I stayed at uncle's apartment as to make sure I'd be up and not miss it. As it turned out, I slept right on through the fucking thing. Woke up about an hour after I was supposed to be there. I was pissed.

Anyways, Fritzy left that Tuesday afternoon. And that night I went for a bike ride to clear my mind and remember all the great moments of the weekend. But right before getting to the main stretch home, a cop pulls up, stops me, and asks where I'm going. As always, anyone out past 10 o'clock is immediately suspected of being a mass murderer. He had to ask it: "You on probation or parole?" That's all that's needed. So after a quick conversation in which he interrogated me on the crime, and after his partner scanned my ID, they let me go.

"How was prison?" he had asked.

"A goddamned nightmare," I said solemnly, but with my usual grin.

The whole state is going to the police. To the prison guard's union. To those big-shot legislators. But, as it is with the American fashion, they'll continue to hide the problem, and put a Band-Aid on a gunshot wound.

Still, the weekend was great. Let's just hope the girl doesn't get pregnant.

Condoms just aren't pleasurable.

Swine Flu Smells Like Bullshit

REEKS ACTUALLY. THE truth is: the United States has always made a habit out of enlisting "boogiemen" to distract attention away from serious issues, or real facts. Osama Bin Laden is a good example of this. After the attacks of September 11th the media ushered in the hysteria of who was at fault. Pointing the finger was simple and garnering public support for war and destroying the jihadist militants became commonplace. Granted, there really is a growing radical Muslim problem. But the facts being omitted are the ones that would incite serious dissent among the public.

We'll push aside (for now) the outlandish "theories" surrounding the technicalities of the actual attacks. Instead, we should simply discern the events leading up to Osama Bin Laden's Al Qaeda network. During the 1980's when the Soviet Union had invaded Afghanistan (after being provoked by the U.S., according to Elitist Zbigniew Brzezinski) the United States decided it would be a good idea to fund and support militant Muslims who were outraged at the Soviet's invasion. Trained in refugee camps, the U.S.-equipped militants won the battle, and thus won their sovereignty.

Who would've thought that the mentality of the militant Muslims might stay with them after the war ended? This is where Osama Bin Laden comes in. A member of the Saudi royal family—who was also trained during the conflict—he went on to organize the loose bands of militants and make his own terrorist network: Al Qaeda. Infuriated after the 1991 Persian Gulf War, in which the United States promised to withdraw its military bases from Saudi Arabia (which it didn't, of course), Osama became convinced that the enemy was Western Civilization—starting with the principle powerhouse: the U. S. of A.

These simple, undisputed facts are shadowed in comparison with the more obvious examples of America's penchant of breeding its own monsters. The Oil Crisis, for instance, is a most sinister brand of evil. Ever since the 1930's, when The House of Rockefeller found huge reserves of petroleum in Saudi Arabia, American presidents have given billions, if not trillions, of dollars of aid to nations who have our interests in mind. No matter what kind of dictatorship it is, no matter now horrendous its human rights record, the United States funds and supports these monsters for the free flow of oil. This has fanned the flames of hatred in the Middle East, and the reason so many of them are now willing to send their sons to Disneyland with a bomb strapped to their chest.

Now ask yourself: how often do you hear about these things brought up in the mainstream media? When do we ever see the human rights records of these nations? Or see reports on how the people hate us? The answer, almost undoubtedly, would be rarely, if ever. This is because the American Elite have given us a "boogieman" to focus our attention on. Instead of giving us the information about how or why the problems are the way they are, we are told to merely be angry at whatever crimes they may commit against us.

This time the momentary enemy was in the form of a flu virus: the H1N1—otherwise known as the Swine Flu. And, indubitably, it did not pass without it serving its purpose: the distraction of the recently released Bush Torture memos.

First given attention early this year, the Swine Flu was given status comparative to that of the Plague, or perhaps even to AIDS. And while the flu did result in deaths, the amount has now been realized to be grossly exaggerated. The reports in Mexico were once in the 100's, and now the official listing is somewhere around 42.

For weeks and weeks we were bombarded with the "latest" on the Swine Flu. We heard about schools being closed down and all the recent death tolls. But did anyone ever stop to think, that if the sickness was so horrible, then why were there only a handful of deaths in the United States? And, most of these deaths came from people already suffering from other ailments.

Regular "everyday" flu complications kill over 36,000 people a year. And the Swine Flu isn't even coming close to these numbers. The SARS outbreak a few years back killed way more people.

Why then all the media hype? Well, I believe the main reason was because during this time the Bush Memos—detailing disgusting torture methods—were being brought out to the public. These memos were released by our current President, Mr. Obama, and again, I believe this was only done with the intent of appeasing civil rights organizations, who demanded the full details of Bush's evil.

Obama routinely iterates that no prosecutions will be handed out. Why would he? After all, Obama is one and the same with the previous administration. He has their interest in mind: the American Agenda, which prevails over all other political discourse.

These torture memos revealed, among other things, the constant and repeated use of waterboarding, insect use, and sleep deprivation. The Bush administration—along with all the other Neo-Cons—have continually tried to justify the use of these methods as legal. The Bybee Memo, for instance, given to the CIA by federal judge Jay Bybee, was written in such a way so as to allow interrogators to use "enhanced interrogation" methods on Abu Zubaydah. Starting with that, the CIA was fully allowed to use tactics condemned by numerous countries and human rights organizations.

If the public were made aware of these things, then perhaps they would push for indictments of Bush and the CIA interrogators. We can't have that, can we? So, to divert attention from these Nazi-type crimes, the elite organized a plot: promote the mania of a nearly-non deadly flu virus.

This is but one example of how we are led like sheep to the slaughter, with complete and utter contentment for the masses, who are spoon-fed bullshit in the form of Swine Flu.

They're Dropping Like, Well, Celebrities...Any Guess on Who is going to be Number Six?

CALL IT SUPERNATURAL phenomenon. Call it superstition. Call it even paranoid delusion. But it always seems that celebrities die in groups of three. Ever since the fateful plane crash that killed Buddy Holly, Richie Valens, and J.P. "Big Bopper" Richardson in 1959, there has been the persistent belief that once one goes, two more are sure to follow. It always seemed that way. Or at least my limited memory on the subject perceives it to be.

But then one morning I realized that it had been awhile since any big celeb had passed on. The last I could remember was probably Paul Newman. And then, the unthinkable happened. It was unexpected. It was startling. And it was mildly engaging. That's right: David Carradine tied his balls up to his throat and strangled himself in order to get a hard-on. I'll never be able to watch Kung-Fu ever again; the spiritual holy man was in reality a sexual weirdo, just like many of us.

Ghastly images indeed.

A few weeks had passed and—in almost a small bit of irony, due to Conan O' Brian's triumphant return to "late night" as new host to the *Tonight Show*—Ed McMahan passed away at the age of 86. A good man and fellow drinker who, as Conan pointed out, had a laughter which became the "soundtrack of the Tonight

Show." I just hope that McMahan caught a couple of episodes of Conan's hosting—as he is the new genius of late night.

Then, on the 24th of June, I found myself in a mild drinking binge, contemplating the evils of government and the endless stupidities of human nature, when it suddenly occurred to me that: there's one more. Isn't there?

Who was to be next then? *I knew!* In my mind there was only one possible person: that timeless beauty who even at her age looked gorgeous in the nude. Ms. Farrah Fawcett. I went over it in my head for a few minutes, about how her condition has been public and well-known. I had just seen a report the previous night.

Sure enough, the next morning I woke up, fired up the computer, and the first report I read: "Farrah Fawcett dead at 62." Suddenly, I felt really bad. Because if I had made a "dead-pool"-like gamble the night before, I would have been a richer man. So instead of spiraling into a guilt-filled nightmare, I decided to amass myself with old Playboy photos of Farrah that I found online, along with a cold bottle of Mickey's. This helped.

"That was three," I told myself. The nightmare was over, at least for the time being. No famous people would be dying anytime soon. Or so I thought.

Then, sometime in the afternoon I turned on the news. The breaking story out of Los Angeles was that Michael Jackson had been rushed to the hospital. "Oh, well," I thought to myself. "These things happen all the time." But then I read the caption at the bottom of the screen: *cardiac arrest*? This could create a bad outcome for the King of Pop. But hell, I'm sure they'll figure it out, right? After all, Michael doesn't go anywhere without his personal medical assistant, and I'm sure he's got a whole assortment of pills that open the heart, close it, and do all sorts of other medical miracles. I convinced myself that Michael was going to be okay, even though I wasn't a fan. He had, as anyone will surely admit, an unhealthy relationship with children.

All he needed was a little Jesus Juice, a couple pills, and his pet monkey; that would surely restore the color to his face. I mean...err...anyways. I jumped back on the computer to look up a few things. Then, about ten minutes later, I get a phone call from my mother.

"Did you hear?!"

"No..." I replied.

"Michael Jackson died."

"They said he was in the hospital right now."

"No, it's just been reported that he's dead."

And sure enough, *TMZ* was right on the money. After a lifetime of amazing talent, a bizarre lifestyle, and several lawsuits, the biggest musical name since Elvis Presley (probably) was gone. "Oh, man." Suddenly I felt even worse; first my prediction about Farrah Fawcett, and then my incorrect prediction that this was going to round out the three celebs. And then I realized that poor Farrah was going to be forgotten in the coming...minutes, if not sooner. International child molester Michael Jackson was going to swallow up the media with his untimely death.

That's what most of his fans neglect. Jesse Jackson might sound sympathetic with all his rhetoric about "his shortcomings not outweighing his strengths" or something like that, but the fact is that Michael Jackson had an extremely unusual, and, in my opinion, very inappropriate relationship with little kids. By his own admission! Sleeping with them, having nude pictures on the bed stand—all sorts of things most parents would look at as unhealthy for anyone else. But Jacko, somehow, was able to make the parents of all those kids who stayed at Neverland Ranch forget about these things.

Was allowing such events to happen a reflection of our age of stupidity or just parental neglect on a large scale? These were not isolated incidents, but ones that occurred when parents let their kids continue to go his house, even after testimony came out.

There could be good to come from this. We are just now

hearing that Michael's children might not be his. They might in fact be become biological results of some unknown person. If this turns out to be true, then years from now those kids are going to be extremely grateful. At least they won't have to worry about being put in a dangerous situation, like being dangled off another balcony, unless the sperm donor turns out to be a Saudi Arabian prince and he gains custody of the kids, in which they might be become little jihadists in the near future. The sick bastard would be destroying little kid's lives even from beyond the grave. But it's best not to think about it now.

So that's four. And wasn't it three's that they di..."*Oh my god!*" Before I could even finish the realization, television pitchman Billy Mays was found dead at his home in Tampa. "What the hell is going on?" my mom asked. One after another. But I'm in serious doubt for one very good reason. Was Billy Mays a celebrity? Well, we've been seeing him for years on television; he's the guy most people mute when they hear his voice come on. And Fritzy thought I'd be glad to hear the news. But—although he was as annoying as a hemorrhoid—it was a sad story.

So, that's now five. There's one more, there has to be! It's the law of...err...superstition...just like Christ. Is it time to play my own deadpool game? Time to take bets? I say Patrick Swayze. The man just doesn't look well. I've also heard that legendary newsman Walter Cronkite is in pretty bad shape.

Ah, what am I talking about? That's sick. Life is far too precious for stupid guesses like that. Forgive me. I'm just in complete and utter shock at the bombardment of celebrity deaths in the last few weeks. I really hope I'm wrong anyways; the old myth is probably just that—a myth. I doubt anyone will kick the bucket anytime soon. Unless that shadow in the curtains is what I think it is: angry parolees who are upset about my essay Cancerfornia, and, alas, I become number six....

In Response to Bruce Cain

THE OTHER DAY I read an article by marijuana advocate Bruce Cain. It was entitled *War Breaks out in the Marijuana Movement*. Cain is an advocate of legalizing marijuana. He is also a protégé of Jack Herer, who in the cannabis world needs no introduction. But to give the briefest of a synopsis for those of you who don't know: both of these men believe in legalization *without* taxation. And, presumably, any attempt to do so without this premise in mind is a cannabis traitor! NORML, *Cannabis Culture*, and of course our brave magazine—along with many others—are regarded as "draconian" and so on. This is my response.

Mr. Cain,

The Drug War must come to an end! I hope that your conviction regarding this bold assessment is as concrete as mine. For thirty-plus years now our families, communities, and liberties have been ravished by the onslaught of needless prohibition. We can cite example after example about the disaster of the 1920's and the subsequent creation of a criminal monster, and how non-violent offenders were and are serving lifetimes behind bars while rapists and child molesters are getting out after a few years. The point is: there is no need to have lengthy discussions about the miserable results—you me, and countless millions of others have agreed upon this.

The question is now obvious: What do we do about it? This is where, after reading your essay, I find myself a bit troubled. Sharp, scathing criticisms over such minor details as government taxation and the exploitation of the private sector have led me to worry if perhaps there is a drift developing amongst legalization advocates. We are at the threshold in which change—real, unprecedented change—is so near to fruition. I wonder if these small details are now going to prevent us from making that devastating offensive blow hit its target.

This response is in no way a counter-argument to your general contention. I very well understand the point, and to a certain extent agree with it. But I wonder if there is a small amount of naiveté in your assessment of who the enemy is. So in case you were unaware, I'll tell you.

The Generals of the Drug War are not merely the conservative representatives who oppose our right to smoke what we want. Emphatically, it is a much larger number of police officers, prison guards, angry soccer moms, and, most nefarious of all, the Drug Cartels. For the last one, you were correct in that legalization would eliminate a huge portion of their illicit proceeds, but what I think you are wrong about is that it doesn't simply wipe them out. The philosophy of "free markets" doesn't apply to gangsters who live to kill. They don't pack their bags and move out of town because business is bad. Undoubtedly, when their marijuana profits go down with legalization, two calamities will take place.

One: The increase in the sale of other illicit substances—with methamphetamine and heroin as the most likely. And two: An increase in more street violence, due to the "lower level" dealers now out of a job and growing bored without their trade. Criminal behavior has evolved from merely being an organized group providing an illegal product, into a mentality which strives to cause social harm. I think this is guaranteed. Granted, the crime rates will eventually drop, but not before a large amount of confusion and chaos ventilates onto our city streets.

Not like this scenario hasn't been played out before. The United States has a long history of breeding its own monsters. Reagan had his militant Muslims during the Soviet invasion of Afghanistan, and now we can see how that played out. And, of course, Prohibition created a large number of criminals and mobsters, many of which were just common folks, driven by the rage of the government impeding upon their lives. When the Drug War ends, you can certainly expect a larger amount of uneducated gangbangers to scratch their heads and start shooting random people. For example: after the repeal in 1933, the Feds had to set up a commission in an attempt to tabulate the confused Mafiosos'. A similar situation is likely to occur here.

Even with all the possible consequences, new measures must be taken. They must pushed, pressured, pursued, and protested into legalization so that we can put an end to this nightmare. But with your essay on how "cannabusiness" will take advantage of this prospect, I fear that a division might erupt between those who advocate legalization because of the way in which it should be handled. This might compromise our endeavor. And besides, where is the revenue going to come from to help fight these bastards? We should address that.

You're quite correct that the private sector will exploit the crop, and soon huge farmlands will no longer be growing corn and watermelons, but instead huge stalks of very legal marijuana. And yes: like any other business they will be subject to taxation and other forms of regulation. Your argument stands that the government shouldn't touch the stuff, and that all private, house-grown crops will be strictly "hands-off" to any Red, White, and Blue fingers. I understand your conviction, but the State could desperately use an extra 1.3 billion dollars to help solve the impending problems mentioned above.

I used to believe that the word "freedom" was a single absolute word that conquered all tyrannical hurdles. Now, I realize that it is a concept which is so much more complex, one that demands humanistic effort—something to constantly progress towards.

Dennis Peron must have thought so too. When he was petitioning for the passage of Prop 215, he had to have foreseen the inevitable consequence that stems from all medical institutions, the one topic that is being most debated right now throughout the nation: they make money. And then they pay taxes. Both business and government take advantage. It's to be expected, alas. But: it was a start. Now, 12 years later after its historic passage, Prop 215 has done something previously thought to be impossible. It has gradually allowed cannabis-sativa to reach an enormous amount of public acceptance.

Today, a far fewer amount of people look at it with such distain, and it has opened a door which might just tolerate full legalization. With this, along with grassroots movements that explore the detrimental effects of needless imprisonment, something extraordinary has occurred. The numbers are all there. The statistics are correct. It is unanimous: the people now realize the futility of the Drug War.

You've heard the old cliché: "My enemy's enemy is my friend." This ancient axiom applies here as well. And at some point it must be determined who exactly your enemy is. Is it the legislators and ideologues who keep pressing for tougher laws, or any single activist who wants to legalize it?

If your answer is neither, then I'll assume it is anyone who wishes to legalize only to tax, which hinders your "right" to grow and do as you please. The contrasting illustration you gave was bathtub gin (or any homemade alcohol). Well, in fact it is legal to brew your own booze—if under a certain amount. Do you believe that alcohol illegality is the top priority for our brave (brave?) men and women in blue? The answer is a reassuring no. Any form of legalization now will soon bring forth the same answer for this scenario.

There is good argument for taxation. Asking again, What will happen to all those armed gangsters who suddenly take to the street in a fit a boredom and anger, the ones who increase the quantity of meth sales? A better question: Who will fund the extra police forces needed to stop them? The State is broke. And to fix the damages precipitated by ridiculous laws might require a few extra dollars. At least temporally. Don't assume, either, that those higher taxes will lead to people buying from street dealers; no one buys illegal booze in large quantities, now do they?

Here in California, we do have a piece of legislation in the works that will alleviate a number of these growing problems. Tom Ammiano's Assembly Bill 390 is likely to come on the table again next year. And its passing into law will bring with it massive decriminalization, tax revenue needed to fight asinine, but dangerous, criminals. We need this Bruce, and I'll certainly appreciate it if you don't hinder this wonderful prospect.

The Drunken Activist

IT'S NOT EASY starting an essay when one is so intensely hung-over. Such is my current status. I feel like a zombie who's trying to type out his last will & testament. And to counteract the aches and pains, I pour enormous amounts of caffeine and yellow dye number 5 into my weakened body, just so I can stop my eyes from receding further into my skull. It's ugly stuff, but important matters demand strong perseverance.

My latest binge began yesterday when I went to a protest in downtown Los Angeles. WeAreChange Los Angeles was having its monthly meet-up, and started the New Year off right by hanging banners over the 101 Freeway at Hollywood Blvd. It seemed like fun, but there was just no way I could go through all of the trouble of getting over there and not indulge upon some of God's nectar; so before heading out, I went across the street to get some groceries: a 3-pack of Budweiser Light, gum, and rolling papers for my tobacco. I was set, almost.

The Metro once again proved itself a valuable ally in this so-called War of Ideas, and it managed to drop me off just two streets shy of my destination. If things didn't work out so well, I was sure the day's events would be made more tolerable with the beer. I'm usually not a Budweiser fan, but it was on sale, and worked properly enough. The hard part was drinking the shit in public. This is where, after admiring the turnout—over thirty people, I estimated—I ran across the street to a 7-Eleven, and promptly paid full price for an empty Big Gulp cup. Running around the back of the store, I popped open one of the cans. Then two. Then three. The dumpsters served me nicely and worked as great cover in this operation of alcoholism. *Now*, I was set.

I headed back before anyone noticed my disappearance. Many of the attendees were on the list, while others, like the homeless kids, or the motorcyclist who got sideswiped on the corner not long after I had arrived, were only there because they couldn't perform the proper maneuvers enabling them to leave.

That accident was a funny scene. Here I am discussing political issues with one of the other activists, and the next thing I hear is the screeching of tires, followed by a nasty crunch, then by several "thump, thump, thump's" as the poor sap's limbs played drums across the pavement. He got right up though—and I've therefore granted myself permission to laugh at it now.

We Truthers acted instinctively, tearing a page right out of Rahm Emanuel's book, taking full advantage of the crisis unfolding before our eyes. Ambulances, police cars, and—stalled traffic. The whole intent of the protest was getting a message out, and we seized the chance to informationalize the delayed commuters. I couldn't say for sure, but if I had to guess, I'd say our DVD hand-out tripled after this little incident. I sleep better knowing there's a more informed public in our streets. Thank God for incompetent LA drivers. Either: they're getting dumber, the traffic is getting worse, or the Truth Movement is growing so strong it's able to stop the average mundane dead in his or her tracks.

At some point during all this craziness, a gentleman came over with a camera and asked if I wanted to do an interview.

"Sure," I said, "but ask me a question first, just to get it started, ya know?"

"Fine. What made you come out today?"

"Well, I was bored." I answered honestly enough. "I didn't really have anything else to do." I told him. I immediately felt that a tinge of betrayal of my own emotions, and rebutted the statement, only to be followed by a series of sentences that conveyed my feelings with issues that I felt were encapsulating our country: the Federal Reserve, the farcical War on Drugs, and so on. Then he asked me the singular, blunt question, "Who's responsible for 9-11?"

Usually I hate this question. Or more accurately, I hate the response that is occasionally rebuked by people with an agenda. I answer honestly every time I'm asked it, but I feel like a Christian who's sitting in Church one day, and suddenly wonders if he's been misled his whole life.

"I don't know," I said. Then explained how I felt the independent research was alluding to the government's involvement. It wasn't impossible, and even if it weren't so, there is nothing wrong with demanding answers to those questions that never received any.

There is something eerie about a protest group that wants every one of its members to believe every single word they say. It doesn't' happen with my group, but it happens quite a bit in many other 9/11 activist organizations; like our "counterparts," the so-called "no-planers." They feel that anyone who thinks planes *didn't* hit the towers are a disgrace to the Movement. People like that want your mind. And will take your body if there's enough room for it. Just check out L. Ron Hubbard. The datum that "the best way to make money is to start a religion" is widely rumored to have come from his mouth. Even if he didn't say it, the credence is found in the whispered insistence that a giant space dragon named Xenu brought life to this planet 75 million years ago. Even with language like that, Xenu can't go two rounds when it comes to "The Church." I mean to say, how many reports do I have to read about former Nazi's occupying the Vatican? All these institutions, once organized and heavily populated, will betray their original purpose. Guaranteed.

After about three solid hours' worth of protesting, we packed up our bags and headed over to a local billiards room right down the street. I was starting to sober up at this time, and wasn't sure if I had enough money to pay for more booze. Still, I went inside the establishment.

It was a nice place, with about a dozen tables, 3-4 parties shooting sloppily on them, and a good, solid 30 foot bar. Naturally, I headed on over, dug into my jeans, and pulled out $2.75; just a quarter shy of the lowest priced drink available— three bucks even, and that's at the end of Happy Hour.

"Short a quarter?" The cashier asked. He must have been sensitive to my situation. I reeked of beer, and he knew I was dry. "No problem. Go get at that man, he'll hook you up"—pointing to the barkeep. I went over, but as turned out, the barkeep was nowhere near as concerned for my problem as the other guy had been. Any time you ask a bartender "what can I get for three bucks?" you're going to get a scorned look, and probably a shitty drink. They know there won't be any tip, even after he went through all the trouble of making the damn thing up for you. I growled a quick "thanks," grabbed the whiskey and coke—not JD—and then wandered off to the other room where everybody was gathering.

They had all separated themselves between a large table, with surrounding chairs, and a smaller table adjacent to the soft couch that I quickly threw myself upon. I took a sip of my drink, and then took in the scenery. There were thirty or more people, all with similar interests in mind: the government is fucked up—in so many ways—and it must be changed, and not by some trumped up campaign mantra.

At times like this, I wonder if the Powers-That-Be know how many people are upset at their actions. Have they any idea that small packs of citizens, from all walks of life, are appalled at the direction our country is going? I'm sure they're well aware of it. And at the same time, I think they are actively ignoring us. Ah, well. It was just about time to go home. Strangely, I had flashback about life in prison. Going in nearly three and a half years earlier, six of those months I was out here, on the streets, and now, I was being active in a world I felt was going astray. "Damnit" I thought to myself, "tomorrow I got an appointment with the court-ordered shrink." I headed back to the train station, crawled onto an empty seat, and watched as downtown Los Angeles faded into a blur of bright lights.

I woke up the following morning positive that I was a new rank and file member of the *undead*. That somehow my body resuscitated itself in the middle of the night; perhaps lightning or something else had jolted my brain into activity.

I began remembering the incidents of the previous day: protests, drinks, porn; not necessarily in that order. I recalled securing an interview with one of the WeAreChange Members, a well-informed guy by the name of Jeremy. I need the story for my next article, and I think—or had thought—that I'd called the editor in the middle of the night, and asked him about it. Again, *I think* he agreed. And even if he hadn't, I'll just presume that he did and write the thing up anyways.

On the way over to the parole office, I started taking wallet-notes of the questions I had in mine. Half-hour later, I walked in, signed in at the counter, took a deep breath, and sat down on an ugly green chair—all while making sure to avoid eye contact with everyone else in the room. My ignoring them didn't quite work, however, and then those ridiculous conversations, so often overheard in places like this, we're again present today.

"Hey homes', I saw your homie Crazy up in Chino," one of them said. "Yeah? Is he over there on east yard?" the other replied.

"Nah, he got into a fight. Took him to the hole."

As impossible as it might seem, discussions like this will go on for hours; new names, places, and circumstances in every sentence. I've been out for almost six months now, and I still can't escape this dreaded atmosphere. Grown men playing "house" with the state penitentiary.

Luckily, my shrink came and collected me pretty quickly, ushering me off into some back room so we could begin our own "discussion." I'm not sure which conversation I'd rather be in the company of: the gangbangers who are enamored with prison, which I don't have to participate in, or the ones I have with my shrink, who is a paid agent of the insidious overseeing organization—the Prison Guards Union.

"How are you?" she asks.

"Good."

"What's been going on?"

She's always very friendly. And at this point, I've come to accept that this is just something I have to do in order to get off parole.

"Well," I say, "I just attended a protest yesterday in LA."

"Really? What was the protest for?"

"We're asking for a new investigation into the September 11th attacks."

She looked at me with her typical narrow-eyed suspicion. It's almost warranted; most of our meetings are all about me bashing our government and its officials, and since I did burn down one of those buildings, she has an obligation to keep an eye on my intentions. I hated that fact the first few months, but now I have come to accept it as a perfectly necessary function in a perfectly defective society.

"Why are you asking for a new investigation? What's wrong with the one we have?" She asks the question like she's supposed to, as a psychologist paid to make the subject—me—appear to be what I am: guilty of everything, inept with regards to common sense, and void of all moral standards.

I answer anyways, immaculately confident in my beliefs. "Actually, there's an overwhelming amount of evidence that points to government complicity. Why were those planes allowed to stay in the air for so long? Why did the commissioners come out and tell us the investigation was compromised? Why was the investigation halted for so long?" Valid points for any rational person. And definitely something that deserves attention when it's concerning the biggest terrorist attack in our nation's history.

"You know, I talk to people who share those kinds of beliefs," she tells me.

"Do you believe any of it?" I ask, hoping she'll show a sign of humanity and say "yes."

"It's not that I don't believe it. It's just. I don't know... *it's heavy*."

"Of course it is. But it's important," I proclaim dramatically. "And it's not crazy like you might think."

"What makes you think I think it's crazy?"

"I know that I'm the specimen in here. I'm the one who gets analyzed. Having a belief that the Government was involved in these sorts of activities...it fuels people like you who are paid to analyze people like me, who is obviously in here for something already questionable...or altogether deplorable."

She looked at me again with her narrow-eyes. Our conversations are like this every time we get together. It's a mental chessboard. Sometimes she traps me; sometimes I trap her. But it hones my argumentation, which is why I enjoy going. I found my answer. I'd rather have conversations with her. At the end of the meetings, we both realize that this is only practical. We won't be friends when this is done; she won't be going to any of the protests, and I won't be writing her any letters.

Then she threw the bombshell at me: "Don't you think that your fellow protestors might enjoy learning about what you did to get in prison?"

She wasn't just hitting a low-blow; she was using my balls as a speed-bag. There are a lot of things that upset me, but when it comes to the participation of American Democracy, I simply cannot stand the criticism. It feels personal. And not only for me, but for the ones who created this nation. Dissention is supposed to be the greatest form of patriotism. These days, it seems like the

United States public has turned into a society of lemmings, and even though *FOX News* thinks the Truth Movement, or the "Birthers"—or even people who believe that Eisenhower had routine meetings with gray aliens—are all crazies, we are supposed to get out there and speak our minds. There's nothing radical about it. *Damnit.* As I explained that concept to her, I subtlety made gestures that the meeting was over.

My shrink gave me all the usual 'good-byes' and whatnot. I made my way back home. Along the way, I continued my notes.

And wondered aloud, kicking an empty soda can:

> *Why is it so damn difficult to make a change in this world?*

Crisis in Copenhagen: A Non-Tiger Woods Story

EVER SINCE LORD Christopher Monckton came out of the woodworks a few months ago warning everybody about a "global treaty" rumored to be signed at the Copenhagen Meeting, I've been stuck on the matter, eagerly waiting for the next piece of information I could get my eyes on. Monckton insists that Global Warming is the greatest hoax ever perpetrated by elitist propaganda, and is leading us straight towards Global Government.

But damn it, how do the Elites always get so lucky? Every time there's a major step taken towards the Global Empire, down goes the celebrity on a drug overdose, or in this most recent case, an outstanding case of adultery. It seems our celebrity-obsessed society has a reflexive impulse to transfix itself on the question of, "What happens next to Tiger?"

Right now, as I type this, 190 nations from around the world are convening (or are ending the meeting) to find the solution of man-made Climate Change. Their much-rumored idea: an updated treaty—akin to the Kyoto Protocols—that will forever bind the industrial world to an obligatory global cap and trade system.

I've been waking up every morning in hope that the mainstream media will have Monckton on, or be pressuring

Robert Gibbs about Obama's tentative, illegal, and unconstitutional signature in Denmark—effectively rendering our sovereignty useless. I go berserk when I see that the story of the day is more "breaking news" about Tiger—usually something heard the day before. But I'll omit the rest of my rant about the incompetent American public from my last draft, and stick to the issue.

The background is scarcely needed; most of the world's population has been sold on it hook, line, and sinker. Global Warming is the modern two-pronged propaganda attack on critical thinking, right along with the farcical "War on Terror." It's pretty simple too: all you have to do is churn out some pictures of melting icebergs and frowning polar bears, and the masses will give their heart and soul to the Climate Change Agenda. If there's even a doubt, they'll be reminded by the subliminal mindfuck of a discreet melting ice cube, and immediately convince themselves once again that Al Gore was right all along. This is understandable. Saving the environment is not by itself a bad thing. In fact, it shows a little bit of sensitivity on behalf of our species—not always a common thing.

However, if we discern the events leading up to these events, and how the scientific contrarians are protesting against the Climate Myth, we might come to an avenue not usually seen by the public eye. It's the avenue that has Al Gore, George Soros, and Maurice Strong making billions of dollars while industrially developing countries are plunged further into debt, all while obeying a stronger, more centralized authority.

You see, Gore helped create Generation Investment Management, a global investment firm expected to make billions off the Global Warming Scare. The scam almost slaps you in the face: the bastards first promote the death of our world, and then we switch on the Cap & Trade system, and suddenly the industries are giving money to international establishments like the IMF, who then give those funds to businesses investing in solar and wind power. Along the way, loans are given to developing nations in compensation for our destroying their economies—and I did say *loaned*. When the interest of the loan is requested, and the nations can't pay up, then comes the pound of flesh: a U.N. vote, resources for cheap, and other such demands. This is the scam of scams.

Lucky for us, the scam is as obvious as that fucking pink elephant in the room, and there's no way they can deny it any longer. George Soros—that great humanitarian—is now asking for a new "executive body" to regulate these policies, just as United Nations Secretary General Ban Ki-moon openly predicts that the final Treaty of Global Governance will be signed next year. And even the first President of Europe, Herman Van Rompuy, is saying that this conference is "another step towards the global management of our planet."

Let us not forget that Lord Monckton was an advisor for former British Prime Minister Margaret Thatcher. For a long time now it has been whispered in the conspiracy community that the "Iron Lady" was removed from office for her refusal to join the European Union. If it's true—and I'm in no way confirming that it is—it would give Monckton a bit more credence, who would have witnessed, and protested, a major grab for more centralization thirty years back. For this, he would have no other agenda except to stop what he sincerely believed to be wrong. You can even tell he's genuine by the way his eyes protrude two inches out of his skull—the man is serious!

Furthermore, Monckton acts as the prominent Climate Change Debunker, insisting that temperatures have not risen at all in the last fifteen years. It might be easy to dismiss one person, but how about the 31,000 scientists—in this nation alone—that have raised their voice and dissented at the very idea of man-made Global Warming? John Coleman, founder of the *Weather Channel*, actually wants to sue Gore for all his lies.

More evidence of this scandal comes from the recent

disclosure at the Climate Research Unit in England, in which thousands of emails were hacked by activist computer nerds. These emails confirmed the conspiracy in front of our eyes, with the center's lead man, Phil Jones, collaborating with his fellow "scientists" to distort, alter, destroy, or otherwise manipulate certain information that would contradict their version of the story. The appropriately called "ClimateGate" is the biggest political tale since Clinton got a blowjob in the Oval Office. And if you don't know about it, then I don't know what to say except a rhetorical, albeit cynical, "why the hell not?"

But, just for the sake of critical thinking, let's assume for a minute that this whole thing is true: The earth's temperatures are rising, and the main culprits are carbon dioxide (CO_2), methane, and nitrous oxide...man made. We use these gases to fuel our civilization, and our entire structure has been based around the disregard of any externalities. Dennis Kucinich would then be right when he pointed out the correlation between "global warming" and "global warring." When we commit ourselves to the Wars for Oil, the war against alternative resources, the ignorance of putting the issues on the table only under the conditions set by Gore and Soros, we commit ourselves to a conversation about "Global Warming"—whether we believe in the notion or not.

Maybe our economies need to start utilizing other resources, before oil runs out, or we give too much to these barbaric Islamic Nations. It's long past time. For instance, we can grow hemp, which can be used to base our plastic, make paper, and weave fabric, and, most importantly, we can start phasing out of this addiction to petroleum with more investment in wind, solar, and ethanol. If we don't, then all we're doing is committing ourselves to more wars, and more problems. For Christ's sake, even if we disprove Climate Change, we cannot rely on petroleum and natural gas to run our engines forever. That means more money to dictatorial nations and Islamic barbarians, who have their heads so far up their theocratic asses they don't remember what extremists they funded last week. But like I said, the externalities have been disregarded in this world. And every time there's an explosion somewhere in the Middle East, we feel the repercussions of our petroleum addiction.

But we cannot rely on Al Gore, who has an obvious conflict of interest with the rest of the world, mostly because who else is making billions from jetting around it—using twenty times more carbon than the average person—while refusing to speak with the press? Watch the scumbag as he shows up at a book signing or some other event; before you can even ask one question about his money-making or offer contrary evidence, he is whisked away by Dark Suits and thrown into a speeding limo. Gore is a vile human being, "A man without a country," as Alex Jones said. He has no loyalty to anything except his bank account. He is the parasite, not the other way around. He should be ridiculed in such a way that would leave him broke and homeless, leaving him on a street corner begging for change.

Alas, I feel it won't happen. Instead we we'll be the ones who'll be hung upside down while our lives and welfare are shaken loose from our hearts and pockets. I think a ballot measure is in order, one that would allow a tax increase consensual and consistent with a democratic government, which would invest much more into building wind farms and solar panels. It would put millions back to work, make us energy independent, and set a good example for the rest of the world. As long as the work and the revenue stays here with hard-working Americans, and not into the hands of scumbag elitists like Al Gore and George Soros, I believe we can do it.

But it must be done quickly, as Monckton is warning that the globalists are in the final stages of creating the nucleus needed to grow a Global Government. It might even be worse than that, as it's now being said that the Era of Peak Oil is well on its way—which would suddenly put a halt to our Civilization.

A Tombstone for the Empire

THIRTY THOUSAND MORE troops. Nobody should be surprised. Instead, well enough expected. This One Party State has only further solidified that adage with Obama's recent decision of more deployments, keeping the Military Industrial Complex, in which this country strives, alive and well. At least our President didn't lie; he did openly state on the campaign that he planned on deploying more soldiers over to Afghanistan. But still, I couldn't get past the announcement; it seemed like a terrible thing to do.

It seemed like such a monumental event—like something out of Lyndon Johnson's own mouth—that I became compelled to attend an antiwar protest in Beverly Hills the other day.

As I traversed through the dark corridors of LA's Metro System, I looked at all the poor and impoverished people; average people, working long hours just to eat, but the all while paying their dues to this Empire. It sickened me in a way I couldn't quite jot down.

At 7:30 P.M. I arrived at the federal building on Wilshire Blvd, almost two hours late. Pouring sweat due to MapQuest's wrong directions, I suddenly came into view of the protest: a mob of demonstrators, picketers, pamphlet distributors, security guards, reporters & T.V. crews, and—never being a real protest without them—angry protesters shouting anti-war slogans into a megaphone.

"Hey, Obama, we say no, the occupations got to go!"

Shuffling my way through the crowd of about a hundred or so, I had little (although not entirely absent) interest in offering my own opinion on the matter. Instead, I was more curious in the participants' reasons, and if they coincided with my own.

After taking a few pictures, I eventually grabbed the backpack of a tall, dirty-looking man by the name of "Jingles" and insisted an interview. "We should dismantle the White House!" he said. When I asked what to replace it with, he suggested "common sense" individuals like Dennis Kucinich, who know what the people want. "We're the most hated country in the world. All we do is police people. That's why these extremists hate us."

Sounded right. But when I asked Jingles about the possibility of Nine-Eleven being an inside job, he sharply responded: "Hell no, those people are a cult." I quarterly agreed, but when he started going into his vegan regimen, and how the animals should be set free and granted driver licenses, I decided it was best to move on. The whole contradictory statement about "being natural" but "against" marijuana legalization also left a bad taste in my mouth.

Attempting to be a real journalist, I tried to get the opinion of even the other reporters. The best I got was the cameraman of *Telemundo*. He told me that the war was wrong and insisted that religion is the main problem. "More people in school, less people out killing," he said.

The most interesting conversation of the night, however, came right after I asked a man in a dark suit and tie if he was with the CIA. He was a solemn-looking gentleman, one whose eyes glowed with a rage that even I couldn't touch. I followed him over to another Vietnam era gentleman, this one wearing a tie dye T-shirt and selling anti-war DVD's. I'm not quite sure how it happened, but somehow that spontaneous encounter turned into one of the most interesting I'd seen since I started attending local protests.

"When I came back, I had people spitting at me, calling me a baby killer. I literally had shit thrown in my face," the suit and tie man said. The anti-warrior, a black man named Clay, retracted, and told him coldly that at that time he was protesting against the war. "I would have rather gone to prison," he said.

Suit and tie stared back at him: "And that was your choice, but when I saw my friends lying dead next to me, I felt it was because you weren't there to take the bullet for them."

When there seemed to be a break in the heated exchange, I tried to interject, asking the reason—that fundamental one—*why?* The man in the suit and tie walked off. Coming from an era in which killing and dying was demanded from your country, he probably didn't want to have some punk know-it-all-kid offer any inquiries, let alone insight.

That left me with Clay, who described this as the "new Cold War," but with the labeling "The War on Terror." "It's a pimple on the ass of that threat," referring to the hostility between the West and the East, "when we had thousands of Nukes pointed and ready to fire at each other."

As I wandered off again, I sort of engraved that image in my mind: two men, one wondering why the other wasn't there to die with him, the other wondering why he had to die at all.

What I really wanted was an interview with the federal buildings' guards. It was important to get a full picture—so I chose those closest to the government. As I approached two burly looking men, I asked if they would answer a couple questions.

"I can't give any interviews," one of them said plainly. "You got your little protesters out here, go ask them," the other said with a tone of condescension. Convinced that he was paid extra to keep his opinions to himself, I gave up asking.

Finally, I heard what I was looking for, from a young man named Ali. He told me that the threat of Muslim Extremists was marginal, but that our occupation was only going to escalate the threat. He also said that the United States actually helped create the Taliban, and supported the repression that ensued.

This is when I decided to verbalize my agreement.

Zbigniew Brzezinski, Council on Foreign Relations member, Co-Founder of the Trilateral Commission, Security Adviser to the Carter and Bush Senior regimes, and top-level global elitist, is on record as stating that the U.S. instigated the Soviet Union into invading Afghanistan back in 1979. Thereafter, we directly and knowingly gave funds and artillery to Pakistan and Saudi Arabia, who in turn funded the Mujahedeen, who…wait for it…eventually turned their Islamic "Freedom-Fighting" prowess into what we now know as the Taliban.

"Zbig" was once quoted as saying:

> What is most important to the history of the world? The Taliban or the collapse of the Soviet Empire? Some stirred-up Moslems or the liberation of Central Europe and the end of the cold war?

Nothing, I guess—maybe except to those who are now calling for more war, and those who are dying in that war. It could be said that the Soviet Union had more of a concern with economics, and thus, more open to diplomatic relations. The radicals we fight now are religious based, and only open to discussion with Allah, who await that conversation once they have successfully suicided themselves and taken with them a bunch of innocent people.

As you might have guessed, the support didn't stop there. In the mid 90's when petro-giant UNOCAL coveted that precious Caspian oil, it began working on a 4.5 billion dollar pipeline. This was helped along by Uncle Sam, who was willing to spare no expense in accommodating those admirable freedom-loving Taliban members, providing arms and supplies to them while they were fighting the Tajik Northern Alliance. Ole' Sam also chose to forgive them while they racked up their human rights violations.

We heard echoes of "law & order" as the compliment to

American propaganda, but in the end the atrocities committed by the Muslim monsters were too severe to sustain a believable deception, and, with a devastating blow coming from democracy, mass protest shut the negotiations down.

But little things like uncooperative killers don't faze the U.S., and Washington drew up the war plans. It's almost common knowledge now that the Neo-Conservative think tank, *Project for the New American Century*, was obsessed with Iraq from its beginning and wanted the removal of Saddam Hussein. The authors would send letters to former President Bill Clinton's office in an effort to start the military offensive. Most striking of all was that the Project stated that it required an event exactly like Pearl Harbor in order to carry forth successfully.

And while Nine-Eleven Truth didn't get much credit at the protest, it can be said that the Event was exploited, and used as a mechanism by the Bush Jr. Regime as an on-the-whim declaration of war. We can forget the weapons of mass destruction claim and use that history lesson in remembrance of how sadistic and inhumane regimes, like Bush Junior's, can manipulate nations into wars, all while making jokes about "misplaced WMD's" in the dining hall. The fat-cat elites laugh as the soldiers die. But no laughter could be heard out here tonight.

Jason Douglas at 411Mania.com brought up two very good points in a recent blog. The first being a question: What if we hadn't invaded 8 years ago? Would we still be sending in more troops?

The second was more of a speculation, one that I'm inclined to think about: at this past presidential dinner, two uninvited guests made their way into the White House, getting within arm's length of Barack Obama, just days before his much anticipated announcement. Was it a: "Don't fuck this up, Mr. President?"

Because the days are over when the Military Industrial Complex needed Lucifer's Lieutenant, Dick Cheney, to pop up out of nowhere and pronounce something about terrorists, and how we have to go after them—right before correcting one of Little Bush's blunders.

Now we have Joe Biden, another veteran of the Senate and a long-time member of the CFR. He manages to stay out of the spotlight most of the time. He's also one of the select few who puts his hand up our President's ass and make him do a song and dance about policy.

The problem is that the policy is always the same: war, corruption, and neo-colonialism; the only thing that changes is the methodology that enables the tyranny to take place.

Bush, sad and blunt as it is to say, was lucky to have intercepted all that prior knowledge of September 11th, thus stopping any possible hindrances to the Agenda. It was that moment that granted him immediate justification to go around the world and bomb whoever the hell he wanted.

What happens today when the American public has no desire for more war? Well, as it happened during the Cold War, you have to manufacture support. This is where, if one discerns the smallest infractions, you can find the subtlest scenarios of "point the finger at the terrorists." The Fort Hood killer, Nidal Malik Hasan, was a perfect example: six months before the shooting, he was put on an FBI watchlist for shouting anti-American, Islamofascist epitaphs. He remained on the list all the way up until that day. Or who can forget any of the countless "reports" of "extremist uprisings," or whatever they're calling it these days?

Not a full-blown tower falling down in Times Square, because the modern American just wouldn't accept another "false flag attack," thanks to the Truth Movement and other activist groups. Now, we get the most arcane illustrations of who the enemy is, or who he is supposed to be. But we know the threat is minimal when even *FOX News* is reporting on the mere one-hundred al Qaeda members in the country; the rest are in Pakistan or somewhere else.

Then, and only then, the deck is stacked, and off we go to

war. But we can't sustain this Empire for much longer. And we might just be venturing into our doom. After all, Afghanistan is called the Graveyard of Empires.

Alexander the Great, the Roman Empire, Genghis Khan, the British Empire, and of course the Soviet Union, have all met their match in that desolate wasteland. The taxpayers will be responsible for selling Uncle Sam his machine gun and accompanying shovel, as this one is bound to be a doozy.

If this is to be the end of the American Empire, I'm glad I participated when its dissenters tried to warn against it.

Race and Power in the American Empire

IN HIS BOOK *The World is a Ghetto,* Howard Winant proposes that racial bondage was never eliminated after its official abolishment in the 19th Century. Rather, Winant suggests that it was simply phased out, and restructured into a different form: labor.

> *The destruction of slavery thus signified both that systems of mass labor would have to be created, and that reform of the extractive and agricultural economies that characterized colonies would have to be undertaken such that the territories could maintain their trade-based linkages to the world economy.*

With the official signatures ending legal ownership of chattel slaves, the obvious next question became: what is the logic behind empire and class hierarchy?

Just like gravity it cannot be denied. White Superiority founded and ruled the United States of America for at least the first three centuries of its inception, and continued right up until the very recent years of the 21st Century. Prior to the year 1870's ratification of the Fifteenth Amendment—which made legal the right of minorities and former slaves to vote—the guarantees of even the basic tenets of liberty were only known to white settlers and male property owners. At the time, to suggest otherwise was akin to blasphemy in the Land of the Free. This tragic truism of America's history often-enough negates the fact that African American slaves were brought against their will to work for white owners.

But oppression often leads itself to another phenomenon: uprising. And with that, an inevitable separation and dislike of the former oppressor. At some point during this institutionalized inequality enforced by the white power structure, Rosa Parks must've decided that she should no longer have to give up her public bus seat for a different-colored passenger. At another, the editors of *Life Magazine* realized that baseball Hall-of-Famer Jackie Robinson would be an ideal first black face to put on their cover. Then, at other times, in different places, social revolutionaries like Marin Luther King Jr. and Malcolm X were organizing mass protests, in hope that someone would listen and change the status quo of segregation and accepted bigotry.

Someone eventually did.

And more than thirty years past the 1963 Civil Rights Act, which granted federally-administered rights to blacks, a 1997 taping of the Oprah Winfrey Show witnessed another, perhaps final, result of this racial struggle. Twenty-one year old professional golfer Tiger Woods declared himself on national television to be a "Cablinasian"—a configuration for the Caucasian, Black, Indian and Asian blood running through his veins. Tiger, fresh off a PGA Rookie of the Year Award and a $40 million dollar advertisement deal with Nike Shoes, was said by Oprah to be "America's Son," and argued by Hiram Perez, the Assistant professor at English Vassar College, to be...

> ...*a figure...that functions to rehabilitate the mulatto in order to announce the arrival of a new colorblind era in U.S. history.*

Although denounced by black commentators, Tiger could, without hesitation or misrepresentation, claim himself to be an authentic product of a culturally diverse democracy, which legally recognizes color-blindness and cannot honestly attribute his superb sportsmanship to any particular racial prowess.

Compare Tiger's example with that of basketball-great Michael Jordan, who's iconic "I want to be like Mike" advertisements for Gatorade rely not on color-blindness, but with the persistent propriety of race-embodiment. Whereas the white man might be stereotyped as a "slave-owner," "hick," or some other epitaph, the black man has consistently been perceived as a sort of god-like he-man with unknown, unlimited physical powers. Michael's Gatorade advertisements command a specific sense of racialization, and not always a friendly one. Perez says:

> Advertising featuring black celebrity athletes typically
> resists humanizing these athletes.

The stigma of racial superiority runs deep in the minds and hearts of insecure persons. Just as a small number of white youths still proclaim admiration of Adolf Hitler without even knowing the unspeakable crimes committed by the Third Reich, a number of black bible scholars attest that Jesus Christ was, in fact, a black man with "His head and his hairs that were white like wool, as white as snow." (Rev. 1:14) These recognitions of intangible occurrences only seek to prove the fluctuant and feeble mindsets residing in each and every one of us. They are, with little doubt, a systemic result of oppressed egos—not always liberties—and fall upon persons possessing an un-dealt with feeling of suppression and rage; usually blamed on another race or minority.

In an imaginary society where all the factors of class-based privilege are eliminated and disregarded for a new utopian world where every individual sees the next individual as a person of absolute equality—void of any unhanded condemnation—there would be no need for essays and discussions on the question of race. In my opinion, as a primitive species, this is impossible at best, and damaging to our way of life at its very worst. Using a mere 2 percent of our brain capacity, we are just barely aware that we are completely unaware of the extent of our avarice, jealousy, and pettiness, and any serious-minded effort to contradict the finite bounds of human empathy would likely result in catastrophe.

This question of social justice need not defeat itself. The best to hope for is a free society; one where law respects individual rights above any color and runs supreme above collective utopians seeking to fit square pegs into round holes. Being a racist or bigot would be permitted—just as many other unsavory vices are permitted, albeit not necessarily welcomed—as long as violence were punished to the maximum extent, and the citizens were keen enough to not allow any persons proclaiming such bombastic racism into public office. Far from being perfect, it would nevertheless emancipate ourselves from any superstitions we might have about forcing humankind to be smarter than it really is.

Coming back down to reality and the everyday nightmare of American foreign policies, one can find that citizenship and class-value is still found to have merit as property and power. Unlike America, whose racial struggle was mostly internal and self-sustaining, the South African Apartheid regime was given an enormous amount of support from external forces. Western forces. In 1948, the Reformed National Party, led by Dutch cleric Daniel Francois Malan, won the national election. This set off a regime that legally and militaristically enforced separation of blacks, from whites. Malan, making no apologies to the world for his policies, was a fervent anti-communist, and was thus granted appeasement by the West. His government also allowed large-scale production of uranium for U.S. sale.

By the mid-1950's, there were several prominent anti-apartheid movements, most notably the African National Congress (ANC). In 1955 they had drafted what would become known as the Freedom Charter—declaring to South Africa and the world that "our country...belongs to all those who live in it." These protestors also rejected racial identity as a basis for mobilization. This regime was allowed to continue under U.S. support up until 1994, when Prime Minister De Klerk began negotiations for its abolishment. In the 1980's the U.S. Congress passed the Anti-Apartheid Bill, which outlawed support for the regime, meeting President Ronald Reagan's veto.

Racial struggle is therefore a struggle from within the boundaries of states, which would otherwise, with time, vanquish if not being oppressed further from external pressure. For a minority group living inside of a nation-state as powerful as the U.S., it would be as difficult as it is to escape the confines of a socially dominant racial superior mindset.

Suggesting that the U.S. government's partnership with the South African regime was contributing to this oppression, at least economically and politically, it maintains that globalization seeks to exacerbate the obvious problem. For many centuries it was simply something one would grow up learning from one's father: a white five year old would not know the difference between morality and equality at the tender young age—it would just be taught to him by his racist father sitting at the dinner-room table who happens to work for Boeing Aircraft or somewhere else. For a young black youth sitting at a dinner table in South Africa, it would also not be obviously suggested that the dominant Apartheid regime was being helped along with its own partnership with the West. To repeat, this in itself suggests that globalization is carried out by military and economic forces, and is therefore something to be warned against.

In the 21st Century, in this brave new world of political correctness, it is taboo for a white man to use the word "nigger." This demonization of the use of racial epitaph is forgotten or left-alone whenever a black comedian is on stage telling jokes about "whitey."

Multiculturalism has morphed into a one-sided justification due to the undeniable fact of racial inequality in America. To his benefit, Tiger Woods truly embodies a person who cannot be prone to contempt by use of these words, and is "above" any honest attempt to do so.

A Magic Plant in the Post-Petroleum World

IN MICHAEL RUPPERT'S new film *Collapse*, the 30-year veteran of investigative reporting elaborates on his conviction that a Peak Oil Crisis is in its beginning stages. "I'm capitalizing on the phrase 'Peak Oil' to indicate that it's a historic event," he writes in his book, *Crossing the Rubicon*. Indeed, the backbone of our current civilization is based upon petroleum production. Everything from the car you drive, the factories assembling them, the food you eat, and even the buttons I'm typing on, are derived from, or made possible in large part, thanks to crude oil.

Ruppert's prediction is based on the fact that the current rapid growth of economies in China, India, and elsewhere, and the subsequent demand for more energy, will leave our planet depleted of oil in about twenty years. Added with the introduction of fiat money, those essentially worthless pieces of paper that are only valued with trust and circulation, a time might be emerging in which that trust must confront a dire situation, one that sees the earth's resources depleted. Here, an economy based on competitive growth will dramatically downsize, leaving us with no commodity qualified in weighing any real value.

If it's true that four billion years of compressed bio-mass have been consumed by the Industrial World in a 200-year period, then it would safe to assume that the human parasite has an addiction.

Unfortunately, that addiction is for the tarry and tricky nectar inside Mother Earth. It might not be renewable, and now, with the possible bleak reality that an entire civilization built on petro-products can perish with the depletion of that resource, society should definitely expect, at the very least, a dynamic change in the way in which current mechanics run the world; no more oil to base the plastics with, and no more fuel to support "across the board" global trade.

My own speculations with such a future incline me to postulate that the major industries will consolidate, with the middle class dying away, and the concept of globalization acting as Orwellian for "controlling the remaining resources." People with accumulated wealth will contend with people of accumulated numbers for the remaining remnants. On the outskirts, nomadic tribes will also consolidate the essentials: fresh water, rich forests, and crops producing a variety of herbs, as well as vital components needed to make fabrics.

In this Mad Max scenario, there is such a crop; one that is both plentiful and renewable, and it is unique in nature in that it provides all the necessary elements needed to make everything from medicine to clothing. That is: cannabis sativa—hemp; referred more specifically in this article as *industrialized hemp*. Prior to the criminalizing of the plant, hemp was a staple of the American economy. Bibles, maps, charts, and the first drafts of the Declaration of Independence, as well as the Constitution are among some of the more noticeable relics of the bygone era. Most ironically, Betsy Ross's original flag was also made from hemp.

Even prior to this, the plant had been used prominently in many cultures around the world for thousands of years. The oldest evidence of cannabis use we have, according to Wikipedia, comes from the Neolithic Yang-Shao culture some sixty-five hundred years ago. Clothes, fish nets, ropes, among many other things— you can be sure—we're made from hemp. Ninety percent of all ship sails—the cargo ships of yesterday—we're made possible thanks to the indispensable usage of that Magic Plant.

And because hemp is capable of full growth in four months, compared to the average tree, which takes twenty years to mature, it could practically replace wood fiber and help save our forests. In 1937, *Popular Mechanics* magazine labeled hemp as "The New Billion Dollar Crop." But today, it is as dead as the dodo in "All-Parts" U.S.A.

"Why?" You ask? Why don't we start growing it?

Well, it wasn't until those business tycoons of the early 1900's, William Randolph Hearst, a newspaper magnate, and Pierre Dupont, a chemical processing owner, who had become enraged at the thought of industrial hemp outsourcing their vast reserves of raw lumber and thus loosing grasp of their monopoly, that hemp became a target in a vicious campaign aimed at criminalizing the precious commodity. Hearst's brand of "Yellow Journalism" (smear jobs) set focus on the evils of "Marihuana"—an obscure word he learned in Mexico that associated hemp with its THC-potent cousin. In truth, hemp has only about 0.03 THC content, making the effort of getting high off it a ridiculous task. "Akin to trying to get drunk on nonalcoholic beer." Alas, hemp did become recognized as a drug, and while counter history remembers it as the "Hemp Conspiracy," society continues to suffer.

An average Google search of "hemp" will churn out about 323,000 hits. Mostly, it is plethora of activists advocating the repeal of all said laws and urging us to begin the widespread cultivation of it. Some sites, like HempOrganic.com, have articulated its efficiency and convenience. While others, like OilEmpire.com, have articles conveying the immediacy of production in order to "cushion the blow" of a Global Collapse.

According to Michael Klare, a respected energy analyst, the energy crunch will start in 2010, and will run indefinitely until a fully functioning transition is in place. He predicts, apocalyptically, that we will not have a suitable alternative in place by the time it happens.

But Jack Herer (RIP), the legendary cannabis activist, and author *The Emperor Wears No Clothes* (the pot-activist's bible), contests, and exclaims that hemp could possibly replace oil as a primary fuel. It is an incredible assertion to be sure, considering the Wars that have been waged in securing such a valuable resource, and the fact that no other American corporation has thought of this yet. However, countries like Russia, China, Germany, France, the UK, and our neighbor Canada (our main importer) have already caught on to the growing economic trend, and have been growing the stuff for quite a long while.

In any case, one notable demonstration of the Magic Plant's tenacity came in 1941, when Nazi supporter and elitist Henry Ford designed an experimental automobile with a plastic body composed of 70% cellulose fibers from hemp. It was found that the car could absorb blows 10 times as much pressure as steel without denting. This is what led Ford to "dream" of the day in which automobiles would be "grown from the soil." For this sole illustration, we should all be collectively ashamed of ourselves to have let hemp industrialization slip away. This is all coming at a time in which scientists are discovering little invisible bits of plastics in our oceans, and Global Warming mongers are crying hysterically about the melting ice caps. Compounded with basic logic—and the acknowledgment that our current System runs on the assumption that earth's resources are infinite—the question must be asked: *What if they aren't?*

Perhaps we are doomed to some sort of cataclysmic meltdown, or maybe my prediction will serve correctly and we'll see more mega industrial cities, like Hong Kong, which will forever compete with smaller communal-based societies, like the Amish. But whatever the outcome, we must be willing to utilize all available resources now in order to sustain any rudimentary form of society. Just like countless other essential commodities are grown, so should be this wonderful weed.

Bemoaning Haiti

IT'S IMPOSSIBLE TO call yourself human if you don't harbor some sort of sympathy for the Haitian people. And even if you couldn't find Haiti on as map (it's just east of Cuba), you would know by now that the nation of 9 million has recently experienced an Atlantic-sized earthquake, killing almost 50,000 people.

It's the biggest story in quite some time, surpassing the Late Night Wars and even California's onslaught of rain and hail. Anderson Cooper, Geraldo, and Amy Goodman have been reporting twenty-four hours a day, seven days a week, from the muddy pits of ground zero. From all the images we've seen, and for all we could have guessed, the nation looks like it literally broke in half.

Though, this is not the first travesty to occur in their rather unlucky history. Because, unfortunately, Haiti is another country, on a rather long list, that has been victimized by United States imperialism. Ever since 1915, when Woodrow Wilson sent 20,000 marines over to start the colonizing—"reinvigorating" Manifest Destiny—the country has been within Uncle Sam's vast influential circle. During this nearing century of control, the Haitian people have had to endure the brutal regimes of Jean Vilbrun Guillaume Sam, "Papa Doc" Duvalier, and Emmanuel "Toto" Constant, and lost countless thousands of loved ones during that period.

In 1990, the Haitian people finally grew tired of their

oppression, and managed to elect the populist priest Jean Bertrand Aristide. Like all predatory animals, the United States acted instinctively, and with the presumed order of King Bloodsucker George Herbert Walker Bush, the Texaco Oil Company funded a coup which overthrew the elected government—sending Aristide packing, and betraying our widely-touted mantra of democracy.

Four years later, in what is now seen as a heroic deed by our government, the Clinton Administration "allowed" Aristide to return; but only under the auspices of "warning" Emmanuel Constant, the dictator at the time, that he had better step aside. The irony is that when Haiti demanded Mr. Constant's extradition to face charges, the former founder of FRAPH (Front for the Advancement and Progress of Haiti), a paramilitary death squad, threatened to divulge his relationship with the CIA. Not long after, Clinton ordered the authorities to release him. They did, and Haiti has yet to prosecute the criminal, or see the documents seized during the political transition, which is presumed to further solidify their devious relationship. Ten years later, in 2004, Aristide was usurped yet again in the midst of political turmoil. He has repeatedly said that the United States and France are responsible.

The humiliation of Haiti only continued when Bill Clinton, now the husband of the Secretary of the State, was appointed special envoy in 2009. It all looked and sounded real moral and ethical, but the truth is much more disturbing: Clinton was yet another who participated in the exploitation of Haiti. While the Super-Rich continued privatizing the flour mills, the peasants who slaved away on the rice plantations witnessed their wages decline by nearly fifty percent.

There is no doubt that this exploitation at the hands of the Global Corporatocracy (a term coined by John Perkins) has allowed Haiti to become one of the poorest nations in the hemisphere, and in a much bigger perspective, these conditions could have very well manifested in the form of muddy huts without much steel framing. These revelations might just make one think differently the next time you turn on the nightly news.

After this devastating earthquake, we have those great humanitarians, Clinton and Bush, who have used the Corporate Media Machine to channel out fairy tales about their good deeds. It's Orwellian at the core, and sickeningly embarrassing for the poor slum dwellers that are so impoverished and uneducated that they don't know they're shaking hands with the ones who abused them.

So yes: as George Clooney, Samuel L. Jackson, and others run their "Hope for Haiti Now" charity—a very good deed, in my opinion—they should also be pressuring for the criminals to face their long overdue charges. Because: this is another glowing example of unchecked tyranny, taking place behind the closed fascist doors.

Obama's "Change" is Stagnant

OUR PRESIDENT HAS an uncanny ability to speak—he's a brilliant orator. After listening to his State of the Union address last month, I almost (almost!) saw him as that unique and groundbreaking politician whose campaign slogans assured us he would change course in this country.

I quickly came to my senses and realized that Obama has not implemented or promoted a single policy which would constitute the concept of change. Furthermore, and as I predicted back in '08, Obama has proved himself to be every bit as corrupt and imperialistic as that former toad who occupied the executive office. This is easily showcased in both domestic policy and foreign policy.

For the domestic aspect, let's start with his cabinet members. First, a simple fact: Every single president in our post-war history has filled their cabinet, to the brim, with members of a secretive organization. No conspiracy, folks. Without going into much detail about each one of them, ask yourselves if you've ever heard of the Council on Foreign Relations, or the Trilateral Commission, or the ultra-secretive Bilderbergers, who demand their attendees sign an oath swearing not to divulge the content of their meetings.

From Obama's cabinet, 9 of them are affiliated with the Bilderbergers, 10 from the CFR, and 5 from the Trilateral Commission; including the war criminal Henry Kissinger. Think about that the next time you elect somebody into office—do you want them meeting in secret, without public or journalistic scrutiny, for days at a time? What a great compliment to democracy.

Then there's the spending. That magic money making machine known as the Federal Reserve—powered by international bankers, and their figurehead, the counterfeiter Ben Bernanke—have recently been given an upgrade by Mr. Change: granted less accountability, and less transparency.

This endless credit card, used by our teenage-minded government, is widely rumored to be the end of us all. After all, the fake dollars printed to support our Empire overseas, or to prop up undeserving corporations, only devalue our currency, as inflationary policies and fractional reserve banking has devalued the American Dollar 95% since 1913. This leads us in head first into poverty, and all while expecting our children to pick up the tab in the future. Imagine the poor laborers who work all day and night to make a buck. The irony is that they are usually supporting their own children, who have to grow up with the expectation of paying off the enormous debt we are putting on them. Nope, no change here.

Let's try our Civil Rights. Namely: the Patriot Act. Not to frighten you, but reading this article could possibly get you onto a "black list." Read the details of the law yourself. By now everyone knows the powers wielded by the federal government. So imagine typing this truism! It's straight out of a totalitarian novel.

As it was not-so-widely reported back in Sept-Nov of last year, Obama has endorsed the extension of the Patriot Act, and all its draconian, Big Brother-like capacities. So here we are worried about the well-being of Guantanamo Bay inmates (with some merit), and yet we don't even care that our government is literally sitting inside of a cave, monitoring a huge computer, watching every move we make. Sigh.

Although there are other issues, I think I pretty much covered domestic.

Now, onto the foreign policy. True, Obama said on the campaign trail that he wanted to send more troops over to Afghanistan. But that isn't the change that most American's want. With the polls showing most Americans oppose our invasions, Obama continues to send over combat troops to eradicate the staggering one-hundred reported al Qaeda members from the country.

It's rather obvious: as with other Presidents and other wars, Mr. Change is fulfilling an alternative agenda. It's the same one that all empires have in mind: nation building. While our infrastructure erodes and decays over here at home, leaving us with potholes in our streets, bridges collapsing on our freeways—not to mention the jobs not being utilized—our government continues to send more troops, spending more money in doing so. This accomplishes very little. We still have bases in 170 counties, each costing us billions every year to maintain.

Obama's propaganda slogans echoed far and wide in this country, resultant in the amazing voter turnout, and a truly historic election. But in the end, he is just like every other politician who gets into an authoritative position. The worst part is he uses his charisma and wit to make us obey, without question, the standards forced upon us by previous officials.

Sorry, no change here, folks.

Glenn Beck is a Reploid

TARGET STORES USUALLY only carry books that have made it onto the New York Times bestseller list. All around the world, protruding out of one of these shelves, is Glenn Beck's master-crap *Arguing with Idiots*. The title itself oozes irony, seeing as Beck has proven himself time and time again as the crème de la crop of lame, ridiculous, yes-men imbeciles who have gone that extra mile in making sure nobody thinks outside the tube.

I mean—*Jesus!*—this guy has switched his position on so many issues, it's amazing that people still listen to him. The only reason I decided to drag myself out of bed to type this column is because he makes $23 million dollars a year pumping out mindless nonsense that nobody, not even himself, believes. And he's only been on the air for a couple years! So I think to myself, damn it: this propaganda agent must be stopped!

Let's look at his recent interview in *USA Weekend* magazine. When asked about Global Warming, Beck says: "You'd be an idiot not to notice the temperature change," then goes on to say that it's at least somewhat attributable to humans, which is a 180-degree turn from everything else he has said before. In the past, global warming debunking has been a focal point of Beck's show. Now he's singing a different tune, snuggling up to the polar bears along with Al Gore.

Same thing happened with the FEMA Camps, those clandestine secret prisons being set up for mass internment once martial law is fully implemented (or so they say). Beck first expressed concern and warned cryptically of an impending fascist agenda. "There's something going on in our country, that is, it ain't good," he says, "I can't debunk them." Somewhere between those comments and the next taping of his show, someone—who's presumed to have a helicopter parked on top the building—approached Glenn and told him that he needed to recant his statements. Beck then got off his knees, hired some guys from *Popular Mechanics*—who are always the experts on these subjects—and simultaneously dispelled the entire conspiracy, while throwing the rest of the believers, or non-believers, under the bus, branding them as "nut jobs" or "crazies" or some other epitaph.

We could on and on. The Bailout? Cut, lunatic, go!—"I think the bailout is the right thing to do…The $700 billion dollars that you're hearing about is not only necessary, it's also not nearly enough." As could have been predicted, Beck quickly switched his position once Obama got into office.

This behavior is commonplace. He's a shill; a Big Government, Big Corporation yes-man who takes his orders from someone of authority. His words are neo-conservative in nature, but to cover his bases, he calls himself a libertarian. And what does this so-called "libertarian" do to honest politicians, like Ron Paul—the only person in the political marketplace deserving of that title? He demonizes him and his supporters. His commanding officers in the FOX Deathstar demand that he repudiate everything Dr. Paul has to say, and he does just that; tagging them as "domestic terrorists" or that they're "taking revolution a bit too literally." I wonder if Janet Napolitano had sent that memo over to Rupert Murdoch's desk personally.

I have only one conclusion: Glenn Beck is a Reploid. That's right: he's a robot with sophisticated bio-flesh fashioned over him. Every morning he's taken out of the charging booth, located in the FOX basement, and is then programmed the entire show into his robotic brain.

That's why his policies and commentary contradict each other on a regular basis. It also explains why he's not at all embarrassed to get up there and do his little song and dance, Viking Helmet and all. Seriously, if he isn't a Reploid, then I don't know what to make of him. Doesn't he go home at night and look at himself in the mirror? Is there no shame? Is there no self-reflection? Does he ever think to himself: "Is this how corrupt cops feel when they sell their partners out for dope money?" Nah, he's a robot—there's no way anybody is that absent from the real world.

But isn't there a better name for androids like him? James Cameron had his T-whatever models. George Lucas had C-3PO. Of course there's Short-Circuit. Ah—I've got it!—we'll call him "Flip-Flop."

There's a name that perfectly suits his behavior. Every time he's on T.V. we can just say, "Oh that's just Flip-Flop, don't mind him, he's not real."

And it would be true.

K. M. Patten

Craig X. for Governor

COMING FROM THE front lines of the marijuana debate is the ever-exuberant Craig X. Rubin: lifelong Californian, UCLA graduate, mayoral candidate, and, most importantly, an ardent proponent of legalization. Born in the belly of the beast, Los Angeles, he has an unyielding compassion for the state he loves.

However, he is one of countless others who have witnessed a drastic decline in the standard of living once enjoyed over here on the west coast. In an email interview, he says:

> I love my city of LA, so I was concerned and still am about the future of my city. We need locally grown food, our own source of water and lower taxes to bring jobs.

This former guest star of the hit cable show "Weeds" (who agreed on Mary Louise Parker's sexiness, but emphasizes her professional talent) has the distinguished honor of contributing to the final lettering of Proposition 215, the bill that officially ratified California as the first state to recognize marijuana for medicinal purposes.

Since then he has run for mayor of Los Angeles, jumping on the platform of ending the War on Drugs.

> People are being arrested for medical marijuana on a daily basis. I was running a legal clinic and now face

years in prison because police officers with valid CA identification and a valid doctor's note joined our clinic.

In another interview, Craig raises the importance of public participation:

If half of the twenty million regular Americans who have expressed their disdain for the current marijuana prohibition gave the campaign one dollar each then we'll have the resources needed to beat Mayor Villaraigosa.

Craig says he also would support ending prohibition across the board, because it creates artificial profit and incentive. He warns:

However, totally unregulated big drug companies [would be] pushing drugs on children as they are already with psychological medications, so I am not totally against regulation of the market.

When asked if he would allow himself to be corrupted by the monolithic influence of the California Prison Guard's Union—the most steadfast opponent of legalization—he says:

No! I just spent seven days in LA's Twin Towers and I believe we torture people here in America. I saw firsthand what goes on in there and you are correct—it is a 'criminal college!'

Absolutely.

Craig, a father of seven, is also a fully ordained minister, who says he loves G-D first, but doesn't like to be called a Christian due to negative connotations. Instead, he likes to think of himself as a follower of the Messiah.

Most, not all, believe in a gentile named Jesus and worship him as a Babylonian sun god. I know the Jewish Messiah named Jeshua and follow him as a Jewish person would. I am very grateful that America is a Christian country founded on Christian principles, but I don't see that lasting much longer because people really don't know the Bible and their history.

He adds that some of the history lost includes passages in the Bible which indicate that the Tree of Life is actually the plant *cannabis sativa*.

The church he operates—appropriately called the "420 Temple"—was raided by federal agents back in October of 2009. He has since been convicted, but is free on permission from a judge, due to gross incompetence from the courts. He could still face prison time.

When it gets down to it, the forty-five year old activist might have inherited that rebellious gene from his own father, who is labeled by Craig as a "Kennedy Liberal and Reagan Conservative." Recalling his father's life, he tells me:

...he studied the aftermath of the Jewish Holocaust. His conclusion was that Jews allowed themselves to be run out of government and that Jewish people in the future needed to be politically minded and involved... My father always gave money to both sides however and taught my brother and I to look beyond the left/right or conservative/liberal paradigm. My interest in politics was twofold because one: I thought I could do a better job, and two: I was upset with how I had been treated by the government officials.

The Wrath of Shamu

THE TRAGIC DEATH of Dawn Brancheau, a forty year old whale trainer at SeaWorld in Orlando Florida, has the media hyperbole machine operating at full steam, looping the same footage for hours at a time and evoking massive amounts of sympathy from those of us unfortunate enough to be paying attention to the regular news, and especially for those who had already come to an obvious conclusion: animals don't write "Dear John" letters before they take someone's life.

Brancheau had been "interacting" with the giant orca, named Tikikum, when it jumped up, grabbed her by her ponytail, and began mercilessly tossing her around. She died from "multiple traumatic injuries," and hundreds of spectators—including many children—found themselves affirmed of what they had been told on the tour: they are, in fact, *killer whales*.

This is not an isolated incident. Killer whales have a history of...well...killing. Tikikum has had blood on his fins in the past, and is personally responsible for the death of at least two other people, one of which was found naked, laying on top of the 12,000 pound behemoth. Apparently, Tikikum just "wasn't that kind of Orca," and didn't take kindly to the drunkard's advances. *The Chicago Tribune* says that the whale is regularly kept in a separate tank, away from the others.

HNL also mentioned the death of at least 22 other people in the past thirty or so years. That's like taking a dead pool bet once a year on who's going to be murdered. Reports of the numbers of janitors murdered by this primitive creature are still pending. SeaWorld says that they are going to keep the whale, despite these findings.

As expected, the trainer-killing attractions have been temporarily shut down. But no worries, someone else's little boy or girl will be traumatized next week when they reopen. I'm almost willing to take the side of Bob Barker—a major animal rights activist, and perhaps an animal in his own right—as he urges the parks to release the whales into the ocean.

Detectives are now investigating this as a homicide. There's merit in that. If I left one of my young nephews with a pit bull, who is foaming at the mouth and sniffing around for something to eat, I could be in the same predicament. Although, just maybe, if put a sign outside the door, indicating some sort of canine attraction—at a $1.50 a pop—I might be able to offer a legitimate defense when the police come and haul my ass off to jail. Prosecutors are much more inclined to give you a break if you tell them there's a business license involved.

But, I think eventually the Florida dicks are going to come up with the same conclusion and dismiss the whole ordeal as a rare occurrence, citing the insurance claim Ms. Brancheau signed before jumping in the tank. Treating this as a homicide is the right thing to do; it just won't result in anything constructive.

Michael Harris, a professional in this sort of field, said in a recent interview:

> Anybody who knows these whales, in the wild, like our whales out in Puget Sound, know that these whales travel 100-miles a day.

He further went on to say:

> I mean, they're constantly on the move. You see them in

large groups, sometimes up to 100 whales at a time...and you see them in the tanks in SeaWorld or other marine parks and there are a handful of them at best.

What he's saying, for those not paying attention, is that these animals are constantly showing more and more psychotic behavior. And in the public arena, it's an obvious danger.

There's a reason why these professionals are warning against the domestication of wild animals. How many more people need to die? Or have their faces ripped off, as in the case of Charla Nash? How long will it be before we see lions being strapped up with leashes and taking a stroll around the block with their 70-year-old owner?

Little Kitty was so sweet; he would never harm anybody— not even after he clawed at my throat and gave me this here tracheotomy.

Jesse Ventura, Always Outspoken: Cannabis Times Interviews the Governor

YOU DON'T THINK your Government is willing to commit high crimes? Seriously don't believe there's ever been a cover-up somewhere? What about old fashioned political corruption or state treason? For Jesse Ventura, finding out these things is just the beginning.

The former Navy Seal, pro wrestler, mayor, and Governor of Minnesota—who might soon add the title of revolutionary to his resume—is currently on a book tour promoting his latest bestseller, *American Conspiracies*. Along with coauthor Dick Russell, Ventura digs deep into the clandestine activities of our government—and its policies—and concludes that the American people need to take back the Republic while they are still free enough to do so.

To achieve this, Ventura thinks we should:

- Eliminate the two-party political system;
- prosecute those involved with torture during the Bush Years;
- open the closed files on Kennedy, along with all the covert activities of the CIA;

- find out what really happened on September 11th, 2001;
- bring our troops home from around the world;

...and, not least of all:

- Put an end to this failed War on Drugs, starting with the full legalization of marijuana in the State of California. "It's the first step in stopping the murder and the carnage at the borders," he tells *Cannabis Times* in a recent interview.

Ventura is all-business, getting right to the point of how the failed War on Drugs costs us a great deal of money and effort for a policy he feels is unachievable, while at the same time financing dangerous cartels.

Cannabis Times: How was your Easter Holiday?
Jesse Ventura: Fine.
CT: I want you to reiterate your thoughts about the War on Drugs.
JV: Well, I think the War on Drugs is identical to the prohibition of alcohol. My mother felt that way before she passed away. It's identical to the prohibition of alcohol: the minute you prohibit something, it doesn't mean it's going away, it just means it will be run by a criminal enterprise. Which will, of course, essentially make the criminal enterprise very powerful and very wealthy, which is exactly what you're seeing happening in Mexico today with the Cartels....Being that I live there for six months out of the year I'm probably a little more aware of it than most people are up here.
CT: Do you feel the effects of it down by where you live?
JV: No. Most of its all by the borders. It's always a hundred

miles from the border—I live almost 800 miles down.

CT: Now, you did say you believe California should "Legalize Marijuana and pave the way." Is that correct?

JV: Absolutely, I mean, for people who even oppose the, well first of all, they should do it for a number of reasons: it would be the first step to stop the carnage at the border. I mean, in the last year 17,000 people have been killed on the United States/Mexico border, due to the War on Drugs. Now, those casualty rates are as big as Afghanistan or Iraq where we're supposedly at war.

CT: When you say "the Drug War" do you mean just marijuana, or are you talking about...

JV: Marijuana is to start. Marijuana is the beginning of the start of us finally taking our heads out of the sand and realizing that, again: prohibition does not work, it has never worked, it will never work, and until we take an adult viewpoint of it we'll continue to face the challenges that we face.

CT: You're including other drugs in this as well then: cocaine and heroin?

JV: Well, not initially, but my belief is that eventually they should be, but not sold openly. There's a difference. Marijuana to me should be treated identical to alcohol and tobacco.

CT: With the same exact regulations...

JV: Yup, same thing. In fact my best quote is this: Marijuana is to Rock 'n Roll what beer is to baseball. So imagine all the people at the ballpark and how they would feel if they banned beer.

CT: You'd have a riot.

JV: Yeah, but again—I don't want this taken out of context. I'm not saying they should put cocaine and heroin out at the 7-Eleven stores where people can buy it and use it. Of course not. My belief is that there should be some mechanism—a dispensary at a hospital, or whatever—where addicts like this can be treated. Because in my opinion, addiction should not be a criminal offense, it should be a medical problem. It should be treated medically, not criminally. Put it this way: you can be addicted to anything. If you could magically take away coffee tomorrow, you'd have murders over it. People who would need their coffee fix that bad in the morning—if somebody had coffee you would see acts of violence in which to get it. You can be addicted to anything. And to me, addiction is a medical problem, not a criminal problem.

CT: Do you see any bad repercussions from legalization?

JV: Well of course there will be. Naturally, there are bad repercussions of the legalization of tobacco and alcohol. There're going to be some negatives to it, but I think that the positives of it far outweigh the negatives.

Chapter 10 of Ventura's book is entitled *Your Government Dealing Drugs*.

CT: With stories of heroin being hidden in the cadavers of our deceased Vietnam Soldiers, to Reagan and Ollie North turning a blind eye to the Contra's cocaine trafficking, to the Middle East and the Afghan poppy fields—which takes place right under Uncle Sam's nose—you'd think there'd come a time in which we would prosecute the people responsible for these illegal activities.

JV: Well, you can't even get them to prosecute people who were involved in the recent torture. How are you going to get them to go back that far in time? You have to live in the Real World—the government does not police itself. Imagine how that works: if you're the government and you commit a crime, then you're expected to investigate the very crime you committed.

CT: I've heard you in interviews talk about hemp industrialization. How hemp can be used for clothing and medicine and paper. Why do you still think that hemp is still criminalized today?

JV: Well it was initially criminalized by William Randolph Hearst—the big paper guy—because he owned thousands of acres of timberland, and he used his money and influence in

Washington to get hemp declared illegal so that we would be forced to buy his timber to produce paper. So always follow the money—because when something like that happens, generally it's because somebody on the other side is going to be making huge [amounts of] money with the prohibition of whatever it is they're advocating.

Ventura recently said that he believes the United States should find a "middle ground" between Capitalism and Socialism, since each operating completely unfettered on its own has shown to fail.

CT: Would you support then, the nationalization of hemp farms so that corporations can't "buy the land" and just sit on it? Taking it under state control so we can industrialize a commodity?

JV: Oh, absolutely. One of the big problems where I saw it come into my life personally was, for about ten years I had a horse ranch. And we would have to use wood chips in the stalls of the horses, and hemp is ten times better. It absorbs the smells better, it absorbs the horse manure, and all the urine much better. And in Canada you can use it, but in the United States you can't. It's utterly absurd.

While the Governor admits he doesn't know much about the Prison Industrial Complex or of any conspiracies in place to keep these substances illegal, he says he's confident that he'd fare well in a debate with someone like Chris Matthews or even Christopher Hitchens if he had knowledge about the subject he was debating.

JV: [On Christopher Hitchens] He's the Atheist, right?

CT: He's an Anti-Theist. He's against the entire notion of a Higher Being.

JV: And that's fine. I'd probably join him on those thoughts a little bit. I'm very much with George Carlin now. I worship the

Sun. He says every morning it comes up gives it great credibility.

A laugh was had at the expense of religious Kool-Aid drinking zealots everywhere. Ventura says he was pleased to hear Obama include Atheists in his acceptance speech. "It was the first time ever I'd heard a President acknowledge, and actually make official, people who don't necessarily believe in God." He also believes the Government should be completely secular. As Governor of Minnesota, he won the National Reward for understanding the separation of Church and State.

JV: Why do you need the Government to tell you to pray? Pray all you want. You don't need the Government to tell you as an individual, "Okay, today is the day you pray." The Government has no business in that business. On the flip-side, if I were to declare "National Prayer Day," then at some point I'd have to declare a "Non-Prayer Day."

CT: What about the Ten Commandments in courthouses?

JV: Should not be there….to me, the Ten Commandments— remember, the majority of those Commandments are not even laws, they're just moral issues. If you could have "Thou shall not cheat" as a law, well then you could have three quarters of this country in jail…you have, "Honor your mother and father." Well, that's not a law; it's something good to do, but it's not a law. So why would you put up the Ten Commandments that are not laws?

On writing his book he says:

> *I found it an interesting book, because we took the side of the Conspiracy, and we came forward with that we felt was the strongest evidence to indicate the Conspiracy was real. I think that anyone who honestly reads my book will see that in all 14 chapters we make as good a case for the Conspiracy as the Government has made for their [own]*

Conspiracies. Because let's remember, theirs are just Conspiracy Theories also. Nothing the Government has [said] has been proven in the Court of Law.

JV: Let's take 9-11, alright?

CT: Okay.

JV: How can we convict someone before indicting them?

CT: Didn't they say, "We have proof that Bin Laden was responsible."?

JV: Why haven't they shown the proof in front of the Grand Jury then?

CT: Six of the ten commissioners came out and said the investigation was compromised.

JV: Exactly. Going back to that, why haven't they indicted Bin Laden for 9-11? They've had 8-9 years to do it...All an indictment is, is the government brings forth their evidence to a group of citizens—who are the Grand Jury—they present enough evidence that the Grand Jury says "there's enough meat on this bone, we'll issue an indictment for murder." Why haven't they done that? They offered no evidence whatsoever.

CT: How does that make you feel about the commentators—like Glenn Beck or Sean Hannity or someone who just takes the official word for granted?

JV: Well, they all do it. Don't just label the Right-Wingers. The Left-Wingers do it too...[Keith] Olbermann, Rachel Maddow—everyone just takes the government's story when it comes to the Conspiracy. You'll notice they'll challenge the government on anything else, but when it comes to any of these events, they're right in lock-step with the government.

Ventura also thinks that there's something "interesting" about people who will protest someone going to the doctor, but who won't protest going to war. "I find that bizarre." Even though he's covered under the Screen Actor's Guild, he says he's still not happy with his insurance. "They won't pay for things, and they won't give me things. The insurance companies run the health care. They tell you what you get, not doctors. They need to take it away from insurance companies."

CT: What do you think about ObamaCare?

JV: I don't know. We're more up in arms about someone [going to the doctor] than we are of sending more people to Afghanistan and more people to Iraq, and probably certainly Iran is in the near future. And we have no problem with that, I guess. Why do you think I live in Mexico?

CT: Why do you?

JV: For the weather, and also because it gives you a great perspective to view this country from the outside looking in, as opposed from the inside looking out.

CT: Do you think more people should do that?

JV: I wish everyone could. They'd get a different perspective of this country. They would find out that we have an ego that needs to be…reigned in a little bit. The point is this: why do have to spend so much on national defense?

CT: Half our budget goes to the Pentagon.

JV: Why do we have to do that…who is out to get us and what have we done? Who's after us? For what reason? Obviously we must have done something to incur this wrath.

CT: Do you think it could have been support for the Muslim extremists back in 80's, including Saddam Hussein?

JV: No, no—it's Corporate America going out into the world and exerting our will on the world. Let me put it to you this way: everywhere else it's called "terrorism," but when we do it it's called "foreign policy."

CT: Or defense.

JV: No, No—we've been practicing terrorism for over fifty years. The first one that comes to mind is our multiple attempts to assassinate Castro. Wouldn't you call that terrorism? They've burned the cane fields of Cuba; they've sunk ships in their harbor. They even have this Orlando Bosch character that blew up a Cuban civilian plane.

Bosch killed 73 people. He was pardoned by Bush Senior.

JV: Aren't those acts of terrorism? If it was done to us, we would call those terroristic acts.

CT: Do you believe we should have a National Health Care System?

JV: Well, the military has had it since World War II? If it's good enough for them, shouldn't it be good enough for you?

As for where Ventura gets his information, he says he reads. "I probably read about 45 books. I average about 15 a winter." Colonel Fletcher Prouty—the real Mr. X—is his latest read. "You learn how every war has been orchestrated since after World War II."

Then there's the educational system.

CT: Should we reform our textbooks and school curriculum?

JV: We need to start teaching the truth, instead of teaching the truth as American sees it. Or the truth that puts America in a good light. When in many of those occasions, we should not be in that light.

CT: All this being said, do you think there's a fringe element in the conspiracy of research? Like say people who say that no planes hit the Towers?

JV: Well of course there are. And that's one of the reasons it's easy to get away with it, because you end up lumping everybody together under one umbrella.

CT: How do you think Schwarzenegger has done as governor?

JV: I don't know. I don't live in California. I wouldn't be in a position to answer that at all. You're from out in California?

CT: Unfortunately, yes.

JV: That's fine, but I would like to appeal to all of you to please pass the marijuana vote this fall.

CT: We're trying.

JV: I've also offered—I don't know if anyone is going to take it up—but I've offered to come do public service announcements. It would also help you're tax situation too. Instead of spending money on it, you'd be getting money from it.

CT: You think we'd spend more on the negative repercussions of legalization? Like DUI's or health bills?

JV: No. Not even close. You'd make billions. If people would obey the rules, you'll have no problems. Do it in the privacy of your own home. Since you're not allowed to smoke anywhere in California, anyways. How do we put people in jail for crimes against themselves? That's what drug abuse is—a crime against yourself.

CT: What about violent crimes on PCP or something like that?

JV: Then prosecute for the crime. I don't care what someone takes, if they commit a robbery then prosecute them for a robbery. I don't give a damn what influenced them.

I took the liberty to offer my own services to Jesse's Show, *Conspiracy Theory*, which was renewed for another season. As for actually having us on as consultants, he said:

I don't know if we'll do one on [these subjects] or not.

Let's hope he does.

Kyleigh's Law is Draconian in Nature and Evil in Functionality

FORGET ABOUT THE Arizona Law, that one just signed into the books with Sherriff Arpaio's blood, which allows state troopers to determine on their own what "probable cause" means while they also demand your citizenship papers. First of all, it's not new: California's finest have been pulling people out of their vehicles for years without the proper constitutional merit. The practice is just making its rounds in today's Brave New World of "security before freedom."

Second, it doesn't come close to the invasiveness of New Jersey's new state-run baby-monitoring program, which has received far less attention. If you haven't heard, the Garden State has just granted Donna Weeks her long-ambitioned proposal: a universal parental system that requires new drivers to place an orange decal on the license plate of their vehicles. It's intended to make the job of locating delinquent teenagers easier for law enforcement.

The law comes after sixteen-year-old Kyleigh D'Alessio was killed in a car crash involving another teenager. Apparently, she was distracted by the other passengers in the car. Her mother, Ms. Weeks, then lobbied heavily for the legislation.

The basics of the lettering run something like this: $4.00 must be handed over for the decal; nighttime curfews will be rolled back to eleven o'clock—an hour earlier than before; only one passenger can ride with the underage driver unless a parent or guardian is present; and cell phone usage will be strictly prohibited, even with hands-free devices. The law applies for all new drivers under the age of 21.

What good will this do? Most things like this are ridiculous right there on the surface, while others have to be read fully to comprehend how dumb they are. For instance, it's not totally understood why parents and/or guardians must be in the vehicle while their under-aged children are driving—unless these parents are willing to jump out of a moving car when the teenager drives off into the opposite lane, or, are reflexive enough to grab the steering wheel in that same chance scenario, possibly increasing the potential for an accident anyways. It doesn't make much sense. Also: aren't you a legal adult at the age of 18? *And even 20 year olds, a month away from their birthday?* It's absurd at any angle.

Groups are already opposing this ridiculousness, calling it an infringement of personal liberty, as well as an insult to other, more vigilant parents, who didn't let their young son or daughter get in the car in the middle of probationary autoing. These outraged citizens organized on Facebook, where they asked for everyone—horny teens, junior gangbangers, and the elderly alike—to place the same decal on their vehicles. That way, the N.J. officers will spend many a wasteful hour harassing law-abiding citizens, only to have to let them go. This tactic is intended to divert enough energy to the point in which the ridiculous mandate will be repealed.

These Facebook pages also raise other concerns.

One page shows tattooed gangsters and murderers with the byline underneath: "These guys won't be required to put an orange sticker on their cars...But I will." Frighteningly logical; and logistical. Gregg Trauntmann, an attorney who tried to overturn the law—with no success—argued that those gangsters and child molesters (apologies for branding all criminals the same) will be more likely to target the teens late at night, as they are now being advertised like call girls in an *LA x-Press.* "Young and Alone," as it says on other Facebook pages already hip to that same sentiment.

While most people seem to be genuinely upset by this law, Ms. Weeks doesn't seem to understand. Fashioning herself as a modern day Joan of Arc or Ellen Ripley on a mission to save someone from something, somewhere, she says:

> *People just need to give it a chance…*

All she's really doing is ripping apart at our civil liberties. I'd love to see her mail box jammed with letters from angry civil rights activists, and then quietly repeating that same sad line.

Lamentations over the death of your daughter will not vindicate your grave injustices, Ms. Weeks—they simply will not. Who is the one that should be placed on trial here? Why do others pay the price for another mother's bad decision?

Maybe instead of legislating nonsense, they could try legislating parental vigilance. Since most laws passed these days gratuitously infringe on our freedoms, we don't have to worry about the family unit or individualism or common sense; we could just penalize parents whose children end up dead at 3 in the morning.

Ms. Weeks can step up and be the first candidate. When she gets done serving her prison sentence, she can help us understand why inexperienced drivers need not allow a car full of raucous passengers to distract one from the road. An accident, tragic and unfortunate as it is, has now led to the punishment of families all over the Garden State. A better lesson would be preferred over more legislation.

How long will it be then before these measures reach the law pages of every county, in every state, all around the country? One can only imagine. New York is already considering similar proposals, as is Alabama and Pennsylvania.

As for me, it makes no difference: California will soon perish and dissipate under the weight of its own stupidity.

I have no fear, like Trauntmann says when asked what he'll do.

> *I'd rather get the hell out of the State before it gets that bad.*

Sharp thinking, sir.

Sharp thinking, indeed.

Discussing High Anxiety, Alternative Medicine, and the Limp of Society with Dr. Gary Archer

I REMEMBER PACING up and down a five foot cell in the last three months, eagerly awaiting the day in which I would be released from prison. There's no fear known to man that can even come close to that sort of horror. The sheer, unrelenting panic of *what if they don't let me out?*

I did, however, make it out of that cesspool. And even though the trees seem greener and the skies bluer, the anxiety accumulated throughout my three-year tenure had reached its peak; society was still a monstrous thing to behold, and it was overwhelming for me.

It was somewhere around this time that my mother had mentioned an acupuncturist she had once seen named Gary Archer. "Acupuncture," I asked curiously, sure that it was something that only Asian cultures do, or perhaps middle-aged homemakers looking for a magic fountain of youth. But after a Google search, and the realization that my stress wasn't going to heal itself, I decided to give it a try.

Now, nearly six months after my first visit, and with my anxiety at an all-time low, Dr. Archer and I have become good friends. He always offers obligatory concern about my smoking and drinking; then checks my pulse; and then we begin a conversation regarding one of the many problems or mysteries of the world. This happens all the way up until he's stuck the last metal pin in my body.

Dr. Archer dispenses a sense of well-thought-out wisdom, and while we don't agree with who was responsible for 9-11 (it *was* the government!), I thought it long past time to have a proper interview with the man.

He was prepared, and immediately attacked me with a barrage of information that was so sincere and straightforward that I had to warn that it would most likely be paraphrased. "Fine," he said. Then told me to make sure my readers got the gist of it.

I asked him how he got started with Eastern medicine.

> *Back in the 1970's, Nixon tried a move in RealPolitiks. He tried to make a relationship with Communist China so as to make their neighbor, the U.S.S.R. (our Cold War enemy), feel alienated. During a dinner with Chinese diplomats, an American journalist, named James Reston, fell ill and had to be rushed to the hospital for an emergency appendectomy.*

He went on to explain how our neanderthalic politicians were amazed that the Eastern doctors were able to alleviate his pain using acupuncture.

From there, our society in the West began to import this practice. Schools propped up and a whole new generation of students were now learning something completely different. Gary Archer was one of them.

He had been in the business now for over thirty years, teaching at such schools as Samra, Royal, and currently at the Alhambra Medical University. As a Dean, he traveled extensively to China, Taiwan, and South Korea. "Not North Korea?" I wondered. "No, just South." He asked me if I heard about the evangelical kid who snuck into the North last week, trying to preach the Word of God to Kim Jong Il. "He'll make good target practice," I quipped. A hearty laugh was had at the expense of a puny dictator.

Dr. Archer then went on with some history.

> *Acupuncture is over 2,000 years old, and it is exclusive to the Chinese—no other culture came up with this idea. Then, when Mao Tse Tung came to power after WWII, he tried to purge the country of Chinese medicine.*

Luckily, due to the phenomenon known as the black market, it didn't last, and the doctors already trained in one practice couldn't be retrained for another. So the officials had to tolerate it.

Then we got down to the meat and potatoes—for Dr. Archer is a vicious opponent of Western medical practices.

> *While Western medical institutions know what surgical procedures are, the Chinese knew what energy is. Our body is a conduit in which numerous meridians thrive. When the energy runs smoothly, everything works.*

He went further with the philosophical:

> *The starting point is realizing that 'the One' created Two—known more commonly over here as the Yen & Yang—and when there's a balance of that Energy, everything works fine. In Chinese medicine, the goal is to find the One.*

He continued:

> *Over here, what do they do? You go to the doctor's office,*

> *and they ask you 'what's wrong?' Then they say 'you're*
> *fine' and give you some sort of pill, tell you to get out of*
> *here....completely sweeping the problem under the rug. In*
> *Chinese medicine, we study pathology. We study a*
> *continuous pattern of human behavior. When we see a*
> *person eating all sorts of disgusting foods and drinks, we*
> *see you running head-first into a wall. We try to say 'no,*
> *stop, come this way.*

He asked me what the number one selling over-the-counter drug was. "Aspirin...?" "Antacids," he said. "Americans eat so much crap. We don't care what happens to our stomachs."

Somewhere in the middle of the heated conveying of Truth, there was a breather, then he continued:

> *Look, what happens to overweight people: they get bigger,*
> *so their heart gets bigger—which is okay, because it's a*
> *muscle, but the valves aren't. So in twenty-thirty years*
> *you're on five different kinds of pharmaceuticals, and two*
> *of them are to suppress the other threes' side-effects.*

On a brief side-note of personal testimony: *He's right!* Look at the way we treat ourselves. We readily assume that the doctor knows everything that is wrong with us. We don't care to question and to wonder if the drugs they're giving us are good for us at all. Not to mention that the pharmaceutical companies are one of the main lobbyist groups in the country.

At this point we decided to gather my father, who I was sure was flirting with one of the cute receptionists in the lobby. As soon as we got in the office, Dr. Archer started back in, all but condemning the way in which we practice medicine in this country. He gave me an analogy:

> *In Western medicine, it's very hard to study—but very*

easy to practice. In Chinese medicine, it's very easy to study—but very difficult to practice.

He expounded:

In western medicine, one hundred people suffering from arthritis is one person—they all give you the same drug. In eastern medicine, one hundred people suffering from arthritis is one hundred people that need to be treated individually.

My pops then asked about Alzheimer's. He answered:

What we find in patients of Alzheimer's is an increased amount of aluminum.

Since our bodies do not produce that sort of metal naturally, I asked what we can do about it.

Don't you use aluminum to cook your food in? What about your deodorant? Check the label. Never use aluminum...with a capital 'N'!

He then brought us to our last point: What about the American public?

Fifty percent have now looked for natural medical cures.

He also suggested that we get the kids away from the computer screens; start doing some more exercise (while they're young), and give them healthier diets.

But I was frightened; now imagining all the people who are at the mercy of the Medical Industrial Complex, and all those unethical CEO's who make billions off of the public's bad health.

Dr. Archer, not helping my anxiety—the main reason I went to him—told us about a study in which they found so much estrogen in the water around Washington D.C., that male fish were actually producing eggs. Estrogen, of course, comes from birth control pills. Another study found enormous amounts of Prozac in water surrounding Texas. "Which the fish absorb; then, when you pop a can of tuna, you put right back in your body," he said.

And I love tuna. But those are horrific externalities that even the most serious libertarians, like me, need to consider. After our two-hour conversation left me wondering what was to come of our society, I asked him his opinion on whether or not the world was going to come to an end. "I don't think the world is going to end," he says, "I think it will continue to limp on as it always has."

My last question was about the use of medical marijuana.

> When we absolutely can't find a cure, we try to palliate
> that person. Marijuana is probably the least harmful out
> of the rest of them…but now, if you go to the doctor and
> tell them you have a tooth ache, it'll do.

That ended our interview, and as I walked outside, I looked at my father and said, "Well, nobody lives forever, I suppose."

Then I sparked up a cigarette.

K. M. Patten

Even Small Town Papers Censor the Facts

I'M NOT A great writer. I don't even think I'm average. As for my educational background: worse than you could imagine. Much worse. No sir, mine's pure conviction: it's the deterioration of our civil rights and the undemocratic processes of globalization that compel my penmanship. Then came last winter, and as I was fixing to do just that, an earthquake destroyed much of Haiti.

It was a time to consider others. But I had no money to give—my paycheck is probably less than theirs, anyway—so I decided to do my part by writing a little essay about the damage Haiti endured under United States Imperialism over the last 100 years or so. It would be scathing, and angry, but informative nonetheless, and important for everyone who thinks Bill Clinton's ambassadorship is an ethical career choice.

First pulling from Noam Chomsky's book *Failed States*, in which the intellectual explains the brutalization of Haiti at the hands of Uncle Sam, and then by playing Google detective (the only information outlet not yet censored), I managed to type a concise Haitian history of about seven hundred words.

The article was sent over to my local newspaper, the *San Gabriel Valley Examiner*. It's a small town rag that mostly deals with community events, budget reports, lost dogs, and a front-page column for the mayor. But: it also has three or four regular columns for the town's most astute commentators. There's a Right-to-Center-to-Left viewpoint on all sorts of subjects. "Why not an independent commentator"—like myself?

But, alas, my little town has been sold on the brand of conservatism they have these days: the "neo" branch. My definition of it: having questions for your government is a treacherous thing that should be held far away from. Fascism and corruption are the political realities that act as safeguards for the mainstream media.

Paranoia rung high for me after I had realized this, although once in a while I embrace that pseudo-sixth sense, and with a knee-jerk reaction, I assumed the role of vindicator. I knew what I was saying was at least 90 percent correct, and it was no worse than the fashion-show media we have on the *CNN*'s of the world. Also on my side was the fact that this paper doesn't have any Jesse Ventura's featured in it, so I hoped that increasingly popular angle might be appreciated on his community rag. It was probably a fifty-fifty shot.

Fortunately, the editor liked it, and his bossman gave permission to try me out with a fresh column. In good old fashioned black and white paper, my article "Bemoaning Haiti" was read—I guessed—by a couple thousand people. Not bad, and what writer doesn't like being in print?

Was it wrong to ask—is it immoral I mean?—to write about such matters? Even if it's ancient history? Is the morality such in our country that we can't even discuss basic facts? The real point: Did Woodrow Wilson not send the troops over in 1915? Was Aristide not overthrown in a U.S-backed coup? Did President Clinton refuse to declassify the documents showing the CIA's connection with F.A.R.C. leader Emmanuel Constant?

Inquiries of this magnitude are supposed to encompass the so-called "Watch Dog Media," a term, I fear, is all but lost in this country. I can at least pretend that I embody the novelistic gumshoe who puts his emotions and ideals on the sidelines while real facts and information come to the public light. With self-encouragement like that in the back of my head, I wrote another one, this time dealing with Obama's refusal to recant Bush-Era policies.

Again, nothing terribly wrong with the basic facts. Obama does have Bilderberger's, CFR members, and others swimming in his administration; he has continued the Patriot Act's eavesdropping capacities; and he has continued with these endless wars. All true, but still, being the pessimist that I am, I had to be surprised when my article was published for a second time. Two for two, and both of which I didn't think would happen at all.

That would be the very last one. I wouldn't know it until about a month later, when I sent in another article entitled: *A Small Study of Globalization and Indoctrination*. My column was dropped from the paper. Someone, somewhere, had decided that I was insane and therefore discarded. Ignorantly, still, I sent in my NWO article. The next morning I received a response from the editor:

> *I'm starting to have a problem with your articles…They're overly conspiratorial…Not everything on the internet is true.*

Then he quoted from a long-time reader who had written him an angry letter, condemning my viewpoints, labeling me as a conspiratorial nut job, and topping off his vitriol by calling me the "Mount Rushmore of Dribble." I was flattered, even when he said that my smartass smirk would "haunt him for weeks to come." What can I say?—I'm confident in my research, and besides, he couldn't last two minutes in a debate with me. Not even close.

Was it something I said? I doubt it; you can never have enough Bush-Bashing. And, as much as the eco-warriors won't admit it—and whatever you might say about the sciences (I don't know a damned thing, myself)—it's true: global tax requirements are the next step in the evolution of technology-based marketplaces. A region's industrial production leads to pollution, which—supposedly—leads to the Greenhouse Effect.

We're all then spoon-fed fear, starting with Bush Sr.'s creepy voice in his New World Order announcements of '90-91—and that we'll die of "foreign enemies," or sun radiation, or insecticidal aliens, or something else if we don't yield freedom and sovereignty over to the internationalists so that we can be protected. And so it is. Terrorists, Patriots, and Global Warming—oh brother! Once it's gone, it won't be coming back. Soon enough, the Banksters and the world's fascist governments will become One. Then, maybe, Jesus will return and things will get even more interesting.

Perhaps not everything I said was accurate. I did call Bush Senior the "King of the Bloodsuckers." He might be a lizard, or he might not be, but one thing is for certain: these Elitists are after global domination. It's not a mad plot from a James Bond movie, it's another natural occurrence of hegemony; first the town, and then the stars.

I have forgotten the preface for this story. Before I even submitted anything in, I sent over an inquiry/solicitation letter. The editor said, "I don't know what you are? Are you on the Right or Left?"

He was baffled.

He couldn't comprehend that I was an independent thinker. Isn't this always the problem? Americans are so divided with these terms. All of a sudden "I can't join your cause because my ideological brain tells me it's against what I believe in."

Intelligent creatures are supposed to question relevant facts. I replied to the editor the only way I could, telling him that I think for myself—weighing each issue on its merits. I'm pro-gun, anti-partial birth abortions, pro-drug law reform, anti-banking cartels, anti-manipulative war, and, because of the oligarchies that rule over nations, I'm sympathetic to democratic institutions (unfortunately, however, most socialism is undemocratic). And if I have to be labeled on either side, it will be with the conspiratorial researchers. At least theirs doesn't talk about the latest celebrity scandal.

If Ron Paul and Ralph Nader can team up to combat growing problems in our country, then why can't we take a cue from them? Not through violence—as Chris Matthews frightens the people into believing that as our means—but by dispensing actual information.

All I was trying to do was do my part in informing the public about perfectly rational, perfectly referenced, perfectly accurate depictions of real-life. Maybe in some fantasy world policy is decided by the President or the American Idol winner or whoever, but for now, it's the scumbags sitting off to the sidelines, and while the people work till they're crippled, they spend their days on golf courses, drinking the best whiskey, and receiving the best health care that fake money can buy.

What a democracy!

Go back to your reality shows, ladies and gentleman, nothing to worry about here.

Bastard Institution: The Results of California's "Tough on Crime" Policies

Bastard: Illegitimate, Bogus, Fraudulent, Having a Misleading Appearance

CALIFORNIA'S PRISON POPULATION has peaked with a 170,000 inmates! To put that in perspective, that's 70,000 past the legal maximum capacity, and more inmates than all of the jails of France, Great Britain, Germany, Japan, Singapore, and the Netherlands—combined, according to journalist Eric Schlosser's essay, *The Prison Industrial Complex*. Inmates are literally pouring out of the facilities; onto the yards, into gymnasiums, dining halls, and elsewhere. This pandemonium is confined to about 35 penitentiaries, give or take, due to the continual rise in prison expansion, in which I'll end on.

Running this network of prisons is the California Correctional Peace Officers Association, the C.C.P.O.A. Do not succumb to beguilement from any talk of "corrections" or "rehabilitation." It's a scam. A brilliant essay written by Ben Carrasco gives a much more alarming perspective on this state union—called by many experts as the most powerful force in the California political arena. The 1980's saw an obvious increase in gang violence.

Added to Ronald's Reagan's obsession with imprisoning poor crack addicts, the expansion of prisons in America grew exponentially. Of the 30-plus here in the Golden State, 21 have been built since 1984. To house inmates, it costs roughly $35-45,000 annually (depending on what report you read). The total bill for running the prison system stood at $5.7 billion in 2004. Less than a decade later, it had nearly doubled.

With a staff of little over 30,000 guards—less than a tenth of the teacher's union—they are the most gracious financial contributors in a land where the best democracy is bought and paid for with cash. An analysis of the C.C.P.O.A.'s campaign contributions gives a very well-balanced account as to why a labor union is so active in politics: any sensible program that might reduce the amount of inmates—and crime—would result in a loss of taxpayer funds, and, subsequently, paychecks.

Take Proposition 5, for example, which was on the ballot in 2008. The measure, officially called the *Nonviolent Offender Rehabilitation Act*, would have required the state to spend more on drug treatment instead of incarceration. The C.C.P.O.A. acted immediately, and the official "Yes on Prop 5" website states that the union threw nearly $2 million to get the measure shut down.

It wasn't the first time they were participants in the legislative branch. In 1994, Proposition 184, known more commonly as the Three Strikes Law, was set to be voted on. Under this proposal, offenders who commit three felonies would be sentenced to a mandatory minimum of 25 years to life. It often does: since it passed, close to 8,000 people have been given a life sentence for simple drug possession. That is, not sales, and not enhancements (IE, merely being under the influence). The C.C.P.O.A was an early supporter of the measure, and contributed some $100,000 dollars to get it signed into law.

The Three Strikes question came up again a decade later with ballot measure Proposition 66. It was a measure that would have amended the law so as to require the Third Strike to be violent.

The C.C.P.O.A. worked with intimidated governor Schwarzenegger, who stated on T.V. that Prop 66 would "release thousands of rapists and child molesters out onto the streets"—a shameful lie. In a very close vote, the amendment did not come to fruition.

These draconian mandates, along with the many other laws protracted or retracted with the Union's influence, are absolutely essential in explaining today's overcrowded penitentiaries. However, before any serious discussion is to be had about renovating the prison layout, one has to give mention to the inmates, and in very specific terms. This is because, in truth, and to the contrary of many prison reform advocates, a large majority of these inmates are indeed dangerous and violent individuals.

Though not all of them: there are about 1,500 inmates locked up for marijuana use right now. Not significant compared to many other states, but with the added total of arrests, salaries, court bills, etc., the final bill comes to over $200 million dollars. Other drug offenders—meth, heroin, cocaine—are where the real numbers come in, with the Golden State locking up a record amount of simple drug possessors, according to information on NORML's website.

Like oil and water, these two brands of law-breakers do not mix. Not at first. But from this, a proverbial hive starts to develop. Young inmates and drug addicts, who, although many of which are just trying to go home, are still human, and thus just as corruptible as the guards themselves. They are routinely subjugated to gang warfare, and, after a while, many come to see it as an acceptable lifestyle.

The facts are simple: compressed criminality never truly leaves the prison bars, and a prisoner recidivism rate that is—quite frankly—unacceptable, becomes the end result of lazy enforcement when it comes to inmate conduct. An average law breaker in California has five prior prison sentences. Perpetual criminality, defined.

This disjuncture amongst the inmates is a design of the C.C.P.O.A., whose internal policy is derived mostly from Julius Caesar's famous words when defining the secret of conquest: divide them first. In a supposedly vindicated effort to tabulate the bewildered and ignorant inmates, the prison officials segregate the races and gangs from one another. Southern Hispanic gangs are separated from Northern Hispanic gangs; Caucasian inmates (who still run as a single unit) without any Skinhead affiliation are labeled as "woods"; African Americans are with Crips or Bloods, etc. Every one of them labeled and separated (very literally) into their own designated cells. This, in practice, promulgates gang behaviorism, with the constant occurrence of rival gang violence taking place in all the prisons all throughout the state. Well-paid guards occasionally have to blast someone in the face with a can of pepper spray.

These inmates are also the cogs for the prison system's wage slavery program. An article ran by the *Sacramento Bee* stated that the P.I.A., the Prison Industry Authority, makes $234 million dollars' worth of products every year; including—but not limited to—furniture, sunglasses, license plates, etc. State law requires the many government agencies to purchase these products exclusively from the prison sector. The inmates are paid nickels and dimes for their work.

A monopoly of union officials and criminal behaviorism is running this state into the ground. The inmate population has always been the Union's bargaining power, and common sense would tell a rational person that they have no intrinsic desire to reduce the quantity of their prized commodity.

Thirty years ago, the average guard's salary was $14,440 dollars a year. These days, with overtime, it's not difficult for a guard to make $100,000 annually, and oftentimes much more. Quite a lot for a state-worker who takes all the funds for himself; never wondering if he or she was the reason the state was financially, and morally, bankrupt. Once again: Why would they relinquish their product?

The Golden State's judicial system is a perpetual prisoner machine, and the C.C.P.O.A. has garnered enormous power by taking advantage of the tired and failing policy of mass imprisonment. They pay off candidates to get into office, and onto their team, and then request giant pay raises to be signed into their budget. Plus, the old quid-pro-quo game does not meddle in partisan politics. Representatives on the so-called "Left" and "Right" are both corrupted by this Union.

In 1994, Republican Pete Wilson received $440,000 dollars from the C.C.P.O.A. At the time it was the largest single donation in California history and it largely helped to win him the governorship. In 2002, Democrat Gray Davis received $2 million from the Union—with the political powerhouse surpassing themselves yet again with another historic money toss.

The next move is as obvious as it is contemptible: both governors signed pay increases for their benefactors. Find a governor who has sternly denounced the C.C.P.O.A. Arnold tried it once, and was instantly greeted with a threat of recall. For the upcoming election of 2010, Jerry Brown, a longtime Union favorite, has once again received the most in donations.

So what's next with this unending imprisonment? Corruption, cronyism, and perpetual criminality led to the next big move in California prison expansion: AB900. Officially called the *Public Safety and Offender Rehabilitation Services Act of 2007*, the bill signed by Schwarzenegger is the largest single prison building project in the history of the world, so says the website CurbPrisonSpending.Org. It will build 53,000 new prison and jail beds at $15 billion dollars—just for construction costs alone. It was passed without a single public hearing.

It is past time for Californians to take back its prison system. Locking up inmates who only hurt themselves is not only a waste of taxpayer money, it is also the prime example of how America has fallen short of its widely touted mantra of Freedom.

K. M. Patten

A Small (Big) Confession

IT'S NOT AN easy thing to admit, and in fact it's an even harder thing to comprehend...for some people. I'm talking about subtle barbarianism. "Subtle barbarianism?" you ask. Of course, we hear of actions that can obviously be constituted as torture from all over the world; such audacious and horrendous events like: beheadings, ethnic cleansing, forced starvation, so on. But there's one procedure that has become so commonplace that it has now reached the domain of obviousness. However, it is no less barbaric.

It is now so widely overlooked that the only time it is perceived as inhumane is when it's happening to a female (more on this in a minute). I am talking of course about circumcision. I'll cut (no pun intended) to the chase and get right to the point (no joke intended either). The most important aspect of this practice is a simple moral truism: in a civilized world the most rudimentary concept of freedom would immediately prohibit any removal of the human anatomy from a non-consenting person.

If discerned for ever so briefly, this becomes a comic-style slap on the forehead, followed by a hysterical "*of course.*" For those not understanding the simple "two plus two equals four" logic: we do not legally or socially or otherwise allow for unnecessary mutilation! It doesn't get any simpler than that!

Nowhere in the law books does it say that when a child is born you are allowed to cut his arm off, right? So the question must be asked as why we allow butchery in other circumstances, especially ones concerning the genitals.

This question is asked, and two answers are almost always given an instantaneous response, both of which are equally inadequate in justifying such an atrocity.

The first reason given is a religious one. Essentially, an Abrahamic mandate—sanctioned by "God"—specifies that circumcision is the method in which Yahweh is able to "mark" his "chosen" people—just as we do today with livestock. This is most likely the prevailing reason for explaining why cutting the end of an infant's penis skin is still accepted. Religious people—and yes, especially Jews (or is it *the* Jews?)—won't allow its forbiddance. Either Yahweh continues to hold a monopolizing grasp on his "vessel," or perhaps parents have just succumbed to such drastic cultural conditioning that they don't understand the freedom being robbed from their child.

If it's the former, the question I pose is this: how do we know for certain that a human being, of just a few minutes of age, is even capable of having a definitive religion? What characteristics determine this? The pretext given: "His parents are." However, if his parents were, say, of a Moloch denomination, and believed in sacrificing live babies to some unseen "Higher Power," would it be tolerated in modern society?

We need no answer, because we're supposed to be "civilized." But this absurd illustration undergirds the argument that a state should always base its constitution on a separation from the Church, as the repressive consequences would otherwise become boundless. Moreover, it's inconsistent to condone barbaric behavior only when the auspice is Abrahamic, while the other "extreme" example of spiraling infants into a huge inferno is condemned. Both are wicked! And both should be outlawed!

The second articulation in favor of genital mutilation is that of hygiene. It is presupposed that by cutting off the foreskin, the risk of contracting an STD is greatly reduced. This rationalization is given far and wide by American pediatricians. My answer is a paradoxical one: If it could in fact be proven that a doctor's hands indeed cause mental trauma and physical torture to a child every time the procedure is performed, I would recommend, by using the same logic given by them, that their hands be cut off before they were able to commit any more suffering.

Savvy to that concept? Before an injury occurs, we take measures to ensure it does not. The only problem is that autonomy and integrity is lost in trying to curb an event that hasn't happened yet. That's not medicine. If it is true that circumcision reduces the risk of STD or bacterial infection (and I'm in no way confirming that it does or doesn't)—let the person decide when they are capable of doing so. Besides, not tending to your ears can also lead to infection. Should we cut those off also?

Regarding vaginas, genital mutilation has been granted solemnity. While American parents chop off the skin on their son's penises, they look antagonistically towards countries who practice female circumcision.

It's difficult even to write, but basically FGM is when any part of the vagina is surgically altered: cutting off the clitoris, sowing the vagina shut—just to name a couple examples (FGM is various, as opposed to male mutilation). The inconsistent moral is blatant: it's okay if it's a male, but not if it's a female. I think Penn & Teller had it right: "Circumcision is Bullshit!"

It's very fortunate that the practice is becoming rarer and rarer. In fact, roughly 80 percent of the world outside the United States is uncircumcised (*intact*); proving once again that America is, and Americans are, an insane, overly-cultured (or conditioned), sheepish, and hypocritical bunch. Hopefully the male species will wake up, and realize that this contention is legitimate. After all, according to the *British Journal of Urology*, circumcision desensitizes the penis by up to 75 percent. This is because there are over 10,000 nerve endings in the foreskin, and, once removed, your libido is working with a mere 3,000. This is why no major medical facility in the world recommends it. By cutting your son's penis, you are only stifling the full potential of his future sex life.

Here then is confession time: I was a victim of such mutilation. More than that, the doctor did a fucked up job. I think he botched it, leaving a huge gaping hole on the right side of my penis. (Alright, it's more of a dimple). I hate it. Whether for insisted sexual preferences or the fulfillment of an ancient blood ritual, what sane man would ever be "happy" that he was strapped down as an infant and had a part of his dick cut off?

Therefore, one can call it cultural mutilation, sexual perversion, religious branding—whatever you like: disfigurement of another human being is as inhumane as it gets. How long is it going to take before legislation is put into place that forbids parents from committing such butchery?

I suggest it be signed into the law very soon, with perhaps felony assault charges handed out to doctors still performing this wicked and deplorable act.

K. M. Patten

My Very Own Green Card

IT'S TRUE. I can testify to it now: The "medical" aspect of marijuana distribution in California is, for all intents and purposes, a ruse—a thinly veiled fixture for the sole purpose of legitimizing the next best thing to complete legalization. Nothing more than a word attached to the end of some numbers vindicate that law. I found this out just a few weeks ago when I decided, at long last, that it would be a good idea for me to get my medical 215 card. It was not hard. It wasn't hard in the least.

With five $20 bills stuffed in my wallet and a folder full of paperwork detailing a previous injury, I headed over to the only place I knew would take care of me without much hassle. The place where neo-hippies and aspiring nobodies go when all else is lost, where fake breasts compliment the organic pot, where even the police get high: my second favorite LA beach, Venice.

The folder was thick. Contained in it was a detailed account of my fractured jaw from a few years back, complete with records of my three-week hospital stint, medications, therapy—all the necessary elements needed to make a half-ass story sound convincing. Depression and insomnia would be easy in selling, I thought, but the migraines would need some FX. The truth is, I could have gone in there complaining about a toothache and walked out with something those hippies in the 60's could've only dreamt of—a little piece of paper, granting me full permission to smoke marijuana, when I want and how I want.

Standing outside the appropriately named "Kush Room," a guy and a girl were doing their best sales pitch. The gorgeous girl said, "Medical marijuana. The doctor is in. Come get your medical evaluation."

The man looked as if he had done some time: white dude with a lot of jailhouse tattoos. As I walked up, he came over to me, and, as if on cue, I started in on my own sales pitch. "Man, I've tried to get these headaches to go away. I just can't do it. I need to try something else."

He seemed less interested in my phony suffering, and more so in how many "customers" he had before nightfall arrived. He spoke plainly and quietly. "The going rate is gonna to be $150 dollars."

"But I've only got 80 bucks," I replied.

Like a good caregiver, he was sympathetic to my situation, and continued to walk me into the main office—a small corner, part of a larger building; wooden floors, a desk, and not much else. The guy behind the desk, an Asian guy, did not ask—not one single time—about my medical condition. At this point I thought I had discovered the trick: as long as you don't walk in and start telling people you want to get stoned, you're in like Flynn.

Then the guy with the tats grabbed a notepad, a pen, and started writing something; trying to keep whatever it was hidden from my view. A second later, he showed me the tablet, saying "this is what I can do for you today." A small printed number with no dollar signs surrounding it: seventy. "Sounds good" I told him. Better than a Kirby Vacuum salesman! Like that, I was set.

I took a seat, and the clerk handed me a clipboard holding together a stack of photo-copied legal documents, the one thing that separated them from street dealers. I must have signed and initialed my name thirty times before it was over.

"The doctor is with another patient. Fill out these forms and he'll be right with you."

"I've got my paperwork right here," I said to him, showing

him my thick manila envelope.

"Oh, yeah...err...you definitely want to show that to the doctor"—faking a slight hint of enthusiasm.

I think it was the first time he had ever seen such an effort. In his mind, he must have been thinking, "The fool...doesn't he watch the news?" I was embarrassed; I had lived in the Golden State my entire life, and never knew how damned easy it was.

At almost the exact same time I finished filling out the paperwork, a door opened up from the other side of the room. A twenty-something Hispanic dude walked out, followed by a tall, thin gentleman—mid-to-late fifties, gray hair, glasses, and with a red stethoscope that hung down between his bleach-white lab coat. Just like me: all the necessary elements needed to make a blatant fallacy appear real. He was a strange man, speaking in a low, monotonic voice. I imagined the Crypt Keeper—stoned out of his mind!

As soon as he saw his other "patient" off he introduced himself. Even his name was creepy: Dr. Sinclair Moriarty. "Hiya, doc...I need your help."

"Come into my office"—which was another cramped room with wooden floors. If it weren't for the sunshine that infused the place, I'd have chocked this building up to a made-over dungeon, perhaps a bondage palace once owned by Jim Morrison. As before, this guy had no inclination about any medical problems I might, or might not, have been suffering from.

"Let's check your blood pressure," he said.

"Its high doctor...I have high blood pressure. Runs in the family."

"That's okay," he assured me. "It won't disqualify you," strapping on the cuff. "I pass everyone."

The entire experience was becoming stranger by the minute. And to break up the monotony, I asked him how long he had been a doctor. "Oh, about 4 or 5 months. Before that I was a general MD. Most people in that field don't know how good this stuff is."

He set the machine up, and began making more scribbles, love letters to his underage Taiwanese lover—whatever it was that these people do to keep the illusion going. I understood all that. More oddly, he put my arm right up against his chest, and, instead of moving his chair a foot to the left, continued writing straight over it. This doctor was burnt out on his own prescriptions, I figured, and it was getting time for me to go.

"170 over 94," he said.

"Ah, it's low today."

"Well, Kevin," he said about ten minutes later, "I think I'm going to recommend you." Which, in California jargon, means he's going to sign my cannabis card, and make me official. It wasn't as if this man was suddenly going to tell me: "You know what? I think you're bullshitting me. I don't think you have an urgent medical need at all! Get the hell out of my office before I call the cops!" No, sir—I could not have imagined that scenario taking place. Not at all.

So I shook his hand, walked outside, thanked the clerk, wiped my hand on my jacket, and made my way over to the ocean, where I rested for about twenty minutes on the sand, studying the paper that now ratified my right to smoke weed legally. After that, I went back to the boardwalk and looked for a store, specifically one that sold pipes. Not long after, I found what I was looking for: "Pipes & Stuff." A family-operated joint (no pun intended), the gentleman came over to me while I was browsing his selection of glass and wood bongs. "What can I do you for?" He said. "I got ten bucks," I replied.

He didn't say a word, but simply summoned me with one finger over to another counter. He pulled out another tray of pipes. A little yellow and blue colored digit caught my eye. "Sold," I said, pulling out a singular Mr. Hamilton. "Have a good one." I continued on the boardwalk, eventually finding my car amongst the surfboards and fake breasts. Along with the two-hour wait in traffic, I felt, at long last, like I was now a true Californian.

And yet, I felt guilty. Not from taking advantage of the state's policy—lord knows they've earned far more than a couple kicks in the ass—but more because of the loss of tax-revenue that could be helping us out of so much debt. I went home, and went across the street to the local dispensary (the only one within miles of my city), and I saw that this place was doing well. And as it states quite clearly on the door: "DONATIONS ONLY." That means that there isn't even a receipt given. There's no official transaction. The sale technically does not exist.

Here's a billion-dollar industry in our backyard, and it's not even being utilized. The more that I think about it, it is a complicated situation, with both its *goods* and its *bads*. For the former: the decriminalizing of marijuana as stopped the enormous influx of pot smokers that had once occupied a good portion of our prisons, costing everyone a lot of money to keep non-violent offenders behind bars. Now we save that money. Even for most people who don't believe in legalization, they also don't believe in sending them to prison, either. This new paradigm has become contagious: more than a dozen states have decriminalized pot since California's historic 215 vote.

That's a good thing all the way around.

For the bad—already stated—a massive cash crop not yet being plucked. While it is legal—for anyone paying attention—no revenue finds its way to these fifty financially bankrupt states. Hopefully, November's ballot measure to fully legalize marijuana will send us into another paradigm. Fancifully, it'll finally be realized that, since prohibition does not work, and will never work, it should be replaced with a more sensible policy—one where industries like this are taxed and regulated.

Ranting About Immunity and War While Standing Waist-Deep in a Lukewarm Jacuzzi

TEN, SIX, TWO-THOUSAND and Ten: For me, a day that started around four in the afternoon with my mother waking me to join her and her ex-husband, my father, for dinner. The regularity of such an otherwise odd thing is a normal occurrence around this household; everyone here is used to it, and nobody wonders why others sometimes look at us funny.

So it is, and probably will remain, and after three full plates of greenery from the Sizzler salad bar, we came back to the house to watch the most popular show in the universe—*Dancing With the Stars*, a program I love to hate and despise and abhor and loath whenever I ponder the downfalls of American democracy. It's almost as bad as watching that evil woman on *CNN*, Nancy Grace, a name synonymous with sensationalism. I made a half-hearted effort to clean my room, if only to read this months' *TIME* magazine—featuring militias and other scary figures—in utter peace, and relative quietness.

It wouldn't be long, however, before their sudden bursts of excitement and laughter resonating from the next room had antagonized me to the point in which I was forced to grab the car keys and dive off into the cold night as fast as possible.

During these fits of frustration, the sauna-area at the 24 Hour

Fitness is a nice place to go. It relaxes me. And often, it's a good place to read, especially at three-oh-clock in the morning. But tonight was not going to be a peaceful night; for it wasn't long before a very deranged and unpleasant individual would confirm for me what I had known long ago: that our military veterans are to be absolutely and always absolved from any form of criticism.

Two separate conversations took place before this confirmation would occur. The first was struck up with another occupant of the sauna regarding my year-long project, the legalization of cannabis. After that routine topic was covered for the umpteenth time, I was asked by a college youngster, who was listening to our conversation, if I could give him any history lessons on the subject of methamphetamine.

"I've been clean for a hundred and sixty-days, and now I'm going to give a speech about it in my class," the bald young man said. He followed me over to the Jacuzzi, standing outside while we had a friendly talk about those dangerous crystals.

Seeing as I was a former user—using it only so briefly—and he had supposedly been clean for a number of months, trying to stay that way, I felt obligated to advise him to smoke as much cannabis as humanly possible; in as long as there were no bleeding lungs and as long as the meth cravings subsided by a noticeable margin. Then I gave him some historical info: "Pervitin," I said. "The Nazi's marketed a brand of meth called Pervitin. Hitler was said to be on a daily diet. That's why he was going fucking crazy at the end." This counseling and discussion didn't go well for the other gentleman sitting in the Jacuzzi.

"You know, it all starts with marijuana," this guy said, interjecting himself into our conversation. "Look at Europe. They're going downhill. Terrorist attacks, all kinds of shit."

I began, "Putting people behind bars for doing nothing more than smoking pot is a ridiculous and tyrannical thing to do in this here 'land of the free.'"

It would be the last time I was able to complete a full sentence, without interruption, during this awkward little powwow getting underway.

"Yeah, but what will they do next? This is the greatest country in the world. I don't want anybody to mess it up with that stuff."

In abrupt fashion—without anyone knowing why or how—the one-sided conversation went from drugs and illicit substances, to an incoherent, almost inaudible rant about politics and world affairs. "Ah man, this is the greatest country in the world. We always go in to liberate other countries. That's why everyone wants to come here. Europe is already gone. They got Muslim extremists all over the place. Terrorist attacks. Blowing shit up. This is the greatest country in the world!" He declared it again and again, slapping his hand on the face of the bubbly green water with every assertion.

To be short, and to the point, and to spare any long-lettered explanation of this talk: the enraged man went into a virtual tirade on how "wonderful" (parentheses due to the fact that he could never say specifically as to why) our nation was, while denouncing every other one. "I travel all over the world," he asserted, frequently enough to make sure that me and the sober student had both heard it at least a dozen times over. It was a vain attempt to make us forget that we had abstract minds capable of out-thinking his nativist ideology.

"The greatest in the world," he said again.

When I suspected a momentary abeyance, I pounced: "Why did the Bush family never disclose their financial and commercial dealings with the bin laden fami....." I shouted it, attempting to connect some dots for him that he was unwilling—or unable—to figure out for himself.

"Ah, what are you talking about?" he interrupted, crying out again with something-something-infallible-ethical-superiority.

When I first got in the Jacuzzi, he was sitting shoulder-high in the water, but with every sentence his face became more embroiled and frustrated, and he would dramatically leap out of the water and waive a finger that was shaking uncontrollably—violently even, like a fuse on a lit stack of dynamite. "This is the greatest country in the world. If you don't like it, you should leave," he said with an index vibrating madly within a three inch spectrum.

I shouted over him that I actually did love my country, but hated, and fought against, what I felt was a government that was deliberately working to undermine whatever freedom we had left. When I asked my question on the moral legitimacy of our wars, he went overboard. "Ah, don't even start with that. I have two nephews in the marines, they're still over there. Been there since before 9-11. Don't ever say that to someone in the forces. If you ever say that to someone in the service"—going over to the side of the Jacuzzi— "they'll do this to you…" He then began beating the wet cement with a closed fist, looking as if he was trying to bludgeon a small animal to death.

The nonsensical show he was putting on parallels other discussions I've had with veterans (which he was not); the sort of unconquerable immunity that is given to them for having served in the armed forces. People who have seen horror and death and bloodshed on a grand scale, and who have, without doubt, been permanently scarred from having been witness to it all. I can only presuppose that the last bit is affirmed every time a returning solder allows for himself or herself the courage to ask a question raised by countless others who have also shared their pain: why did I go to that battlefield? For what reason?

War is not a simple question to ponder. And I certainly won't give my naïve thoughts on it. But there's an observable paradox whenever one says that the "troops fight for your freedom and democracy." That is, if they have indeed done so, can I now use it to question the next war? Was this fulfilled after World War One or Two, Korea or Vietnam, Iraq or Afghanistan? When will I be able to use that Freedom and Democracy?

Liberation! New game plan. But if say, "I wish to liberate this or that country," then wouldn't there need to be an objective, factually-correct debate involving all parties capable of making those important decisions, while being honest to those who have to pay for them? If honesty and facts are to be discarded for a whimsical declaration sure to ensnarl entire nations for years to come, then what the hell good is democracy in the first place? And on a side note, one should never equate country with government.

With this asshole, I never got to state that point, as he seemed to be getting a slight arousal from his literal chest-beating and bitter statements. "They're still reading your emails," I said to the angry man in the green water, now looking as if he was about to start foaming at the mouth.

"Nobody is reading....who's reading your emails?" he blurted.

I didn't get the chance to reply, but for those paying half-attention, the Obama Administration has continued with clandestine provisions permanently endowed within the Patriot Act text.

Ah, but what the hell.

The greatest country in the world.

The greatest.

A Personal Reflection of Proposition 19's Failure: How I Could Have Become a Victim of Section 4

EVER SINCE READING Section 4 of the Proposition 19, the mandatory criminalization that, for some reason, had to come with legalization, I have been on edge, and on guard. I now think my suspicions had merit.

In the morning following Proposition 19's defeat, I, a fearless cannabis reporter, found myself in a situation where a real-life nightmare had almost become reality. I could've woke up in a cell today. As it was, and now deceased, Section 4, Subsection C of Proposition Nineteen read:

> *Every person 21 years of age or over who knowingly furnishes, administers, or gives, or offers to furnish, administer or give any marijuana to a person aged 18 years or older, but younger than 21 years of age, shall be punished by imprisonment in the county jail for a period of up to six months and be fined up to $1,000 for each offense.*

I think to myself: God forbid if some agent of the State bursts into my room at 8:00 in the morning, demanding answers to questions being directed to me and my partially naked girlfriend.

In so many words, the measure tells you it's a serious offense. *Don't do it.* In actuality, a first time offender would probably be sentenced to six months and be out in less than thirty days. Not that big of a deal. That's not exactly the case, however, if your name is currently listed on the state's ridiculously long parole sheet. In that situation, your ass is going back to the slammer, doing at least eighty percent.

As a parolee in his mid-twenties, the idea of recreational cannabis smoking with someone under the arbitrary legal age should be embedded firmly in my thoughts, inducing a deathly fear of ever even considering so. If, by chance or by fate, Proposition 19 passed, and Section Four became a reality, caught smoking marijuana with an underage "toker" would find me right back into some cold cell way out in a lonely desert 300 miles from home, eating food that is indecipherable from cooked dogshit and listening to some child molester whistle in the shower. I should know better after doing three years.

But, alas, sey-la-vi, and as always: a beautiful girl is a beautiful girl; with all their temptation and blood-sucking capacities. Like the very best buds in the world, they're capable of corrupting a man's motivations, and making him do things he wouldn't normally be inclined to do. Clarissa. She's beautiful with long black hair, small brown freckles across her cheeks, a rather prominent dimple on her chin, and who stands at least three inches taller than me. She's eighteen, but Clarissa has been smoking pot long before meeting any disgruntled cannabis reporters. There's no need for suspicions and confessions; one can guess the first time and get it right without deflection: I get high with this girl as often as I can. It makes my day, and I figure, in the eyes of any quacked out "doctor" selling med-cards down at the beach, she's just another medical patient with headaches or back pains or something.

For the two of us, the night of November 2nd seemed typical, if not somewhat bland. Maybe even strange if one were to take into consideration the crystals sparkling on top of our magic bud. Something someone gave me called Super Silver Haze, which had rendered our sense of style completely useless. We rocketed around LA in a convertible Mustang—my mother's—enjoying the setting sun and trying our very best to look like two lazy and adventurous Californians who were high on THC and low on petroleum. Occasionally my video camera would be pulled out and I'd ask the driver stopped next to us if they had voted for Prop 19. Many yes's. Few no's. Weird reportage, but with so little resources, I must make do with what I have.

Still, I couldn't forget the thought of failure lingering in my head. With an odd feeling of precognition in my mind—somehow knowing that the measure was going to fail and be sent into a political abyss—I took off to Hollywood to see if there were any cannabis-creatures walking down the street. I've met one before, giving the measure some serious backing, and I thought that perhaps there might be supporters out there doing the same. This is what the initiative really needed—some proper public support.

Ah, but there weren't many cannabis-creatures out tonight. I felt despair in my heart. The victory sex was canceled, and my grand idea of a successful celebration with legions of public enforcers flipping off Sheriff Lee Baca after all of the votes had been counted—it would just not happen tonight. Marijuana would not be legalized in the streets of Los Angeles. But I didn't expect it. There was no money behind the damned thing, and, after all, nobody wanted to imagine stoned bus drivers picking up their children from school.

We drove back home after the boredom had taken hold, turned on the TV, and settled into the night with some fluffy and comfortable green mounds. The blankets were also very comfortable. I put two holes in a green apple, broke a toothpick in half for my bowl, and smoked some more of that wonderful silver cannabis, allowing some douchebag *FOX* news reporter on TV to confirm for us the fate of the measure. *Destruction*. A long, smooth leg stretched over me and I fell into dreamland, or something that could be remembered as such. The apple full of beautiful herb rolled off my hand toward the foot of my bookshelf, which also held the remaining weed in an old copy of *Cannabis Times*.

The next thing I remember was my brother pounding at my door at 8:30 in the morning. "Hey, Kev, are you awake?" He was using his forearm. Something was afoot. My black computer chair was wedged against the door handle. I have no lock, but at least nobody could get in. "Hey, Kevin. Wake up."

All of a sudden the tone of voice changed. "Kevin, open up, it's Ms. Lyons." (My parole officer, whose name is obviously changed.)

Christ! Didn't this woman come by a couple weeks ago? My first instinct was that this probably wouldn't turn out good. With a maniac compulsion to escape her power to send me back to prison, I grabbed the magazine, funneled it together, and poured the remaining marijuana right down my gullet, washing it down with stale beer. On her third "open up!" I had kicked the girl awake and demanded that she take the apple and lighter.

I removed the chair and let her in. "Oh, that's why he's taking so long,"—she actually said aloud—"he's got a girl with him." She walked in like she owned the place. "Is this your girlfriend?"

Partially awake, tasting like hangover and freshly-cut grass, I muttered a "no, not really" and took the small bottle she was handing me. Mandatory for all those on parole: random drug tests via piss in a bottle. "One of them, uh?" she said, telling me to go to the bathroom and pee in the tube while she took a little look around my room.

I peed, put it in a bag, and silently hoped standing in front of the mirror that by the time I had opened the door back up, Ms. "Lyons" would be in my kitchen waiting to ask me how I'm doing. I had to remember, aloud even: the measure did not pass. I should be alright then. We were just "medicating," after all.

I opened the door. Clarissa still sat on the floor wrapped in blankets and smiling half-heartedly. The poor girl might be traumatized by all this. The PO was standing in the kitchen, and performed her routine "how are you doing?" session before leaving me be. I breathed heavily and jumped in the shower to begin scrubbing away at the stink of irony. It could have turned out a lot worse.

The whole thing really doesn't make any sense to me. Why, more people should have asked, if marijuana was set to be legalized to those over the age of twenty-one, does Prop 19 penalize persons who are offering to a legal adult? Those between the ages of 18-21 are also subject to have their lives destroyed simply for offering cannabis in front of someone under the age of an adult.

Section B reads exactly the same as C, although the responsibility of punishment weighs on an eighteen year old. That immediately denotes suspicion amongst those who wrote the measure, and assumes that those under twenty-one will be able to easily acquire large amounts of marijuana, neglecting a main argument for Prop 19: that the "playground pushers" will be taken out of society, making it difficult for teens to acquire cannabis. Someone stood to gain from this, it seems.

From information available on the California Correctional Peace Officer Association's website, there are close to 100,000 people under the age of twenty currently on parole. Marijuana, plus a teenager, plus an underage cousin or nephew, could very well equal another incarceration. Terrible formula.

And, I just found out on the third of November that my endorsement of this measure almost betrayed my efforts. I could have been in jail that day, as with many others. Looking back at it now—and only now—I'm glad it didn't pass. I've changed my opinion, slightly, amidst so much personal reassurance. Prop 19 was pseudo-legalization, and nothing we should accept as acceptable.

Cannabis suffered a horrible blow at that year's election, but in the end, the real casualty was personal responsibility, subverted yet again by someone else's idea of morality.

It's safe to assume the Police State will still weigh in via one form or another. If it's not the Prison Guards, then it'll be the Police Force. At least it wasn't the Feds, who I was certain were already prepared for "Operation Golden State Takeover."

As for me, am I ashamed? Should I be? Truth be told, smoking with her is not likely to weigh heavily on my conscience. As a matter of fact, the next cannabis initiative I endorse will include not only eighteen year olds, but also the rest of the country.

Experiencing the Geminid Meteor Shower

IN THE EARLIEST hours of December the 14th, I decided on a whim to drive my girlfriend fifty miles from home to Silverwood Lake so that we could witness the year's most grandiose cosmic show: the apex of the Geminid Meteor Shower. We ascended a dark, rocky pathway—far, far above the actual lake—and prepared a rudimentary "blanket bed" on the top of my old Pathfinder to lay and watch.

We were up there for over quarter-hour after midnight before anything was seen. Then, in perfect surprise fashion, we saw one: a brilliant diamond darting across the night sky. Then another. And another. The cosmic show commenced. All throughout the valley, gorgeous beams of light dashed across the darkened hills. Each could be followed for at least three seconds or more. Some looked neon blue; others gave off a yellowish hue. We were, as they say, awe-struck.

The meteors come from the asteroid 3200 Phaeton, which has been traced back to the constellation Gemini, explaining its namesake. Scientists have long been puzzled about the appearance of Phaeton, which exhibits an orbit similar to that of a comet, but without the dust tail so symbolic with others.

In what is regarded as a truly remarkable characteristic for an asteroid, Phaeto spews grains of space rock—the Geminid

Meteors—which usually come from passing comets. Another interesting aspect of this "object" is that it passes closer to our sun than any other accounted for. This has led to a couple of discussions, the first always being a series of alternative theories that attempt to explain Phaeton's unusual galactic qualities. One explanation places a new-born Phaeton as originally being a...that's right...comet, which eventually, it is theorized, burnt up due to too many passes around the sun.

I lay quietly and summoned renowned anthropologist Joseph Campbell, who reported a mythology that is perhaps more interesting than the science. In a popular tale found in Greek literature, Phaeton, meaning the "shining" or "illuminator"—or something like that—was the son of Phoebus, the God of the Sun. After an exhaustive search across Persia and India to find the Sun Palace, where his father sat upon an emerald throne surrounded by his most loyal followers—you know: Day, Month, Year, and Century—Phaeton requested of Phoebus a seal of proof, declaring to the whole world that he had a son.

Not wanting to let his little boy down, Phoebus immediately promised anything that the lad requested. What he didn't expect, however, was that young Phaeton wanted to drive his father's Chariot of Fire across the sky for all to see. "You are asking for more than can be granted," Phoebus told him. "Each of the gods may do as he will, and yet none, save myself, has the power to take my place in my chariot; no, not even Zeus."

With Phaeton still adamant to take his father's vehicle for ride, Phoebus had to agree. Not heeding his father's demands to stay in the middle of the path to avoid causing damage to the Earth below, Phaeton at first grazed the "heights of the sky"—freezing the Earth. Then he went too low, burning most of the rest. Zeus eventually had to intervene, tossing a lightning bolt at the chariot which sent the reckless youth descending into the ocean, leaving a tombstone bearing euphuisms about bravery.

Phaeton (err, I mean 3200 Phaeton) was first discovered in

1983 by a group of astronomers looking for the parent body of the Geminids. They realized, sooner rather than later, that they had found it. They come like clockwork every year, and this year they shone as wonderfully as they have for at least the last few thousand years.

As for the many stories and theories, no one should discount any of them. Mythology and pattern-seeking gets the best of all of us. If born into another epoch, I likely also would've grabbed the first rock in sight to carve an interpretation of how the gods were engaged in some sort of fierce battle amongst the stars.

As for this evening, I just cuddled up to watch the brilliance taking place in our atmosphere.

Uncle Sam: Pervert and Dictator

IMAGINE THIS: IT'S Christmas time and your mother from up north has invited you and the family to come and spend the Holiday season with her. She's so excited about seeing the grandkids, she's even bought the airline tickets. Upon arriving at the airport, you see an unusually large number of police cars, freighting in their backseats what appear to be normal, everyday people who, like you, are just trying their best to make their flight and visit their out-of-state family members.

"No big deal," you think as you shuffle in the security line, paying no attention to complaints echoing from the sea of tired travelers. Finally getting to the front of the screening process, you notice futuristic-looking machines, each containing an individual person. Adjacent to the phone-booth-things you see two overweight security officers wearing TSA attire that are rigorously and thoroughly feeling all up and down the other travelers.

After a brief argument with the wife about who's at fault for neglecting to investigate exactly which airports had the new body scanners, you decide to send your sixteen-year-old daughter and ten-year-old son through the machine while you and your wife receive the "advanced pat-down."

"No one's going to touch my kids," you assure yourself as you and your wife begin lining up. Suddenly, the atmosphere turns into something dreadful. A day that started off thinking about nothing more than your vacation is now one where your wife is being groped by a large woman with a tattoo on her arm that reads "I Love Beavers" while your daughter raises and lowers her arms at the command of a group of men standing behind a monitor. They laugh and point and snicker while staring at the screen that shows off that push-up bra her mom bought for her birthday.

And then your son goes in; in at which time the group of men shift their attention to another one of the screens—except for one little man, who stays behind. He's weird and creepy and sports a strange grin on his face. You want to protest, but the larger man behind you has his hand going side to side along your testicles, and you are unable to find the words because you are frozen in fear and trembling at the serpentine scenario unfolding before your eyes.

After it's all finished, you're given clearance to continue onto the plane. Being the man of the family, you feel the irresistible urge to raise a complaint against these sick people. And before you know it, you're in the backseat of a cop car, being told that you will probably be facing heavy fines with your name going onto a federal government terrorist watch list.

Is this only a nightmare? Or have you forgotten sitting in your High School English class reading George Orwell's prophetic *Nineteen-Eighty-Four*, quietly thinking to yourself that Winston Smith's totalitarian society—controlled with thought crime and camera screens on every street corner—was only some figment of an author's imagination; that it could only happen in the literary world and most certainly not here in the Land of the Free.

Since the Naked Body Scanner issue has been covered by every newspaper, TV show, radio program, webzine and magazine in the world, you would surely know by now that— no—this is in fact the new American reality.

Just a mere few weeks after the controversial extravaganza went live on the media market, the abuse of these porno scanners began their inevitable documentation. In November alone, over

900 complaints against the Transportation Security Agency (TSA) have been filed with the ACLU.

Among disturbing examples: a man stricken with cancer who became so distraught that he urinated on himself; a woman who was subjected to a full groin search after her feminine napkin produced a burly image on the screen; and a young big-breasted girl who says she was targeted out for "additional screening" by TSA agents, rather obviously she says. "The TSA agent used her hand to feel under and between my breasts," another woman said, "she then rammed her hand up into my crotch until it jammed into my pubic bone."

The background for this evasiveness starts on December 25th of last year, when 23-year old Umar Farouk Adbulmatallab boarded Northwest Airlines on a flight headed from Amsterdam to Detroit. Umar's intention was to ignite a plastic explosive device strapped into his underwear. With an intervention that turned out unfortunate for Umar, and always advantageous for the government, the Muslim terrorist had his plot thwarted by vigilant passengers.

Interestingly, just days after the incident, our War and Empire-obsessed Congress awarded multi-million dollar deals for two of its military contractors. One, Rapiscan, was given $173 million. The other, L-3 Communications—a favorite amongst the Complex's accommodators, receiving $5.1 billion from the Pentagon in 2006—had this time reached an agreement worth $165 million.

Further solidifying the cozy relationship between our elected officials and the multi-national corporations that pull their strings (Journalist Nick Turse's book *The Complex* is a must read on the subject) is the fact that L-3 Communications has doled out more political cash this election cycle than at any other time. The Center for Responsive Politics has found: $466,300 between January and October 2009—a 26 percent increase above the company's 2006 contributions. Of that, Representative Bennie

Thompson (D-Miss), the chairman of the—*gasp!*—House Homeland Security Committee, received $8,000 from the L-3 Communications PAC.

The TSA is a tentacle of Homeland Security—itself part of a larger, world-wide Complex. One of its original designers, Congressman John Mica (R-FL), called it a "bloated, ineffective bureaucracy with over 66,000 employees." With an annual cost that started with $0.7 billion in 2001, ballooning to $6.9 billion in 2010, Mica could be right, seeing as they couldn't even prevent Umar from boarding an airplane, despite the suspicious and unanswered fact that he had no passport, no identification, and was already listed on a terrorist watch list.

Ah, but we needn't fear now. There won't be any more Umar's or Osama's; no more scary Arabs out to kill us; or multivocal terrorists out to destroy our Freedoms. Instead, the threat comes from federal thugs who are so brazen they now tell you that you are under their control. The list of such ambiguous apprehensions wrought upon us by the government to instill fear is petty and illegitimate compared to the genuine tyranny they now take advantage of in the wake of such beguilement.

Take for example the growing concern raised by a number of doctors and scientists who warn that such radiation exposure could result in adverse health effects. In April, a group of such learned individuals from the University of California at San Francisco sent a letter to Obama's science and technology advisor John Holden. To wit, the letter disclosed some concerns you'd usually have when being pushed through a machine that generates radiation waves.

Close contact, they say, could present an increase in cancer—especially in the case of elderly persons—as well as mutilated sperm cells, and of course the dangers posed to children still in their mother's womb. They emphatically added that such machines have not been verified as safe by independent research. Don't worry though, the government never—ever!—fucks anything up. As a test of sorts, the next time you're put into a body scanner, ask the TSA agent behind the lead wall why he's standing behind it in the first place.

Paul Craig Roberts, creator of Reaganomics-turned maverick empire-hunting essayist, has also made things a lot clearer in regard to the "terrorist aspect" with one of his recent articles. "If Americans were more thoughtful and less gullible, they might wonder why all the emphasis on transportation when there are so many soft targets." Craig continues: "Shopping centers, for example. If there were enough terrorists in America to justify the existence of Homeland Security, bombs would be going off round the clock in shopping malls in every state. The effect would be far more terrifying than blowing up an airliner."

Indeed, as might have been foretold, John Pistole, the FBI agent-turned Administrator of the TSA—and all-around scumbag—has said that the time is nearing when we'll need to protect trains and subways. How long will it be before that trip downtown for groceries turns into an all-day event, filled with Body Scanners and armed goons on every bus and train station from Pasadena to Manhattan?

Since there are only sixty or so airports in the country currently using the scanners (only about two percent) one can only assume what this scheme is all about: incremental implementation of complete government control over our society. Pistole has repeatedly said that the screening process will not change anytime soon. In that case, it should only be expected to get worse.

And what have all these draconian mandates brought for Pistole and Homeland Security Chief Janet Napolitano aside from endless amounts of scathing criticism and a lawsuit filed by Harvard Law Students, who say, correctly I think, that the scanners and policies of the agencies involved are in contempt for violating the Fourth Amendment which prohibits unreasonable search and seizure.

Actually, the worst of it isn't even known.

Not yet.

A letter sent to Representative Thompson specifically stated that the machines had the capability to retain and export images. Apparently, this happens quite often at the facilities where they train new employees. Naturally, the letter stipulated that it was for "testing and evaluation only."

Unfortunately, the human factor tells us something entirely different: that the corrupt, minimum wage-earning federal agents—at least a couple of which have had serious sexual offenses on their records—are more than able and willing to commit insidious acts upon the rest of us. While it may or may not become an epidemic, the question must be asked: Why should we trust them in the first place? And ultimately: How long before underground websites start propping up that deal in smuggled "scanner-porn?"

What then, is the difference between a TSA agent who gropes and fondles and peeps at men, woman, and children, and this guy named "Python" I knew upstate who was doing five years for feeling up his female patients while they were under anesthesia?

The answer: one waves a big, bright flag, deals in billion dollar bills, and has the backing of the U.S. Federal Government.

The other is just a weirdo, without a badge, who happened to get caught doing something which would have otherwise been seen as illegal, let alone immoral.

Getting Paranoid in the Land of Secrecy

THIS PAST NOVEMBER, WikiLeaks founder Julian Assange dumped another 250,000 pages of previously classified documents into the hands of mainstream reporters, who, without a modicum of verification, began typing the memos into news reports. Since opening the website in 2006, the 39-year-old, Australian-born Assange has fashioned himself as a prevailing force for democracy: an icon of transparency and crusader against all forms of government secrecy.

In the past, he released thousands of documents and videos depicting American soldiers massacring Iraqi civilians; along with a copy of the *Standard Operating Procedures for Camp Delta*, which said that some inmates at Guantanamo Bay were off-limits to the International Committee of the Red Cross; as well as taking his turn at bashing Sarah Palin.

But not so fast. Assuming that a big-government State like the U.S. is no stranger to deceitful activities, the question might be asked simply as a forewarning: Could WikiLeaks ever become sabotaged by the people it fights? What if, instead of dealing mortal blows to the Establishment, the Establishment—with its long history of covert operations—has now found a way to re-program the website from a democratic tool, into a pseudo-official carrier of key information that might otherwise prove useful to the secret state? Deliberately handing out intel that would be needed to garner public support or divert attention elsewhere.

As speculative as it might sound, it's probably unwise to dismiss such a theory out-of-hand. During the 50's, 60's and 70's, the FBI surreptitiously worked to undermine the efforts of socialists, Civil Rights activists, and anti-war protesters through an operation known as COINTELPRO—short for Counter-Information Program. The plan was to "expose, disrupt, misdirect, discredit, or otherwise neutralize" the activities of these movements and their leaders.

One such deployment, code-named Operation Hoodwink, was designed to incite organized crime against the Communist Party, in hope that the mob would carry on its own form of disruption to the CP. A tactic used by the Bureau was to falsify information and send out memos to group members to drive wedges between them, even going so far as to print their own newspaper to discourage new membership. In 1968, the Indianapolis office of the FBI created a newsletter called "Armageddon News." Its purpose was to "prevent any non-leftist students from being duped into joining the groups of the New Left." These revelations came out years after the fact, when sued by the parties mentioned.

In the case of WikiLeaks, we find one such well-publicized topic that is very much in line with the American Agenda. A "concern" that can be read in almost any random American newspaper—Target: Iran. The fears of American politicians with regard to Iran's nuclear program appear to be vindicated, it seems, now that the greater Middle East has reached a similar conclusion. Egypt, Jordan, Bahrain, the United Arab Emirates, led by our longtime "ally" Saudi Arabia—who was also accused in the data-dump of being the primary funder of al Qaeda—has declared Iran to be a rogue state and in need of serious reprimanding. Saudi King Abdullah urged the U.S. to "cut off the snake's head," even feeling threatened enough to purchase $60 billion worth of armaments from Uncle Sam, including F-15 fighter jets.

The Iranian situation is a complicated lot. As said, any old rag today will have the latest article conveying the urgent threat of President Mahmoud Ahmadinejad and the Islamic fundamentalists who run the State. What those rags won't say—not usually—is the other side of the story; the history that includes the CIA-funded Operation Ajax which overthrew democratically-elected Prime Minister Mohammed Mosadegh in 1953, replacing him with the brutal regime of the Shah and his SAVAK police force. This oppression eventually led to former CIA agent Ayatollah Khomeini's 1979 Revolution, which put Koran-inspired leaders in the Shah's place once he was disposed. These events helped create the animosity between the two hemispheres today that might've been avoided back then.

The latest development of this 60-year war is the recent admission of U.S. and Israeli intelligence in creating the Stuxnet Computer Virus, which was intended to shut down Iran's computer systems. President Ahmadinejad has publicly admitted that a cyber-weapon had affected their nuclear program. Two scientists were also murdered during this time by hit-men on motorcycles, a tactic used by Israeli's Mossad. Preliminary results of these attacks have worked in favor of those who instigated them.

The Iranian press, controlled by the State, will attempt to draw a different picture. Here, Ahmadinejad is a well-mannered diplomat committed to friendly relations and open facilities, who declares that "most world governments have recognized Iran's nuclear rights, and only a few Western countries are using the language of force." And while the verdict isn't in yet on the sentiments of the real international community (not the one constructed by *FOX News* or *MSNBC*), it is true that Iran is trying to make friends: Lebanon, Kuwait, Azerbaijan, and one in particular that stands out above the rest—Turkey, the now fading-friend of the U.S. and Israel.

The secular state of Turkey has been an equivocal ally to the U.S. During the 90's, with the aid of the Clinton Administration, Turkey expanded its terror-campaign against the Kurdish people, eventually topping Columbia to become the top recipient of U.S.-aid (save always for Israel). After the immoral invasion of Iraq in 2003, however, the leaders of Turkey sided with 95 percent of their population in opposing the U.S.'s proposal of using their nation for "front door access" into Baghdad. It was only then that we began hearing about the crimes committed by Turkey that killed thousands and displaced millions more, while neglecting to mention the fact that it was never reported beforehand, because the atrocities were carried out with Washington's vast military apparatus, answering the question as to "why not?"

The tide has changed slightly since Uncle Sam gave the Turks the big Red, White, and Blue middle finger—continuing to use their massive airbase in Incirlik for "front door" entry and, supposedly unbeknownst to their government, a portal of transportation for suspected terrorists; some 24 flights, according to the WikiLeaks documents. The CIA torturers claim that since 2002, the government of Turkey has allowed use of the airstrip for their "Operation Fundamental Justice"—that is, rendition program—up until February of last year.

As can be seen in recent years, the nation of Turkey has broken ranks with Uncle Sam, and has now openly called for better relations with Iran, welcoming it to the 21st Century and condemning U.S. pressure to enforce more sanctions that seek to curtail its nuclear infrastructure.

Revelations of that caliber do not help Uncle Sam's goal of worldwide hegemony. Surprisingly (or unsurprisingly to us conspiracy-minded researchers), the WikiLeaks data-dump disclosed that Turkey was now a terrorist-sponsoring rogue state, whose open border policy was directly responsible for weaponry getting into the hands of Iraqi insurgents. Strangely, an early report from the *Jerusalem Post* also claimed that the U.S. was supporting the PKK, the Kurdistan Workers Party, which is listed as a terrorist organization. This has all yet to be verified.

Those cables were soon followed up by direct criticism of Turkish Prime Minister Recep Tayyip Erdoğan, who is said to be an incompetent fool at running his military. Says one of the cables:

> Dutch Foreign Minister Bernard Bot was 'disturbed' by Erdogan's admission to him 'that he could not stop the flights [out of the Aegean region bordering Greece] because he did not control the military.'

Then came word that the Prime Minister had been holding Swiss Bank accounts. Eric Edelman, a former U.S. ambassador to Turkey, in a cable sent to Washington on Dec. 30, 2004, wrote:

> We have heard from two contacts that Erdoğan has eight accounts in Swiss banks; his explanations that his wealth comes from the wedding presents guests gave his son and that a Turkish businessman is paying the educational expenses of all four Erdoğan children in the U.S. purely altruistically are lame.

Erdoğan has said the information is bogus, and swore to resign if found true. He's even threatened legal action against WikiLeaks.

It might be forgiven if the end assessment of these disclosures is little more than a government-sponsored ploy to curry war-time hysteria, while simultaneously discrediting those who disagree with our foreign policy. H. Michael Sweeney, "Professor Paranoid," has similar thoughts. As a personal privacy and security expert, webmaster of Proparanoid.net and author of three books on the subjects of disinformation and mind control, the Professor shared similar theories with me.

Twenty-newspapers started publishing lies about Germans cutting off the breasts of Belgian women [during World War II]; wasn't true, but it fueled fervor for and favor of entry into the War [II]. The same thing happened in the Kuwait rescue verses Iraq; CIA brought in a shill Kuwaiti 'nurse' (who was really the daughter of wealthy Kuwaiti royals) to testify before Congress that Iraqis were bayonetting babies to steal incubators. Was not true, but we went to war thinking it was.

As for what Professor Sweeney thinks about Julian Assange and his WikiLeaks, he says,

I think Assange is both legitimate and a dupe at the same time. His matters are somewhat parallel to what happened to Pierre Salinger in the Flight 800 friendly fire matter. Someone fed him sensitive information and he ran with it. But it had been a set up. In the Wikileaks case, the setup took form of two CIA 'hookers' who filed complaints against him. By shutting down his U.S. server and having him arrested, he is not in any position to manage the WikiLeaks defense against escalating verbal hype designed to have us believe him un-American, unpatriotic, and a kind of terrorist; and by association, thus, we all must be who challenge government wrongdoing and date publish proofs of our charges. It was a set up for an assault on Free Speech.

The Professor continues:

In Pierre's case, he was set up with information deliberately put onto the Internet prior to being issued to him, such that he could be made to seem the fool. The source of information did not materialize in the promised

form, and he was left holding the bag, allowing the entire 'friendly fire movement' and, more importantly, the internet, to be indicted as a 'rumor mill.' Never mind that we who kept banging away eventually gathered enough evidence that we forced the entire NTSC investigative team to resign rather than answer questions at a public hearing. You didn't read about in the newspapers, of course. Once more, it was an assault on Free Speech.

That's true in this case as well. As the Professor points out, there are several grabs for the First Amendment now commencing in Congress. Libertarian Bob Barr wrote a piece at his "Barr Code" column, reiterating fears of a new Sedition Act. "If the congressional critics of WikiLeaks founder Julian Assange have their way, a new and revised version of the Sedition Act may be in the offing," he writes.

As for what I think about Julian Assange, the man himself— who knows? He has spawned as many critics as he has fans, and both groups may very well have their own good reasons. From the former circle, however, we find a much more verbose assortment of individuals who wish to dissect the website and its webmaster for their own purposes.

Some quite literally.

Representative Peter King of New York has called for WikiLeaks to be branded a terrorist organization, while the always reliably idiotic Bill "I-might-as-well-be-a-Nazi" O' Reilly has said he wishes Assange was hit by a drone strike.

Suspending these ridiculous statements for a moment or two, one can reflect on what is known for sure: The United States Government, as with any other tyrannical state, is prone to secrecy. That truism is contradictory to our proclaimed democracy, for starters, and demonstrably detrimental to our well-being throughout our history.

Whistleblowers are not traitors, terrorists, or anything else.

They should be praised, not condemned.

With that being said, Assange plays the part of an international playboy rather well, obviously enjoying his James Bond lifestyle. All that media exposure can make a skeptical mind wonder: if he is really saying things the State doesn't want to be heard, would he be given as much airtime as he has been on the Corporate Media Machine?

One last bit to reflect upon.

A man who writes articulate essays regarding the ill-effects of State conspiracies apparently has no place in his heart for a nation that was never given a proper answer as to why 3,000 lives were taken on the morning of September 11, 2001, yet, at the same time, brags about holding onto information that evidently proves little grey men in flying saucers exist, and are amongst us. "It is worth noting that in yet-to-be-published parts of the Cablegate archive there are indeed references to UFOs," Assange says, embracing the so-called "cablegate" meme.

Whether true or untrue, the words of the late conspiracy researcher Jim Keith serve well in dispelling such bombast disinformation:

> *An analysis of current UFO stories, including those of flying saucers and the recent element of 'underground alien bases,' suggests that they may be cooked up to conceal actual realms of experimentation and manipulation by the government or other control factors.*

In summary, I recommend healthy doses of skepticism for everyone.

Even for Mr. Assange.

Proposition 19: Who Said What, and Why

PROPOSITION 19 HAS been defeated. The Tax, Regulate, and Control Act was the first legislative attempt in nearly thirty years of Golden State history to legalize and commercialize cannabis sativa for recreational use. Until another attempt comes up, pseudo-legalization in the form of medicinal cards will remain in place.

An abbreviated history of drug policy in the U.S., and of cannabis particularly, summons unusual tales in the early 1900's, about "Hindoos" coming aboard San Francisco ports, with their hashish smoking and strange attire. In the meantime, a certain "loco weed" from beyond south of the border was making its rounds in California pharmacy journals.

From there, government proxies Dr. Hamilton Wright, a narcotics expert and a man considered by many to be the "architect" of prohibition policy, and one Henry J. Finger, a prominent member of the California Board of Pharmacy, began laying the groundwork for prohibition, which came in 1913 with the first state law banning hemp production. At the end of last year, the U.S. government had thrown nearly $40 billion dollars at law enforcement agencies for their cause, state and federal funds put together (as documented by the DrugSense.org website). This was justified with an oft-pronounced objective of stopping the use of illegal substances, while somehow reinstituting another brand of socially-acceptable behavior, and to ultimately declare victory on this "War on Drugs"—considered by many to be near-superficial, and completely compromised by all parties involved.

Even with such an enormous amount of time, money, and effort being put forth in order to stop the use of marijuana and other illicit substances, the outcome has remained abysmal: 20 million people in the U.S. continue to smoke pot regularly, with 2009 seeing a slight increase in that percentage. Marijuana prosecutions that year were at nearly 900,000 people, one of the highest numbers in years. Tokers, pot smokers, and people who legitimately need cannabis to treat life-threatening ailments remain the number one target in this nebulous drug war.

And for many constitutional experts, our rights, specifically the 4th Amendment protecting private property, have been bent or broken altogether to reconcile the many declarations of this "war," the people in which it affects having no understanding as to why it is being carried out in the first place. "The War on Drugs is the most common reason for the use of extreme tactics by local police," asserts constitutional expert Judge Andrew Napolitano.

The end result of this New Age Inquisition? Gangster-run institutions, both legal and illegal, sheriffs and hoodlums, north and south of the border, which have monopolized and now control every facet of a very lucrative and pivotal marketplace— the drug economy. Every one of these people sustaining a moderate income from the current policies in place.

Although everyone has heard of these numbers before— shown long ago to be ridiculously unproductive—a debate on the issue has only recently been heard by those living in California. Discussions about this issue can regularly be convoked when speaking to one of the countless thousands of non-violent offenders currently imprisoned in one our many penitentiaries. Opponents of the historic measure wanted to keep marijuana criminalized in the new century, for arguments made decades before, and proponents today were thrilled that such an initiative was finally set to be decided on, although with occasional naiveté.

Mike Meno wanted to see a change in this nation's drug policy. As media consultant to the Marijuana Policy Project (MMP), one of the largest and most influential marijuana reform organizations in the country, Meno had been appearing regularly on news and commentary programs, lobbying for the passage of Prop 19. "MMP has endorsed Prop 19," he told Cannabis Times a few months back, "not only because it [would have been] a huge step forward from a national movement to end marijuana prohibition, but more immediately it would bring an end to nearly a hundred years of failed prohibition in California."

Meno emphasized that out of half a million people going to the emergency room for drug illnesses—legal and illegal—marijuana is responsible for the least amount. Coming from the side of the opposition to defend their monopoly is the impenetrable Alcohol Industry, which contributed to Prop 19's defeat. Meno provided Cannabis Times with the numbers: $10,000 from the California Beer and Beverage Distributors. Critics immediately contested that they were simply trying to kill the competition.

Although "Big Booze" denies any intention of doing so, insisting only that Prop 19 is "misguided" and "poorly-written," the industry continues to market colorful cans with such brand names as Loco 420 (lots of caffeine, sugar, and alcohol) and Earthquake malt liquor (tall can with 12 percent alcohol-content for 99 cents)—favorites amongst the delinquent teen culture. Alcohol deaths annually claim around 100,000 lives, with that whole debate ending in 1933. The tobacco and fast food industries won't be detailed.

Other opponents of the measure were those who earn a living from such prohibitive legislation: law enforcement officers. In fact, a domino-reaction to legalize cannabis around the nation—as happened with Prop 215 in 1997—could spell endgame for law enforcement personal everywhere, leading to millions of layoffs. To stop such an occurrence from happening, generous donations poured in from the likes of the California Police Chiefs Association, with $30,000, and another $20,500 from the California Narcotics Officers Associations.

Los Angeles County Sheriff Lee Baca decreed himself as a sort of "leader" of the opposition. "The medicinal marijuana program that voters authorized years ago has been hijacked by underground drug dealing criminals who are resorting to violence in order to control their piece of the action," Baca said, adding that Prop 19 would have burdened officials with too much work. Pointing to hypocrisy within Baca's statements, a letter to the *LA Times* contends: "When doctors write inappropriate prescriptions or patients seek them, Baca doesn't say that the pharmaceutical industry has been hijacked by criminals."

"They have a vested interest in keeping it illegal," Meno said in agreement, who also acknowledged the potential Prop 19 had in damaging the Drug Cartels right across our border. "This is why former Mexican Presidents have come out and called for legalization." True, experts pointed out a vulnerability in the Mexican economy that might not be able to accommodate for full-scale legalization. Despite this, former Mexican President Vicente Fox has said that Mexico should "consider legalizing the production, sales, and distribution of all major drugs." Current Head of State, Felipe Calderon, had also expressed a desire to see an objective debate on drug legalization, before metamorphosing into just another politician in line with the status quo.

A report from the *Sacramento Bee*'s Tim Johnson confirms the fear, as drug production in Mexico climbed 35 percent in 2009—the highest rate in nearly two decades. In 2001, cannabis farming in Mexico's Golden Triangle was around 10,000 acres. That number has now almost tripled. Like opium in Afghanistan, cannabis remains a pivotal part of the Mexican economy, and accounts for nearly 60 percent of the Cartel's drug revenue. "If they vote 'yes' to approve full legalization," says Jorge Hernandez Tinajero, a political scientist at the National Autonomous University, "I think it will have a radical impact in Mexico." Since it has never been tried here before, nobody can say for certain. "Is that much going to change in a regulated market?" Meno asks me rhetorically. Except for sweeping the rug out from under the murderous gangsters, "probably not."

Not everyone sees this as a good thing, however. Victor Cass held a different opinion on Prop 19. A member of the police force in Greater Los Angeles, Cass believes that the measure would have sent a negative message to the younger generation, and to the world in general. Taking a personal standpoint against the measure, he spoke to *Cannabis Times*.

> [*The U.S.*] *stands for a lot of good stuff: freedom, democracy, rugged individualism. I don't think one of the things we should stand for is legal drugs...It just sends the wrong message to people. I know a lot of people have debated the merits of marijuana organically, and I'm different in that I don't argue the merits of marijuana smoking per se; I'm arguing about the message to our young people—and around the world—the message to the people in this country that wish to undermine the fabric of our country.*

As noble and honest as Cass' statements are, two explicit pieces of irony can be made clear. One: "rugged individualism" could be, and often is, defined in such a way that includes putting what you want into your own body, harmful or not. "There's a whole part of our society that loves the outlaw figure," Cass says. "They love Jesse James and the Sopranos. They love this 'barefoot bandit' even though he's a criminal who steals from people. They take rugged individualism a bit too far." The other bit of irony in his assertion is the evidence suggesting that our highest officials have actively played a role in undermining that sacred fabric. Allegations against former National Security Council member Oliver North sought proof of his involvement in Contra cocaine trafficking. Senator John Kerry's Subcommittee on Terrorism, Narcotics, and International Operations in 1988 concluded that "numerous references to drug trafficking [can be found] within Mr. North's own notebooks."

"If you want to smoke weed, smoke weed, just don't ever tell our young people that it's okay," Cass says.

Another concern opponents have is the potency of the Tetrahydrocannabinol (THC) in the marijuana being grown. Forty years ago, hippies smoked joints that were between 1—4 percent THC. Reports now read of that amount going up to ask much as 10 percent for most strands nowadays. As for the Mexican cartels, Cass says it's no time to wave the white flag of defeat, but admits that undermining their influence is difficult. "If I had the magic answer to that, I'd be a billionaire, working for one of Obama's agencies."

Now-former Governor of California Arnold Schwarzenegger had largely been an enigma in the debate, although he was one of the first prominent persons in the State to openly call for one. On the one hand, he writes an OP-ED plainly stating that legalization will not bring forth the revenue needed to fix the state's financial crisis (insisting the blame on egregious pension plans for State workers), adding that Prop 19's passage would have been a "laughing stock" to the country. Then again, at the time of this article, the Governator's signature of SB: 1449 will have acquired more tickets from pot possessions of less than an ounce. "It's already like this in everything but name," Arnold said, who defended his action on a taping of the *Tonight Show*.

"The biggest question mark right now," Mike Meno warned, "is what the federal government is going to do." Indeed, both the Bell salary scandal and the San Bruno fire have brought with them federal probes. When it comes to drug policy, and the long history of indictments and prosecutions, be prepared for something never witnessed before.

One last guaranteed negative that was sure to come from Prop 19 would have been Section 4—criminalization. Sale of marijuana to a minor, starting from someone 18 years of age, is a felony punishable up to three, five, or seven years. Thousands of parolees under the age of 21 are currently on parole here in the Golden State, living in environments that could have very easily been interpreted as a "potential" for sales to a minor. "If we were all good parents who raised their kids with the values you and I may have," says Cass, a recipient of NAMI California's 2010 Criminal Justice Professional Award, "if teachers were teaching properly, if social workers were doing their jobs, if coaches and clergy were doing their parts, you wouldn't have this Drug War."

As truthful and optimistic as it sounds, that's not the reality.

Legalization: Still a Good Idea

MORE THAN TWENTY years ago, drug-reform advocate Todd Austin Brenner wrote that "complete legalization of marijuana…would be the real test." He further went on to argue that "drugs causing permanent addiction, such as heroin and crack, would be banned from sale. Instead, these drugs would be offered free of charge at clinics where addicts have been registered. Simultaneously, these addicts would be helped in trying to overcome their illness and would hopefully be cured."

The digital timepiece at DrugSense.org still remains quite clear with the implication. Counting only since the start of 2011, the U.S. government has spent nearly five billion dollars on the Drug War, state and federal efforts combined. Nearly 115,000 of those arrested are cannabis users, fifteen-hundred of them already locked-away. Meanwhile, usage remains undaunted.

Notice the hint?

No matter how much money the taxpayer spends and no matter how many are arrested, we get no closer in stopping the use of cannabis or any of those other readily available substances. That's the addictive nature of drugs, ill-defined as that word might always be. Rather, the numbers given above are more reminiscent of dollar signs floating above a given prison official's head as he ushers his "product" into an iron cage. He or she with said-badge would laugh if reading such a suggestion, lest they be found guilty of profiting from crime.

A New Problem Coming into View

Accepting the corporate view of the world, non-participants of this debate would respond apathetically. However, this monster is evolving. Nowadays, the voter-block has been stirred ever so slightly while law enforcement officials begin to realize that they're not the only ones with big numbers in their paychecks. Both of these amnesiac bystanders could notice the column permanently placed in the *Los Angeles Times*: "Mexico Under Siege."

Stealing the morning edition from my neighbor's recycling bin, the effort failed me not: Uncle Sam, now considering putting armed troops into Mexico, where almost 230,000 people have been displaced from the Drug War. Congressman Michael McCaul (R-TX) has recently convened in the House to consider placing the Mexican cartels on the international terrorist list. With America and its UN partners now deciding when our country goes to war, it's unlikely to raise a suspicious eyebrow anywhere in the civilized world.

In a recent report for *Cannabis Times,* I quoted numbers given to me from the Marijuana Policy Project's very own Mike Meno, who says that over 60% of the Cartel's drug revenue comes from pot. David Bienenstock at *High Times* reports 40%. In either case, underground sales of cannabis fund just about half of that Mexican Mafiocracy south of the border—an unconfirmed multi-billion dollar number. And yet, with no clear objective in mind, the criminal-factories here in the U.S. continue to operate.

Criminal factories? Yes, the "Hydra-Theory" of drug lordship: once one goes down, two more take his place. The only way to slay the beast for certain is by removing the source of his power— or might that be powder? —the white stuff you tried to warn your kid about, whom, if the laws were slightly altered, would not be greeted by any narrow-eyed strangers carrying shoe-boxes outside their school. It's long been known that these beasts breed inside the secretive Prison Networks, who are left unrestrained from taking tax-dollars to their bank accounts instead of rehabilitative services.

Exploring Alternatives

Obvious as this failed policy seems, even a minimally persuasive reform-advocate would have to plead with their neighbor for an honest conversation about the matter. The trouble is worth it, *because there actually is another option.* This idea is foreign, perhaps like eating fragrant meat at a low-key Korean restaurant downtown, but—who knows?—it might just work.

Ostensibly, the reform always referred to is the transferring of responsibility: taking drug distribution away from the black marketers, and, with public and parental vigilance, entrusting the task to somewhat more conserved hands who can keep an eye out for who gets what and how often. After recognizing the evidence that undesired products don't go away with any wizardly pen signatures, and that costly prohibition has in fact had the opposite effect, this by creating even more criminals inside the less-than-transparent penitentiaries, it would not be difficult in conceiving.

An academic study by Alex Stevens—asking "What Can We Learn from the Portuguese Decriminalization of Drugs?"—reports that since 2001, when their government decriminalized drugs and focused on treatment instead of incarceration, the amount of Problematic Drug Users (PDU's) actually dropped—slightly, but significantly enough to warrant more consideration. "Using data from the Netherlands, the U.S., Australia, and Italy…They [citing another study] concluded that the removal of criminal penalties appear to produce positive but slight impacts. The primary impact was reducing the burden and cost in the criminal justice system."

Stevens also emphasizes that, contrary to the widely-held notion that the removal of sanctions would increase the amount of users, it did not happen.

With the countless studies showing cannabis to be far less harmful than tobacco, alcohol, fast-food, pills and other bad habits (many of the studies government-funded), a strong indication persists to recommend the plant be allowed to flourish naturally for personal consumption, with understandable limitations on the amount of 420 cafés sure to prop up there afterwards. Harder drugs—the ones you dare not even whisper—would be manufactured and handled pharmaceutically, with a Netherlander's approach of treatment instead of incarceration.

Concerns

In the weeks prior to Prop 19's vote, the CIA-funded RAND Corporation published a study called *Reducing Drug Trafficking Revenues and Violence in Mexico: Would Legalizing Marijuana in California Help?* Their final report said that the measure would not cause significant damage to the Cartels.

Amazingly, the statistics provided by the think tank left out one important fact that was pointed out by Meno. While Mexican exports of pot are estimated to be anywhere from 15-30 percent, the gross domestic production of Cartel-operated pot farms here in the U.S. is roughly the same. Weed is very easy to grow, you see, and besides, why let California's perfect crop weather go to waste? The end result left unmentioned by RAND: it's impossible to eradicate such an easily-grown plant; only attempt regulation at its commercial value via distribution.

In the case of addicts and dope-fiends, breaking into another's personal property is usually to fund the ghastly habit, with alcohol and speed occasionally causing social disruptions involving vehicles and rose gardens. Giving it away for near-free to the Zombies (I mean addicts!), and placing them into specialized areas (like parks or dormitories), might alleviate the public burden of DUI's and assaults. Ultimately, it is vastly more humane, far less expensive, and certainly more controlled than sending a non-violent offender off to the prison Factory.

So, did Prop 19 bring forth remedies for this perpetual madness? Perhaps it helped. Bienenstock's *High Times* article reported that "Exit polls showed that youth turnout was up 16% over 2006, the last midterm election in California, and that a whopping 64% of those under twenty-five supported Prop 19." Statistically impressive, but from a personal standpoint, I recall little talk amongst the college-bound. One such conversation took place inside of a Jacuzzi:

"Yeah man, it sucks the measure didn't pass," a well-to-do psychology major had said to me.

"Well, did you go and vote?" I asked.

"Nah," he shrugged.

Oh, well then...

Questions Requiring Answers

Since the Drug War affects all neighborhoods alike, an objector of such reform measures who takes the time to have this little chat (Jacuzzis or elsewhere) should be required to answer the following questions:

- How do you intend on making all this money and effort worth our while?

- Are you willing to send another non-violent drug-user off to the Criminal Farm?

- Maybe we could publicly flog the creature in Times Square hoping that it'll scare others from doing so?

- What about raising the deficit a little more so as to pay the pensions of a hundred-thousand gangster-minded prison guards?

- How about asking Ben Bernanke to print another trillion dollars to fund Mexico's oncoming civil war?
- Or, what if we just blow-up the entire fucking peninsula—all the way to the Panama Canal?

These decisions are lost on those possessing hearts accustomed to punishment as an absolute, even if the crime is hurting oneself and the outcome is a zombified drug-addict obtaining five new contacts once he is put in his cell.

Since Proposition 19 was defeated, this revolutionary debate has, predictably, been placed on semi-hiatus. Presumably, it will pick up again once another thousand people are either decapitated or incarcerated or otherwise had their lives ruined.

This reformer's argument is best summed-up by Peter Gorman at *Skunk Magazine*, who placed a well-said rant in a recent issue:

> *For decades, voices of reason have been calling for an end to the War on Drugs, through legalization, but what with the billions of dollars in black market money to be made annually, most of which at some point goes through US banks, and billions more spent on weapons and ammunition, the prison industry, law enforcement, prosecutors, rehab—hell, even methadone...well, those voices of reason seem to be whispering into a very large pit. Nobody making the money is listening.*

How true Mr. Gorman. How sadly, consequently true.

The Loughner Question: The Media's Portrayal of the Arizona Shooting

WHILE MAKING THE declaration that "the revolutionaries from the revolution are in control of the land and laws," Jared Loughner saw it as justifiable grounds for walking up to Gabrielle Giffords at her supermarket rally in Tuscan and opening fire, hoping that it would later be understood that it was needed in order to push the world past A.D.E. Or, its Peak. Giffords survived, thankfully, but six others did not.

I watched the tragic news unfold from the first day. A "psychotic, murderous rampage," Shepard Smith affirmed, in what would become the only credible report on *Fox News*. Details of Loughner's behavior were quickly established. For the past couple of months he had been leaving cyber-prints all over the web, the most publicized of which was his scrolling manifesto found on YouTube. A diminutive, plain text, with words that were always structured in a kind of limerick, were set against a solid-colored background with the most melancholiest of sound pleading from the beyond the speakers. Reading it in the dark by myself at three-o-clock in the morning, it was all the more unsettling.

Loughner could just say something like, "If you're receiving a grade from Pima Community College class then the grade you're receiving is unconstitutional because of the Bill of Rights"— affording the viewer a fully-drawn conclusion that he was being mistreated. In his mind, this retardation of elementary discourse was vindication-enough for him to prove his thesis with spilled blood. While a great many of us question his actions, it's a fair guess that he is probably doing the same: sitting in his cold dark cage, wondering how others don't understand *why*.

The Freedom to Speak

There was another group left out of the discussion: those who were concerned with civil liberties and the Constitution, who at that point, in the earliest hours of the breaking news, were hearing something entirely different than the endless commentary. The patriots, basement bloggers, zine publishers, street activists, and conspiracy theorists saw it coming like a tidal wave over the horizon, and could do nothing to stem the flood of disinformation about to be witnessed: a tidal wave of media magicians, arm-chair experts, and jaded politicians, who were going to tell us all how *bad* things were and what must be done to prevent the next psychopath from striking.

The first of these characters was Arizona's own Sheriff Dupnik, who at the very first press conference took the opportunity to denounce the "vitriolic rhetoric coming from the people in the radio business and some people in the TV business," invoking that America has "not become the nice United States that most of us grew up in." The awkward and inappropriate statements of Dupnik were only the first of a great many more to come.

An early online-surfer of such bombastic nonsense was Kae Davis, a writer at the Green Celebrity Network. While using her column to directly blame the Sarah Palin crowd (more on her in a second), she nevertheless correctly stated in her article that "the assassin has been reading philosophy and logic books but failed entirely to understand that if you assert a premise that simply is not true, that no matter how cogent your argument, no one is going to believe you."

Exactly.

But when she stated that everyone assumes he is "an asshole who employed the strategy of terror to both humble and make a mockery of all things right about our American government," I felt a compulsion to oblige Ms. Davis with my own thesis. If, as an illustration, I said that she was fundamentally wrong about this situation, and that the government of the United States was using the shooting in Tucson to generate a panic in an attempt to curtail Constitutional liberties, I would (and should) be expected to present evidence.

Inserting that in a minute, it should be noted not as coincidence but instead as another earmark in the recent attempts to derail freedom on the Internet, that on the day before the shooting (January the 7th), CBS reported that the Obama Administration was in the process of drafting legislation that would give everybody using the Internet a federally-registered ID card. So what? Who cares? Well, after much insistency that it was not a national ID card, gadget guru Damon Brown, writing a follow-up piece at CNET, warned:

> *If each individual had a universal ID, it would be even easier to access his or her information. Aggressively targeted marketing using private data and evasive, extensive files on user habits could become the norm.*

In fact, several pieces of legislation have been introduced in our Congress over the last year or so that would essentially reduce net anonymity and give sweeping authority over to the Feds. The DISCLOSE Act of 2010, for instance, would "radically redefine how the FEC regulates political commentary. A section of the DISCLOSE Act would exempt traditional media outlets from coordination regulations, but the exemption does not include bloggers." If operating from any foreign institution, significant influence on elections, via federal regulation of money put through the blogosphere, would not be allowed. The mass media, being home-grown, is not subject to such rules, unless there exists a 20 percent stake in an external institution. National boundaries notwithstanding, bloggers typing anywhere from Moscow to Beijing—if ever defined as having "significant influence" on the government—would be forced to disclose those financial contributions.

The Combating Online Infringement and Counterfeits Act, another attempt, would "Black-list" Internet domain names with broadly defined language of "infringement activity." Websites publishing scoops about a politician's adulterous sex affair could then wield a sabre of "intellectual holdings" and request court-approval to shut down any website trying to republish the story. Neglecting critical reservations made from the ACLU, the Entertainment Industry, worth an estimated net of some billions, favors with Patrick Leahy (D-V), the co-author of the legislation.

Yet another tentacle reaching for our Bill of Rights is The Protecting Cyberspace as a National Security Asset, which would grant President Obama (or any other paid-for executive) the authority to shut off the Internet in the event of a cyber-attack. Say, from a superpower like China, or an activist group like Anonymous, or anybody else one might hear on tonight's report. Quoted in a *PC Magazine* article, the bill's co-author and main promoter, Senator Lieberman (I-CT) noted that "right now, China can disconnect parts of its Internet in a case of war... We need to have that here, too."

Getting to Ms. Davis's conclusion, the mass media machine, in collusion with the government elites who fear uprisings such as that in Egypt (and who subsequently author freedom-eroding laws to prevent information from turning into organization), deliberately injected a massive dose of influential hysteria into the tragedy when they quoted—the very next day—an undisclosed individual working at the Department of Homeland Security, who

186

first tipped off *The Huffington Post* that Jared Loughner might (key word might) have been affiliated with a white separatist movement calling itself the American Renaissance.

The founder of the organization, Jared Taylor, quickly went on record to condemn the attacks and reveal that Loughner had never even been a subscriber. After recognizing it as the lie that it was, *Fox News*, the *Associated Press*, and the *NY Times*, fearing for being labeled as defenders of racism, refused to retract their initial reports and repudiate the DHS's claims.

But that's not all. The Loughner Question, as it was at this point, quickly applied itself to the Second Amendment and an individual's right to possess firearms. Sarah Palin, the Tea-Partiers, and any other person imploring "gun remedies" were taken to task for "inciting an atmosphere of violence and hate." Or something like that. Even the most moderate libertarian would have been appalled that individual responsibility was never even considered for placement in the equation, which became more or less a game of pong played-out between talking-heads stationed on the top of media empires, refusing to report the stated concern of Constitutional freedoms.

The Result of Hysteria

Such unchallenged fear-mongering can soon lead to a disillusioned population, already lethargic from watching reality shows, and are not likely to protest when the said-laws floating around in Congress are about to be given a signature. Positioning the situation in contrast with the escalating chaos in Egypt, and the Mubarak Regime's intermittence of the Internet, a rash of solicitude would be warranted here, stateside, from vigilant commentators.

With such deceitful claims of group affiliation, like being part of a racist movement (usually funded by the same elites), it can easily be compared with other behind-closed-door types who employ similar tactics of division. Comparatively, by the same reasoning, I can say that the two smoking packages that showed up in Washington in the days preceding the Tucson shooting were the concerted actions of someone at the CIA—this as an effort to create yet even more chaos—and it would not have to necessarily be true in order to gain reputability; merely stated.

Forgiving my pseudo-academia, an objective analysis would report that Jared Loughner cannot be singled out for his deranged, incoherent language while the government of the United States stands guilty of the same offense: making bold-faced assertions without the gratitude of evidence. Why exalt such blatant propaganda? Unless the trial provides tangible evidence (which might also become questionable), Mark Potok could have very well put the final nail in this coffin. In the courtyard of his Southern Poverty Law Center, Potok—brandishing a very large paint brush—stated that the rhetoric emanating from Jared Loughner's hate could have come from anywhere. From Marx, to Hitler, or even New Age hero David Icke.

The next move?

Tragic events like this always lead to the introduction of new laws. This time we have Rep. Robert Brady (D-PA) who is promising a bill to outlaw any speech or symbols that could be interpreted as threats to members of Congress. Furthermore, Rep. James Clyburn (D-SC), wants us to "rethink the parameters of free speech." Rep. Louise Slaughter (D-NY), with finger pressed firmly on the document-shredder, promises to look into ways to "police the airwaves more effectively."

"Frankly," Slaughter says, "what I would like to see if we can all get together on both sides of the isle...Democrats and Republicans, to really talk about what we can do to cool down the country. Part of it has to be what they are hearing over the airwaves." Rep Peter King, (R-NY), has also just introduced legislation that would make gun-toting a crime if one-thousand feet from a federal official. No word yet as to how this is expected to play out in the real world.

The only man who was brave enough to stand up for liberty was the father of nine-year-old Christina-Taylor Green (synchronistically born on 9-11-01), a victim of Loughner's rampage. During an interview on the *Today Show*, John Green said that, "This shouldn't happen in this country, or anywhere else," then bravely added what no talking-head dared to: "In a free society, we're going to be subject to people like this. I prefer this to the alternative."

A New World Order?

One of those cryptic, global elites often spoken of, Zbigniew Brzezinski, the geostrategist (and a conspirator's best friend) now giving his opinion on the Egyptian crisis, has stated that the global world now requires...

> ...[an American] society dominated by an elite whose claim to political power would rest on allegedly superior scientific know-how. Unhindered by the restraints of traditional liberal values (founding liberal values like freedom), this elite would not hesitate to achieve its political ends by using the latest modern techniques for influencing public behavior and keeping society under close surveillance and control.

Hillary Clinton, a more prominent elite, told her friends in the United Arab Emirates that Loughner was an "extremist" (not a psychopath), and signified that both nations "have the same problems."

Today, two months after the deplorable and senseless attack, it should be widely known that Jared Loughner was not *only* a devil-worshipper. Nor cross-dresser. Or drug-riddled psychotic. But also a patsy, whose ideologies might never be clearly defined except by those desperately attempting to brand him as *this* or *that* for their own purposes.

With no weighty assurance for any particular mindset, he was the perfect tool to fire-up rhetorical debate, rebuking Kae Davis' description.

Remarkably void of any human empathy, Loughner was unaware that actions like his are used by governments keen on stopping the very suggestion of the kind of uprisings now being reported on in the Middle East. Nonetheless, when stating that "they" were controlling the grammar, he was probably too stupid to realize what THEY actually were trying to do—graciously helped along by his sick mentality.

The Drug War Grows Appendages

IN ADDITION TO well-established laws already requiring the arrest of "controlled substance" violators, police personal in the states of Indiana and Kentucky have just been granted *carte blanche* in deciding whether to enter a suspect's place of residence. Warrants no longer need to be requested, and any "presumption" otherwise has been made clear by the Supreme Court for all Americans to know and learn from: if police ever become curious of what's inside your home, there will exist a permanent set of "exigencies" that overrule the Fourth Amendment.

This comes in the wake of two historic court rulings. The first, *Kentucky vs. King*, started in October of 2005 when Lexington police conducted a "buy-bust" operation in which dealers of crack cocaine would be indicted after selling dope to an undercover cop. After following one such entrepreneur back home, officers were overcome with the aroma of burnt Ganja emanating from the apartment complex, and, believing those inside to be destroying vital evidence—the stated exigency— exercised pure jackboot strength, kicking in the door. It happened to be the wrong one.

Instead of their presumed suspect, police found three people sitting on a couch, one of whom was smoking marijuana. Crack cocaine, scales, and several cellphones were adjacent to them. According to *High Times*, Hollis King was sentenced to eleven years for intention to sell dope. The Supreme Court of Kentucky soon overturned this conviction because the evidence was illegally obtained, due to the absence of a warrant.

The U.S. Supreme then pronounced the final judgment, agreeing that it was legal for police to enter due to the "circumstances." Justice Scalia, speaking for the majority, stated that, "Everything done was perfectly lawful," asking snidely, "It's unfair to the criminal? Is that a problem? I really don't understand the problem." Scalia added, "The one thing that it (law enforcement) has going for it is that criminals are stupid."

Stupid, yes, but not always treasonous.

Justice Ginsberg, the lone dissenter, wrote: "How 'secure' do our homes remain if police, armed with no warrant, can pound on doors at will and, on hearing sounds indicative of things moving, forcibly enter and search for evidence of unlawful activity?"

In the Hoosier State, officers were responding to a domestic dispute at the residence of one Richard Barnes. Barnes, refusing to let unauthorized police enter his home, eventually shoved an officer who believed himself exempt from 4th Amendment principles. Predictably, Barnes was Tasered, arrested and charged. In this case, the final ruling came from the Indiana Supreme Court. After unanimously agreeing that the police were in violation of the law and had no business in the home, the court decided in a vote of 3-2 that the "right to resist an unlawful police entry into a home is against public policy and is incompatible with modern Fourth Amendment jurisprudence"—so stated by Justice Steven David.

Justices Rucker and Dickson dissented: "In my view," said Rucker, "the majority sweeps with far too broad a brush by essentially telling Indiana citizens that government agents may now enter their homes illegally—that is, without the necessity of a warrant, consent, or exigent circumstances." Indiana Sheriff Hartman has mused that "...he would use random house to house searches if he believed it was necessary."

These new appendages of the Police State have given

ammunition to an already well-equipped Drug War, a formidable opponent who, according to the documentary work of Charles Shaw, has a current employment of 2.4 million people—more employees than Wal-Mart and McDonalds combined.

The prison syndicate stranglehold on this once free land might soon find out once and for all that the mission of stopping drug use has been compromised from within. The recently arrested Sinaloa cartel member Jesus Vicente Zambada Niebla listed in a sworn affidavit his true employers: the U.S. Department of Justice, Drug Enforcement Administration (DEA), the Federal Bureau of Investigation, Immigration and Customs, and, my favorite, the Department of Homeland Security.

Niebla is expected to testify against them.

Even more so, the "higher-up's" dissolved any hope for drug sentence reform, instead deciding to amplify provisions of the Patriot Act, just given a 5-year extension. These policies, which constitute life here in "New" America, show yet again that the ruling caste of America in the year 2011 is no different than any other administration that came before it.

And, perhaps, much worse.

Cindy Sheehan's Anti-War Cause gets Condescended

LAST MONTH, ANTI-WAR activist Cindy Sheehan appeared on Dr. Drew Pinsky's new *HLN* program, responding to the death of Osama bin laden and expounding on her statement that "anyone believing in the death (of Osama) is stupid." Having positioned herself in a spot where most people would automatically decry her as a crazy, Sheehan defended herself rather well, lucidly telling Drew that it's "pathetic to just accept these pronouncements from our government like they're the truth," adding inquiries that ought to be answered, like where the DNA evidence is proving it was him.

But pure skepticism with an admitted absence of empirical evidence from anywhere wasn't enough for Dr. Drew, who, under the guise of agreement, was actually condescending of Sheehan's radical position—ever so subtly—by constantly asking if her activism was the way she coped with the loss of her son Casey, who died in Iraq back in 2004. "Sometimes I tell people dealing with depression, or trying to find meaning in life—or grief—service can really make a difference," Pinsky said.

Consistency is not Dr. Drew's strong point. At no point, neither on the program nor in any article (as far as I can tell), did Drew ever wonder aloud about a noble, albeit controversial question: how does George W. Bush cope with taking this nation to war under a lie? Does he go running? Relapse into alcoholism? Battle man-eating pretzels? Contemplate the secrets of universe?

Indeed, he probably does all of the above, with the exception of the very latter. These diagnosis's must've been lost in Drew's one-track mindset of a presidential decision outweighing a mother's mission of justice; no doubt perceiving Sheehan only as a woman who handles her anguish through protests, and not as someone who sincerely wants an end to American imperialism.

But Sheehan is in good company.

According to legendary prosecutor Vincent Bugliosi (the man who sent Charles Manson to prison), the case against George Bush is simple. "With Bush, we have hard, hard evidence that he just deliberately took us to war under a lie," Bugliosi told me in a recent interview. In his book, *The Prosecution of George W. Bush for Murder*, he makes the legal case against the forty-third president by evidencing many of the lies put forth by the administration preceding the invasion of Iraq.

For example: Bush discussed flying U2 reconnaissance aircraft over Iraq, falsely painted in UN colors, hoping to "provoke a confrontation" with Hussein if war was not immediately agreed upon in Congress. These contingency plans were recounted by David Manning, the chief foreign policy advisor to former British Prime Minister Tony Blair, who was visiting at the time.

As recently quipped by radio host Jack Blood, the Bush administration is easily interchangeable with the current one. Sheehan, responding to President Obama's statement that showcasing dead bin laden photographs is "not who we are," told Dr. Drew:

> Barack Obama has been drone bombing North Waziristan in Pakistan. He's increased [the bombing] three or four times the amount that George Bush did. To say 'we're not the kind of people to put grisly photos, but we are the kind of people that drone bombs innocent civilians.'

This policy can be nothing but bad news for the U.S., with thousands if not millions dead; a debt number that adds up to an incomprehensible total; China's recent warnings that more attacks on Pakistan will be construed as an attack on the Communist state; propounded even more so with all polls showing that Americans want out of these wars—forever plural, it seems—it might just be time to reconsider the Empire.

Where was Dr. Drew's coverage of all this?

Something else considered for not bringing forth proof of Osama's death: if evidence was delivered dutifully, it could have very well been the beginning for new calls of troop withdrawal, since, after all, the mission stated in the aftermath of 9/11 would have finally been accomplished.

Alas, that is unlikely to happen.

Why Don't We All Go-Topless?

AUGUST, THE TWENTY-FIRST: it was a rebellion against clothing. Dozens of topless protesters marched down the Venice Beach boardwalk calling for an end to sexual inequality, and a submission to simple reasoning which insists there is little difference between male and female areolas. "It's promised in the 14th Amendment" is the usual legalistic jargon.

It was one of about a dozen demonstrations taking place throughout the country, all of them organized by the appropriately named GoTopLess (Dot-Org). That group, comprised mainly of Facebook junkies and bloggers, was started in 2007 by a Frenchman named Claude Maurice Marcel Vorilhon, otherwise known as "Rael." Cult-watchers and UFO enthusiasts will remember Claude well from his humble background: a former race-car journalist turned extraterrestrial abductee. Aliens came to Earth, the story goes, for the sole purpose of meeting Claude and transporting him back to their homeland planet, some 25,000 years more advanced from ours.

Savvy observers already know this tale.

Claude came back; pronounced himself as "Rael"—the messenger of the aliens; said they were coming back; blah, blah, blah. He also attested that the aliens—the 'Elohim'—had scientifically created our species in a laboratory, and, as such, were exculpated from ridiculous earth laws that discriminate between body parts. Extraterrestrials or not, Rael provided a sound, undebatable premise for scores of men in need of an excuse to watch lovely, young women show their tits. And thank God for it, because I needed the story.

Arriving ten minutes late due to the clogged artery known as LA traffic, and startled by the surprisingly small amount of people aware of the protest, I made my way around the back alleys looking for the commotion. Then I found it: what we call a "sausage-fest"—with a ratio of men to women around 5-1. All the good-looking girls were huddled in the front of the mob, where microphone activity was taking place. It was the very extent of this "protest," and I recognized it immediately as a publicity stunt.

Trailing behind, and already a bit frustrated, I turned my camera on and spun around just in time to see them coming into view: two massively hanging breasts, accompanied by another, smaller set of tits, not any less lovely. Acting like some sort of cheap, voyeuristic porn producer, I began ducking in and out of the crowd with my camera, getting as many clips as possible; running back and forth between clearings in front of the many businesses and the sand-covered bike trail running parallel to the boardwalk—capturing as much of the action as I could from above the shoulders of spectators.

In desperate need of cameraman, I agreed to pay $10 to a Venice beach bum named Paul. "I'm here for as long as you need me," the supposed Arts-major had promised, not yet given his Mr. Hamilton. Together, we worked our way through the moving crowd, some-fifty or more people, some holding signs, a few men wearing red bikinis, and a far-fewer amount of woman top-free—except for the mandated taped nipples—and all of them moving diligently down the pathway shouting colorful boob chants. "Free your breasts, free your minds!" they vociferated, almost inducing me to take my own shirt off. Upon the sixth or seventh round of it, I decided to move in for the interviews.

Spying one of the beautiful babes in crowd, I tapped a slender, tanned shoulder and requested of the pretty face to let me point my microphone at her and ask a few questions. "Well, what brings you out here?" I asked. "It's go topless day!" She said it like it was Christmas. It wasn't really an answer, but it worked in the midst of all the belligerent nudity. "Are you part of the alien cult that organizes this?" "No," the petite, small-breasted girl said. "Do you know what I'm talking about though?" I asked again. "No."

"That was fucking pointless," she told her partner. "Sorry," I said, thinking about how redundant and stupid my questions must have sounded. "You're not welcome," she said back to me, the jiggling little ass bouncing back into the crowd.

Still bouncing back and forth between the sides of the crowd, I met up with another writer who was doing a story for the *LA Weekly*. "Everyone is talking about how this is a political event," the reporter shared, "and I think it's an event run by an alien cult." "It is!" I exclaimed. "It's run by the Raelians." It was sobering to find at least one person realizing it. After all, how many more participants could answer the question of "what are you protesting for?" with "it's Go-Topless' day"?

The freedom fighting exhibitionists soon stopped and gathered into a small circle; podium in the middle, and signs around the outer edges. "Go topless, go topless, go topless—go!" bellowed the tall, bikini-clad man standing on the soapbox. He was one of the two main organizers for the group. His partner, an-almost mature woman with smaller breasts covered with plastic nipples, was giving interviews on the outside.

"It's about being equal. If women don't have the right to be topless, then men should have to wear a top wherever a woman has to," she told to one of the other inquirers. "Hasn't it already been approved in Washington? Nadine Gary?" she averred, referring to the president of GoTopLess. "Oh yes. It is legal to go topless in Washington!"

I eventually gave my provisional cameraman his well-deserved $10. "You'll stay with me, right?" He assured me that he would. Unsurprisingly, the bastard was gone less than twenty minutes later. Unperturbed by the idea of trust, I took some more pictures, had a few more conversations, and then made my way out of there.

It should be noted that these protesters were not doing anything wrong, or even illegal. They could go topless every day with taped nipples and get exposure for their cause. They could run around with no tapped nipples and risk being arrested and fight it in court. Maybe they could support sympathetic candidates.

There was a lot more that they could have done to achieve their objective of equality in law.

But, then again—no matter what was said—it was a titty party, not a political demonstration, and all I could imagine was Mr. Rael sitting back in front of a computer screen admiring his fine work.

Occupying Los Angeles

ON OCTOBER THE first, 2011, hundreds of activists gathered in Pershing Square and began the first of their marches down the bustling Los Angeles streets. It is the first day of "Occupy Los Angeles," and it is expected to be a very long and exuberant protest. The protesters eventually stopped in front of City Hall, their new camp site. "By their expectations, it's going to be days," a police officer told me when I asked how long the occupation was expected to last.

I showed up around nine-thirty, almost a half-hour before the march began. There were already a few hundred people displaying signs, others designing them, some more handing out literature, and then those just standing around, anxiously expecting democracy in downtown LA. "It's the banks and corporations that are in charge!" yelled a man on a microphone. "Banks say 'get back' we say 'fight back'!"—"Banks say 'get back' we say 'fight back'!" The crowd chanted it again and again in timely sequence.

The overall objective of this protest depends on who is asked. Indeed, one of the primary organizers is the ANSWER Coalition, a group seeking "an end to war, and an end to racial inequality." And, as clockwork, the "vast majority of the occupants are socialistic and communistic," said Brian, a member of the Industrial Workers of the World.

A much smaller fraction wanted to see an end to the fractional reserve banking system (the group of people in which I am most inclined to agree with). "I want to bring awareness to the Federal Reserve, because I think they're interconnected, because the Fed prints the excess equity that gives the politicians the power to spend the money on wars," was told to me by Oscar, one of the few "anti-Fed" activists at the Plaza.

Following the marching demonstrators alongside the street was the "Peace Mobile," a double-trailer truck equipped with a high-powered stereo system and adorned with American flags and harmonious slogans. There were plenty of colorful characters also to be seen in the vicinity.

A website group named TheBillionaires.org stood by the street with another megaphone. The caricaturized ensemble were dressed as rich oligarchs, complete with top-hats and dollar bills protruding from the pockets of their tuxedos. They "thanked" people for giving them billions in bailout money. "Thanks for the bailout. Couldn't have done it without you." Laughter followed, leaving a feeling of quiet disgust.

After the protestors settled in and around the City Hall courtyard, the bongo drums came out, and the people began their presentations of dissent. The rest stayed on the sidewalk with banners, appealing to the cars driving by. For their efforts, they were greeted with many honking horns.

Another group out there was one that would rather not be labeled as much: Anonymous. "One should not be Anonymous, one can only claim to be anonymous," told me a Guy Fawkes-wearing gentleman. Every few minutes I would see a Fawkes mask pass me, usually worn properly on the face, other times behind the head. By far the strangest group of all the attendees was the pro-Obama crowd—consisting of a single man. And I might have seen another supporter wearing an Obama '08 ball-cap. *FOX News* reported that the Wall Street demonstrators have gathered more people from when the Occupy protest started. On the East Coast, they've been out there for weeks.

Where is this headed? Time will tell.

Occupying the Highways

"THE OCCUPATION MUST live!" someone yelled the night Occupy Los Angeles got raided. There was no way that the authorities were going to let the Occupation live forever. True, many had become complacent, and bored, and decadent—*me included*—but the level of national awareness of corporate tyranny had been raised by several points, thanks in large part to these protests. If this trend is to continue, and the goal of shaking things up is to be taken seriously, we must carry forth.

But where? And how? For the longest time, I've wanted to traverse the open highways and meet the ghosts of Jack Kerouac and Hunter S. Thompson. If it weren't for an unfortunate DUI, I probably would've already been out there. There are many legends about dissent on those long, lonely highways, and it was so important to do the same today, as revolution draws nears and we attempt to solidify our name into History.

Enter: "Yum-Yum," a guy whose name is as juvenile as his behavior. He was an eccentric, crass, and occasionally monstrous individual who's less restrained in exercising his personality than most others. When I told him that I needed a driver, he was all the more willing to help out. The "Gathering of Love" was suggested for our destination, in Florida, a gigantic group of hippies, freethinkers, and spiritual something-or-others.

There're already a few groups driving around the country with that same idea in mind. But make no mistake: we're better, more ravenous, more resourceful, more revolutionary.

We left on Christmas Day, right after another bout with my tyrannical landlord. "You are not allowed to give showers to people off the streets! If your mama wants to take them in, she can! Give me your pool key!" She screamed it for all the nearby tenants to see and overhear. I tried to tell her that I was trying to forego the pagan holiday of Christmas and actually do what Jesus Christ had said: help people. "Some Christian."

Tyrannical Trudy was referring to my partners, who were standing on the sidewalk watching the woman in the heat of her tirade: Yum-Yum, Dizzy, and Pirate. The second was a black kid, twenty years old. He was someone who could switch between chortles and calmness. Pirate was aptly named because of his goatee, trench coat, and magician's hat, which actually had a functioning, spring-loaded feature. I met them both through Yum-Yum, who I first met during the LA Occupation. I had taken home and slept with their mutual friend and fuck, Skittles, some big-breasted, bespectacled girl who enjoyed whiskey as much as she did cock. Yes, people do adopt these names and lifestyles. But they're all "lesser" people than Mrs. Community Despot, so no worries.

The vehicle for this excursion is my 1987 Nissan Pathfinder, a reputable machine in its day. She's got 155,000 miles on her, room comfortable enough for four, and a maroon red that looks quite appropriate here on Planet Mars.

All the windows are dark, with the back windshield proudly displaying three well-placed bumper-stickers. One of them advocates Ron Paul for president. I am, after all, a libertarian anti-socialist freedom fighter. He's got my vote, not because I support his views, but because he supports mine. AntiWar.com is right below him, a good resource for those people attempting to educate themselves on Empire and escape the plethora of bullshit propaganda coming from the likes of *FOX News*—who I warn against with my last remaining sticker that reads: "Turn Off FOX,

K. M. Patten

Bad News for America." The three of the stickers have a purpose. Roving activism.

"But how will you get gas?" my family asked. That's a fair question for this sort of randomness, especially when there's no immediate funds. If one were to Google the word "spanging," you'd come up with a definition that says something like, "The act of asking for spare change." Gas jugging is the same thing. Neither are really an act of hustling so much as an artwork of humility. And the trade works well-enough in every location we've been to so far. *So far*. Before leaving we managed to hustle up one half of a tank, enough to get us out of San Dimas.

The first stop was to be Las Vegas, taking us a grand total of eight hours, crawling along the 15 freeway. At this late an hour, we guessed an accident was causing the delay.

A rest stop outside of Barstow showed no sign of help, as all the bathroom doors were locked and...*occupied* (a word to be used ironically and emphatically from henceforth). Around the back was urination central, with scores of men—and some women—pissing into the cold wind. Two bummed cigarettes later, we were back on the crawl. I have no radio in my car, and my laptop only has a few songs, one of them being "First of the Year," by *Skrillex*—appropriate for the occasion. Over and over it played, breaking up our little conversations about drugs and sex and all things unrelated to the Cause.

Arriving at the Nevada state line around 1:00 in the morning, we went into Whiskey Pete's. Yum-Yum went to play the slots and get a drink. I went to the restroom. There was commotion outside the adjoining ladies room. "Why the fuck do you need your purse?" a man shouted. A heavy Filipino accent mumbled something and laughed drunkenly. "Why do you need your wallet? This is the why I don't trust you."

As I finished washing my hands, I turned the corner and saw the man pointing fiercely to a lady sitting on a stool. "I'm gonna fuckin' kill you bitch," he said without a hint of humor. She

205

continued her drunken giggle. I remembered being told in Folsom State about the amount of dead bodies buried out in the desert. I'd hate to one day read about this poor mail-in bride being another casualty of Vegas.

We left the borderland casino; drove to downtown Las Vegas; settled in the Circus-Circus parking structure. It was sometime near two 'o clock. The Strip was mostly dead.

We had tried hustling for funds, me offering to do backflips for money.

Nothing. Not even beer change.

I eventually retired in the front seat. Yum-Yum and Pirate came in around 6ish. Four people sleeping in a small SUV isn't the most comfortable thing in the world, but it'll have to make do.

For some 3,000 more miles.

K. M. Patten

Why I Occupy: Testimony of a Libertarian

ON SEPTEMBER THE 27th, 2011, an email arrived from Bruno, a fellow *We Are Change* activist. "Join Forces with Occupy LA?" Because the New York Occupation had received mixed coverage from the Networks, I was only vaguely aware of what was going on. It seemed like a good-enough idea: get a tent, some supplies, and camp outside the Los Angeles City Hall, where the authorities and elites can experience the worldwide polarization between society and its ruling governments.

"To hell with the Elite," I thought, gleeful at the chance to obliterate lame, ill-conceived concepts of tyranny. It was finally time people were awakened from their trance. Bruno is a good man; his judgment was all that was left to seal the deal. My emailed response stated quaintly: "I'll be there."

Ah, but grievances—the very reason for protest. Mine were many, and monumental, and contrary to those I knew would be at this occupation: communists and statists, public union members and immigrants demanding "free" everything. It was time to educate people on why they should cease their support for the Monster.

"A monster?" someone had asked me. *Yes indeed*, everyone at Occupy Los Angeles had seen this Creature before the eviction came. On one of those long, boring days, well into the

207

occupation, an artist named Scott Olsen stopped by and took advantage of a 20-foot-high wooden barricade which was set up to stop us from defacing the park fountain. When he was finished, a menacing, purple-skinned, multi-tentacled beast was revealed for all of us to learn from. Its name upon a concrete crown said: *Federal Reserve Bank.*

As Christ might have foretold to John, the Creature held the power to give measurement to weights and credit, and with that, all the resources needed for aggressive expansion. "The Fed"—as the modern incarnation of central banking is known—was an often discussed topic here at the Occupy. Once, an anti-bankster advocate named Mary Mark came by and gave a lecture on the subject. "The People's University," which consisted of a white plastic tarp, was a much different setting than what she was used to as a teacher in the local area.

We discussed how the bank remained as a silent entity in its near hundred years of existence. How Henry Ford once remarked that if the People ever discovered its true mechanism there would be a "revolution before tomorrow morning." It only took many decades after Ford's death that he would become partially vindicated out on the front grass of LA City Hall.

Responding to my question about how far back in history the banking dynasties go, Ms. Mark referenced a book called *Babylon's Bankers*, by Joseph P. Farrell, dealing with the ancient alchemy between money and a brainwashed society. "The Rothschild's actually claim descendancy from one of these bankers," she said, adding that it was, "Just a claim. Just heresy."

"We are conspiracy theorists," I assured her.

A well-educated gentleman named Alejandro jumped in: "They were the descendants of the Nobles who wrote the Magna Carta in the year Twelve-Fifteen," he said. Alejandro had declared his sovereignty from the United States Corporation, another nebulous subject he knew a lot about. These were the kind of discussions I planned to evoke while camping out here. Not just a definition of freedom. Not just an interpretation of liberty, but a discovery of what it meant to actually *be free*.

Recognition of the criticisms of the Fed is a good place to start on this journey. They are widespread, and damning. Leftist commentators frequently report on First World banking policies in the Third World, referred to over there as economic terrorism. Over here, Austrian economists like Ludwig von Mises explain the need for market control regarding currency and interest rates. Eager conspiracy theorists also speak on this subject, explicating the most valid and verifiable conspiracy of all time. Honest researchers and journalists have just stood back, reiterating the basic facts.

None of us are alone on this crusade. There are many out there—and some here at the Occupy—that anticipate the Creature's demise. Another opponent is history. Despite being popularized by that collective, interactive brain known as the internet, a lot of the information that's exposed the Fed is, like the battle itself, somewhat dated. Author and lecturer G. Edward Griffin did a marvelous job documenting it all in his 1994 book, *Creature from Jekyll Island*.

The battle against central banking goes back to the founding of our Republic. Jefferson, Madison and Paine were enlightened men who believed that it would wreak havoc in a Free Society. Although unpopular in the Occupy camp, Ron Paul is in line with this tradition and remains a champion against monetary tyranny. As such, his presidential candidacy is almost always advocated on one of my many signs, much to the dismay of others. At a Paul rally in 2008, Griffin stated that "Ron Paul is the only candidate who can win for America." Au contraire to my fellow Occupiers, I tend to agree with him.

Orwell observed that everything follows once "Two & Two" is allowed the correct summation. So here's the first *Two*: a State, by definition, is sovereign. It has boundaries in which its administrators can legally operate. The primary responsibility of the State (and in my opinion, its only justification) is to uphold Natural Law—commonly referred to as due process—and to punish its abusers.

However, the primary function of all states, as with any government that facilitates it, is to forcibly collect taxes from the citizens (sometimes called stealing), and to distribute the wealth in one direction or another; hoping that the allocation will be noble, and righteous, and "good."

This function also happens to be its main defect. Government is, as libertarianism explicitly points out, a monopolization of force, consummated by a piece of paper stating the authority as an absolute. The Founding Founders always intended, therefore, for minimal government, reasoning that truly free individuals resented such controls. After all, how often does someone wish his or her neighbor were caught stealing? Or telling someone else how to raise their child?

The articulation from Austrian theorists argues that central government planning in the economy will always end with mismanaged funds, and, eventually, runaway inflation, inevitably happening once governments appropriate more money than they have taken in. With the help of crafty machinations, the State can also use credit—not actual currency, which is defined as a medium between desired commodities—to finance endless, mindless programs, this at the expense of enormous deficits. Griffin correctly labels the process of inflation and loss of purchasing power as a "hidden tax."

Adam Smith wrote in *The Wealth of Nations*:

> *The statesman, who should attempt to direct private people in what manner they ought to employ their capital, would not only load himself with a most unnecessary attention, but assume an authority which can safely be trusted, not only to no single person, but to no council or senate whatsoever, and which would nowhere be*

so dangerous as in the hands of a man who had the folly
and presumption enough to fancy himself fit to exercise it.

Smith believed that taxation was only for contribution to a State that granted protection to those enjoying their wealth—not to give the wealth.

This is because governments don't run businesses. They run states. When markets can no longer afford to pay either bills or employees, it has to readjust finances. In contrast, when governments can no longer pay for their programs or employees, it just prints more money. Credit is debt. And debt is expected to be paid off by future generations. When not kept on a short leash, government's ability to tax and to allocate becomes a boated, debt-ridden monster that can artificially afford anything from welfare to warfare.

But the scenario is much worse in today's world. Putting the other *Two* in this equation is the fact that our government now employs a private, offshore corporation to finance state programs. Recent alternative media attention has exposed the Fed for being an agency that operates completely independent of the U.S. government (the resources of which technically depleted since the Civil War), and revealed the central bankers for what they really are: a group of international financers who are allowed to use our namesake in purchasing worthless government treasury bonds. They are now granted with the near-limitless power of creating new money while also being allowed to carelessly place it into the economy.

Ostensibly, the purchase of our Treasury Bonds is an IOU on behalf of the government, as every dollar printed is legally binding tender, also known as a receipt.

Don't think so?

Look again. The bills displaying the faces of our ex-Presidents say "Federal Reserve Note"—not U.S. dollar. If you decide to call anyone with an expression of your disgust, don't expect the Fed to answer.

These "Banksters" are an anomaly in an otherwise simple equation that should always equal four. Instead, our representatives say it equals five, leaving us absent a great truth that hides a fascistic smile. Along this path to financial tyranny, greedy politicians decided that it was morally acceptable for unborn generations to bear the encumbrance of paying back a secretive cartel of unaccountable, unelected bankers. The debt is some-trillion dollar number, and counting. "I wish it were possible," Thomas Jefferson said, "to obtain a single amendment to our Constitution—taking from the federal government their power of borrowing from privately-owned corporate banks."

Don't worry. The things our government pays for are inexpensive, like military empires (sarcasm noted).

In the libertarian movement, a majority believe the Creature should be given tighter chains while plenty of others want it killed. Despite, however, being told about its uncanny ability to consume economies, many occupiers are willing to drink endlessly from its magnanimous nectar, which tastes oddly like cheap paper.

Milton Friedman was correct in one of his last interviews given in 2006: "Socialism used to mean the ownership and operation of the means of production. Nobody gives it that meaning today." Not at all. Socialism today has become symbiotic with out-of-control statism, as most Occupiers demonstrate. The usual diatribes heard from Occupiers include "May I please have some free education? How about free health care? $50 an hour? Please."

They beg the Master (corporate parasites that feed off the wealth of a population raped by state power) for some sort of mercy. Embarrassingly ignorant, considering that the quality of everything dramatically goes down while the deficit goes up.

Socialism has become a bastardization of its former self, similar to an underserving corporation which has no place in a truly free enterprise system. Well-intentioned Communists will forever stand incorrect on economics.

Some people are more successful in trade; others will always toil harder for longer hours. In a free society, we have the right to experiment in the market to see which best fits us. "No difference," I would tell the many interviewers in the park, "between a greedy union and a greedy corporation." To give it one last analogy: if I steal money from the reader of this article, and give it to one of my friends, that does not make that person a capitalist. And always remember, corporate welfare outspends social welfare 5-1.

The raid on Occupy Los Angeles took place on November 29th. Reportedly, twelve hundred officers stormed City Hall just after midnight and made nearly three hundred arrests. Scott Olsen's mural has since become the subject of ownership. Does the city own it, or the People? The last I heard, we were getting it preserved.

Olsen's depiction of the Monster Bank held some sound advice: "Take the Power Back."

Much like the mural itself, that seems to be completely natural.

America: The Exile Nation, A Review of Charles Shaw's *Brainchild*

IN THE EYES of award-winning journalist and activist filmmaker Charles Shaw, a vast amount of American citizens have become exiled within their own country. "Three million incarcerated; seven and a half million on probation or parole; thirteen million with felonies; sixty-five million who can't pass a background check. They're exiled from the fruits of our society. From our basic moral contract," says Shaw, speaking to me on a long-distance phone call.

His documentary film of the same name is described as an oral history of the War on Drugs and the American criminal justice system, which Shaw says is more akin to "a gigantic economic engine." The film—available for free online—begins with a voice-over reminding us of a time when people believed that prisons had a justified purpose of rehabilitating prisoners. This documentary depicts a different, more realistic scene: warehouses that are used by bureaucrats, politicians, and unionists, all dependent on nonviolent criminals for modern day slave labor.

As the film chronicles, the crime rate between 1910 and 1970 was relatively immutable. Then, in 1971, President Richard Nixon famously declared his "War on Drugs"—an amplification of funding for federal narcotic laws already in place. Shaw concurs that at the time there was a problem with inner-city violence:

Cities were cesspools. Crime really was an issue. That's not a Left-Right thing. If people were scared to go outside, they were scared to go outside. And they were definitely scared.

Interviewed during the course of his two-hour expose are many experts in the field of practical policy. Mark Kleiman, a Ph.D. teaching at UCLA who wrote the book *When Brute Force Fails: How to Have Less Crime and Less Punishment*, agrees with Shaw. Kleiman originally advocated the building of more prisons to compensate for the increase in crime. Viewing it in hindsight, he says he feels a bit like the "sorcerer's apprentice," wondering where the "off switch" was. As Kleiman explains, drug war enforcement starts off with a "presumption of futility."

Whereas taking a burglar off the street will result in one less person stealing, the effort of taking a drug dealer off the street has no direct benefit, as the dealer's clients will simply find another person to give them what they want. It expands the underground market of narcotics by inviting more opportunities for other dealers.

A personal testimony of criminality and life-behind-bars comes from a baldheaded man known only as Steve, who quantifies the absurdity of sending a seventeen-year-old to prison with a bunch of hardened thugs when his "crime" was only being in possession of marijuana. "Not only is he going to get hurt, you're going to turn loose a lunatic." He adds that prison is ninety percent psychological, ten percent physical. "The bruises go away, but the psychological part damns people for the rest of their lives."

As these stories progress, the real-life nightmare is elucidated for all despots to admire. One convicted drug offender spent sixteen and a half years behind bars for owning a piece of property which held his friend's cocaine. The police let the other man go. Another man, admittedly guilty of something, tells us that the

American government employs more drug informants than the Stasi did under Soviet Union rule; and, that more blacks incarcerated than during South African apartheid.

The social dilemma is best explained by an attractive New York physician who uses a cookie jar as an analogy. If, she explains, you leave a jar of cookies on top of a shelf and tell a child not to eat them, there's a good possibility that child will find their way up there and eat them anyways. On the other hand, if there was an open discussion about not eating the cookies, because of health or discipline or whatever, the child just might be more respectful.

"More than anything," she says, "our nation's drug problem is a public health issue. It's an issue for the therapist. The psychiatrist. The medical doctors." Quickly the scene turns to another man with only a singular name. "Dimitri" tells us about his own heroin addiction and the unfortunate death of his young wife from endocarditis—a heart infection resultant from sharing dirty needles.

Adding to this insanity is the endless news reports, columns and studies—coming out every day—that assert this very same principle. A very recent, brave column by James Bloodworth at the U.K.'s *Independent* was titled: "The Prohibition of Drugs Has Been an Abject Failure with a Devastating Human Cost."

After citing the usual abysmal numbers—you know: $15 billion spent last year by the U.S. government, along with the mere 5 percent of the world's total population who use drugs—Bloodworth added, "Most opponents of prohibition would refrain from claiming that legalization would provide a definitive solution to the problem of drug abuse. What we would argue, however, is that decriminalization (at a minimum) is, unlike prohibition, not mired in political fantasy. Those of us who believe prohibition to have failed live in the real world—a place that will always be, and always have been, people who experiment with drugs."

Admitting to his own narcotic experience years ago, Shaw

tells me how the law finally caught up to him in 2005 in his hometown state of Illinois. He ended up spending a year incarcerated. "Non-violent offenders have absolutely no place inside of prison," he asserts firmly. "But that's not to say that everyone locked-up is a victim." Having spent a lot of time around law enforcement, he's convinced that Chicago has the most corrupt police department, explaining how they would "railroad" Latino suspects who were convicted for crimes they had never committed. "By far the worst." Once getting out, Shaw became deeply immersed in politics and activism.

The forty-two year old creator of the Exile Nation Project now spends most of his days traveling and promoting his film. His upcoming book, *Exile Nation: Prisons, Politics, Drugs, and Spirituality*, comes out in May. It is an extension of his written work online. *Alternet, Huffington Post,* and *Reality Sandwich* are a few of his outlets in which he writes about current events, the environment, and national affairs.

During our conversation Shaw also made clear a great misconception about private facilities: "I'm an expert here. I've been out there and have actually talked to the people, to the families. They will tell you it's more humane inside of a private prison." Being the progressive that he is, it was painful for him to admit that, like the Justice System itself, the unions that serve it have become distorted from all their original intentions. "I think it's like 90% state unions in the country [that run prisons]," he notes.

Discussed in example was the California Correctional Peace Officers Association (CCPOA), a public union often referred to as the most powerful special interest in the Golden State. These Puppet Masters "have so much influence," Shaw tells me, and "they can shape public opinion very easily." He stated how many people, when presented with options to reform the system, are often overwhelmed by rhetoric that denounces such measures as being soft on crime. "And you know what?" he asks solemnly, "It works every time."

When the California Supreme Court upheld a court order last year mandating the release of 46,000 inmates, Shaw was surprised. "I thought they would overrule the order. It shows you how fucked up it is over there. Even the Courts have gotten into it."

Governor Jerry Brown, a longtime CCPOA stooge, was once quoted as saying that "the Drug War is one of the games to get more convictions and more prisoners." Brown should know, having had several closed-door sessions with Union leadership and refusing to even consider Proposition 19's passage.

On the Presidential candidacy of Congressman Ron Paul, a consistent libertarian long opposed to the Drug War and vehement critic of fake "compassionate conservatives," Shaw comes across indifferent, although not entirely spiteful. "I'm advocating a withdrawal from the entire System," he says, adding that if Paul wins the election "the decision will fall down on the States, and the 'red' ones will go one way, and the 'blue' ones another way." Texas? "Not gonna happen."

More critical were his comments on current President Obama. When asked if he supported him, Shaw says: "Absolutely not. Obama's presidency should finally put to rest this idea that politicians are going to do what they say. It's the System that needs to change."

He went on crucify Obama's hypocrisy, who first stated on the campaign trail that he would not enforce federal medical marijuana raids, but then, last October, ordering a crackdown in California. "I'm pretty sure [Barack Obama is] CIA. Yeah....he's CIA."

Marijuana's Tipping Point?

A Chat with Dr. Christopher Fichtner, Author of
Cannabinomics

WHEN DISCUSSING ANY illicit substance, health and safety are usually the first concerns. If marijuana were legalized, more people would use it, it would lead to harder drugs, our youth would become decadent and depraved, and our great society would come to an end—so says the average prohibitor.

A bold statement like this is neither helpful nor accurate when discussing such an important issue, the likes of which already prosecute nearly one million people every year. Although you wouldn't hear it from one of these advocates—who are now in the minority—three different angles of the same topic are today coming together, all of them leading to the irresistible conclusion that cannabis prohibition must come to an end.

The cover of Dr. Christopher Fichtner's book, *Cannabinomics: The Marijuana Policy Tipping Point*, has all of the trajectories nicely depicted. There's a stethoscope, showcasing the medical benefits that countless studies have proven; a judge's hammer, alluding to the failed Drug War; and money, because "cash crop" is not just a catchy saying.

Fichtner believes that the converging of these revelations is at last marijuana's "tipping point"—that Rubicon that must soon be crossed, when cannabis can finally be freed from the terrors of government persecution.

As he laments in his book's forward, quoting from Dan Baum: "Just Say No finished the job…of closing the debate. Don't talk about why people use drugs…Don't talk about the tendency of prohibition to promote violence…Don't talk about the lives, taxpayer dollars and civil liberties sacrificed for the Drug War…Don't talk about the medical potential of illegal drugs. Don't talk at all. Just say no." He hopes that by merging these different angles he can bring about a new language, which he has named "cannabinomics," and that it will reverse the popular trend of criminalization, allowing people to finally realize the obviousness of such a backwards policy.

I first received the book from his publisher last year, and met with him at his office in Hemet, California not long afterwards, where he has been a practicing psychologist for many years. He greeted me wearing blue jeans and a black shirt, unshaven. "Hey Kevin," a smiling face said, shaking hands. I followed him into his back office. Crammed bookshelves were everywhere. I set up my camera and set it on the table directly in front of him. "Dr. Christopher Fichtner…" I said, first asking how he got involved with this subject. "Well I'm a psychiatrist," he started, "and I finished my training in '91. I started working for the VA (Veterans of America) System—treating veterans with PTSD in Illinois. A coalition of several groups were trying to pass a medical marijuana law in 2003 or so."

He recalled, as he does in his book, his meeting with Julie, telling me about her multiple sclerosis and how she used edibles to help calm her symptoms. "She told a very compelling story," Fichtner said, who watched her give testimony to the state legislature. "She was a major influence, who even schooled me on the use of the word 'marijuana.'" The true professional as he is, he prefers the term "herbal cannabis" over any other because of the negative connotations. "High," a fortuitously used word, has so many "degrees of it," he says. "There's a euphoria that would be extreme, and it can lead to giddiness, an inability to interact in a reasonable social manner." I added, "But not dangerously though." He emphatically agreed: "No, not dangerous, but there's a mood elevation, which is just a reduction in anxiety, a feeling of greater well-being."

Curious about his profession, which requires prescribing large amounts of psychiatric medication, I asked him at what point he would suggest cannabis as an alternative. Unsurprisingly, I learned that Riverside, the county where he currently works, doesn't have a policy supporting such recommendations. "I've done a few outside of that on a private basis—not very many," he answered.

As a medicine, Fichtner says that it's "always okay to talk about cannabis, as long as there's a defined problem, like major depression; bipolar disorder; PTSD." As a matter of ethics, he says he's first "...gonna go with the meds that are FDA approved. Herbal cannabis comes in when someone says, 'I haven't been able to tolerate this, but have experience with cannabis and found that it is helpful.'"

Drug War proponents need not panic.

Having this conversation doesn't mean anybody wants to allow cocaine vendors to set up down the block, or have businesses named "Heroin R' Us" directly across the street. Such demagoguery is not allowed in the offices of Dr. Christopher Fichtner. Everybody already knows that the ingestion and consumption of strange substances can hardly be good for one's health.

Anyone can tell you that.

But the list of such substances can grow upon closer inspection, and can come to include many things you might or might not consider to be dangerous. "Smoking is never good for the respiratory tract," Fichtner says, "but when you go look for the relationship between lung cancer and marijuana, you just don't find it the way you find it with alcohol and tobacco."

Several times in the book he mentions the potential of substituting the two big killers with cannabis. Discussing a 2009 university study, Fitchner tells me that it "[dealt with] Squamous cell head and neck carcinoma, cancer—which alcohol and tobacco are major contributors to. Once they factored out the influences of those two, what they found was not only was there no positive relationship with cannabis, [there was] a statistically significant inverse correlation. In other words, those who used marijuana were less likely to get head and neck cancer!"

Dealing with the Drug War in his book, Fichtner introduces us to "Garry," a medical cannabis patient whose Southern California home was invaded by federal goons. Garry sustained serious injuries, was no longer able to work, went on social security, took more pain pills, and eventually had to foreclose on his house—all part of America's new standard domestic policy, with menacing faces like Gil Kerlikowske and Eric Holder standing close by, approvingly. In the book, Fichtner compares America's collective attitude to this war with Professor Jerry Harvey's tale of The Abilene Paradox—or, as is summarized, "The tendency for groups to embark on excursions that no group member wants."

I asked him the general "up-or-down" question: "Do you think the Drug War is a failure?" He answered with a familiar sense of obviousness: "Oh yeah. So many have spoken to that. They just had the Global Commission, and then pursuant to that you had Jimmy Carter who also wrote in June—maybe it was even the day of—the 40th anniversary of Nixon's War on Drugs. Jimmy Carter wrote a piece in the *New York Times* talking about how it's been a failure, harkening back to 1978 when he first said we oughta implement the recommendations of the Commission [on Marihuana and Drug Abuse]...that did some very good work under President Nixon, who just paid no attention at all to them."

Why would there be any disconnect between the President and his Commission? Well, the unanimous conclusion made by

Nixon's staff was that marijuana should largely be made legal, and the president had other plans.

Bringing the results of this policy up to date—to a sort of social reckoning—Fichtner cites several popular headlines throughout his book (including the *LA Times*' permanent project), concluding that: "What *Forbes* magazine called the 'Mexican Meltdown' competes with the economic crisis, healthcare, and our foreign policy more broadly as the news item most likely to be updated on the front page of major American newspapers." The latest development? As of May 13th, forty more decapitated bodies dumped on a major highway near Monterrey; the Zetas claiming responsibility yet again.

I asked his opinion on whether or not there was an underlying reason why "drugs" were criminalized so harshly. "Well, first of all," he answered somewhat sharply, "I think partly the way out of this is to stop talking about 'drugs' in a generic way."

While praising the work of LEAP (Law Enforcement Against Prohibition), he said they had habit of doing this. "It's too big a conversation to have; too big a piece to bite off. I think the conversation should start off with specific substances, rather than lumping them altogether...Coming back to your question—what do I think is sustaining this?—I think it's partly the failure to parcel-out the language." Dr. Fichtner thinks that instead of just saying "drugs" and being done with it, a person should resist the urge to be overly presumptuous when considering this question. "Then we ask: 'cannabis vs. alcohol; cannabis vs. tobacco; cannabis vs. opiates'; and so on. Cannabis is something we'll look at fairly quickly because of its relatively favorable safety," he says.

Although a newcomer to this discussion, Fichtner was surprisingly articulate and well-read on the topic. He thinks that because of its "inclusion clause," California's current medical policy is the best in the country. With other states having specific guidelines, the Golden State has almost none. I told the doctor about my experience getting a medical 215 card; about the price drop from $150 down to $80; and the odd parallels between a California "caregiver" and a Kirby vacuum salesman.

Again with naïve professionalism, he told me that people he knew in the industry "at least favored it for medical use," adding that most doctors "who do really good check-ups [and exams] believe cannabis should be sold over the counter." As the Devil's Advocate, I reiterated the sentiment: "Maybe you and I wouldn't look at it that way, but for others that's borderline recreational use." Fichtner made clear that his concern was more for patients willing to try it for themselves, instead of worrying that someone might get hold of a substance far less harmful than those already available. "It certainly opens the door to recreational use, but there will be a percentage who uses it recklessly and it could lead to other problems, and you'll also have a percentage who will substitute it for alcohol or tobacco," he says.

Finishing up that question, the doctor stopped me to ask one of his own: "Which is more important?" he asks, "the probability of some users who may not exercise good judgment, and that the system may be abused? Or the possibility that a lot of people who are being denied access for its therapeutic benefits [could get it]?"

If it has not already been made clear, Dr. Fichtner believes people ought to be allowed to make their own decision. "People with all these diseases are usually on a cocktail of different medicines each with their own side-effects, so when you're on a cocktail, you have to add all that up," he says, rhetorically asking, "Why you wouldn't want to consider a naturally occurring substance" that has "an array of structural-related molecules that do different things? Some of them elevate mood, some reduce anxiety, and some of them may even have anti-psychotic and mood stabilizing properties." And not known to be dangerous!

Cannabinomics, he believes, could become a language known to both liberal Democrats worried about Civil Liberties, and libertarian Republicans concerned with State's Rights. He ends his book by saying that marijuana is "the low-hanging fruit of drug policy reform and medical marijuana is so ripe it's falling off the tree."

A question that escaped me during our discussion was Fichtner's reportage on the progress of Savitex (RT), which he talks about throughout his 227-page book.

The GW Pharmaceutical creation, Savitex is a lab-grade synthesizing of several cannabis components. Popular in Europe, the drug has been given an exclusive patent by the U.S. Government. An interesting thought of the doctor's was that "our federal government currently actively denies American cannabis producers the opportunity to enter into the business in the open marketplace, in which the demand for cannabis—for medicinal and personal use—is quite high."

He also admitted to me, somewhat remorsefully, that the issue of hemp was only briefly mentioned in his book.

I had one last question: "Will you sign my copy?"

He smiled and thanked me for reading it.

"Here's to finding a better way to manage medicinal herb in America!" he wrote.

The Bohemian Grove: The Elite's Conclave in the Woods

Bohemian Beginnings

BOHEMIAN. WESTERN AUDIENCES might have images of Hunter S. Thompson, or even Robert Downey's portrayal of Sherlock Holmes: eccentric, unkempt and unconcerned-types. Wikipedia gives a definition of Bohemianism as: "The practice of an unconventional lifestyle, often in the company of like-minded people, with few permanent ties, involving musical, artistic, or literary pursuits. In this context, Bohemians may be wanderers, adventurers, vagabonds"—*or even warmongers*.

Circa early 1870's San Francisco: in this emerging "golden city," literary icons of the day desired an exclusive retreat. This club's official annals state the reason as being for the "promotion of social and intellectual intercourse between journalists and other writers, artists, actors and musicians, professional or amateur." Ambrose Bierce, Edward Bosqui, Bret Harte, Jack London, Mark Twain—and others—routinely met at what was named the Bohemian Club, a place for similar minds to have a drink together and brainstorm without interferences from the outside world.

Less than a decade passed before these so-called "men of talent" encountered a problem. As founding Bohemian member Edward Bosqui reflected in a diary entry, "the members were nearly all impecunious, and it was soon apparent that the possession of talent, without money, would not support the club."

The resort was depreciated, and to subsidize it the Bohemians decided to invite a financial element. These were the "men of wealth," who quickly endured criticism from some club members.

The numbers ascended rather quickly, from 182 members in 1874 to over 550 in 1887—now complete with friends and family of the Crocker banking cartel, one newspaper tycoon named William Randolph Hearst, Mr. Arthur W. Moore, a Bay Area shipbuilder, and at least fourteen Army and Navy officers. Certainly aware that they had dishonored the "Spirit of Bohemia," the original 'BoHo's' viewed them repugnantly. Nonetheless it worked, and the club remained open.

During this period, this very unique group of "talented and wealthy men" began making yearly treks to the ancient redwoods in Sonoma County, some 80 miles north of San Francisco on the recently completed North Pacific Coast railway. The beauty of the Russian River must have caught the eye of the Bohemians, who quickly struck their claim right beside it. At the time, the undeveloped Grove property was a diminutive hundred and sixty acres. In 1913, a dispute with a prospected real estate project compelled the Club to purchase hundreds of more acres, continuing right through the decades until 1944 when it reached its present size of 2,700 acres. Now they had as much privacy as they wanted.

Was this an early sign of conspiracy? Perhaps it compounded the already clandestine nature of the club, which had arguably taken an oath of secrecy twenty years earlier when it proclaimed Saint John Nepomuck (pronounced NAY-po-muk) as their Patron Saint. For refusing to divulge the Queen's confession of adultery, Saint Nepomuck was executed by orders of King Wenceslas the IV, ruler of 14th century (Czech) Bohemia. Today, a statue honoring his legacy stands in the Grove property; index finger still pressed firmly against his lips as a constant reminder for the requisite vow of silence.

Newspaper coverage on the Club was also on the decline as the propensity for elitist membership was gaining leverage. From 1900 to 1915 the *San Francisco Chronicle* had run nearly 400 stories on the Bohemian Club, making it one of the most highly publicized clubs in the San Francisco Bay Area.

In the early 1930's, with the membership list at nearly 2,000, the group had raised nearly $800,000 to be used as an upgrade for their Clubhouse. Either because of the sensitive environment during the Great Depression, a massive general strike in San Fancisco, or the growing desire for more anonymity, the grand opening in 1934 was, unlike the grand-opening twenty years prior, now selected for the back pages of the paper.

The Grove property began shrouding itself in mystery. For the first fifty years of its existence it had been comparatively accessible to outsiders. But now, as the Grove garnered a reputation for being a paradise amongst American presidents (notably Teddy Roosevelt and Herbert Hoover), exclusivity began to rear its evil head. The first recorded rejection of outside publicity came in 1949 when the *Saturday Evening Post* requested an interview. Even despite the publication's "conservative" tilt, the Club's board of directors voted in the negative. Kevin Starr, historian for the Club, was even once quoted as saying that "...the Club has nothing to gain by talking to the press." During the course of my research I began to wonder—like many others before me—was something more insidious taking place in the Land of Bohemia?

Wearing the Devil's Slippers

It would be a couple of decades before curiosity was raised about the club that Hoover once called "the greatest men's party on earth"—which subsequently became the title of John Van Der Zee's 1972 title. A waiter at the Grove, Van Der Zee was one of

K. M. Patten

the first of many "inside testimonies." Drawing from his account
and others, a young, if not slightly obsessed sociology professor at
USC, one G. William Domhoff, began an exhaustive study of
these elusive resorts. The starting point for all Grove researchers,
his 1974 underground classic, entitled *The Bohemian Grove and
Other Retreats: A Study in Ruling Class Cohesiveness*, detailed many
things few knew about this strange place.

For starters, the membership list has consistently remained
between two and three thousand, all of whom are men, as the
club holds a very stringent policy forbidding women as regular
attendees. With a few exceptions, the members are also almost
exclusively Caucasian. Most members come from California, with
New York coming in second, and Washington D.C. as third.

Although not entirely, it is by and large a Republican event. A
very common way to denote the Club's social status is by pointing
out the fact that every GOP president since Hoover has been a
member. It is confirmed that Teddy Roosevelt was, but various
conflicting reports state that Taft, Harding and Coolidge were
here as well.

Other corporate executives are tabulated in Domhoff's "List
of Heavies"—gained from a 1968 membership list and a 1970
guest list—and it reads like a "Who's Who" of American power.

At that time the list included presidents, directors, chairmen
and VP's of such corporate behemoths as Wells Fargo, Bank of
America, Douglas Aircraft, Standard Oil, Union Oil, General
Motors, and Lockheed Martin. In 1983, Domhoff published an
update of his analysis, and found that of the top 800 corporations
in the U.S., an average of 25-30% had at least one officer or
director at the Grove. Colleges across America have faculty
members in their ranks, with the University of California holding
the most. Ray Kroc, the man who made McDonalds what it is
today, was a member; as were Barry Goldwater and William R.
Hearst, Jr. and Chief Justice Earl Warren. Democrats? President
Jimmy Carter and Robert Kennedy have been photographically

documented.

Notable members and guests of more recent years include Former CIA agent and reputable conservative intellectual William F. Buckley; "The Most Trusted Man in America" Walter Cronkite; of the Rockefeller banking dynasty, David, Laurence, and Nelson; Former Secretary of Defense Casper Weinberger; Former Director of both the FBI and CIA and current Chairman of Homeland Security, William Webster; Former Attorney General Edwin Meese; Former VP Dan Quayle; Federal Reserve Chairmen Paul Volcker and Alan Greenspan; Former Secretary of Defense and Vice President Dick Cheney; Speaker Newt Gingrich; Chief Justice Anthony Scalia; Former Secretary of Defense Donald Rumsfeld, and, not to be forgotten, the indicted war criminal Henry Kissinger—names and titles that no Rogues Gallery is complete without.

This is just the tip of the iceberg. Bohemians are themselves members of various camps inside the property, which number about 130 in total. This has caused a few street activists to label Bohemia as an "Occupy for the One Percent"—except that they perfected the craft well before late 2011. When walking and golf carts are not an option, an oversized safari-type vehicle that carries upwards of twenty people serves as the 24-hour transportation system.

Although the Grove property remains open year-around for members to enjoy with their families, the real show begins during the second week of July, when a sizable portion of the world's power brokers (sans the wife and grandkids) gather to enjoy some extravagant fun. Then: plays, variety shows, shooting contests, art exhibits, swimming, nature-riding, policy-chatting, drinking, prostitute-ordering, and mock-human sacrificing—are all in due time.

What!?

Truth *is* stranger than fiction, and even if this place does not warrant the title of "conspiracy" (because two thousand people can hardly be defined as such), this essay seeks to make clear that this, both a headquarters and playground for the elite, is too dangerous an institution to lose track of. At this juncture that main question arises, which is to estimate possible outcomes of having powerful people gather in such an incredibly informal setting without the element of media scrutiny.

An immediate clue to this answer resides in the seeming contradiction between their official mantra, "Weaving Spiders Come Not Here," and their daily Lakeside Talks, which give members and guests the opportunity to address their constituents about various political, economic, and social issues. The club's mantra comes from Shakespeare's *A Midsummer Nights' Dream*, first appearing on an 1875 club flier, and has always been seen as the Club's way of dissuading members from engaging in formal agreements.

One wonders when presented with a list of past Lakeside Chats, which have been acquired almost every year by a life-long peace activist named Mary Moore. Living in the nearby town of Occidental (a few miles from the microscopic town of Monte Rio, where the Grove property is), Moore formed a coalition of activist groups to do battle against the "Grovers" in 1980. Her activism has always revolved around halting war and nuclear power (more on this in a second), and continues to emphasize the importance of the Lakeside speeches to give an indication of what is discussed.

She gives an example on her OccupyBohemianGrove.com website (which seems to have gone defunct). In 1982, German Chancellor Helmut Schmidt's speech writer told protesters outside that he had just delivered a speech that might well end his political career. "Through our sources," Moore writes, "we learned that he had delivered a Lakeside Chat, saying he had ordered closer ties with the Soviet Union, whose nuclear arsenal was no theoretical, far away object, but something sitting on his country's border, literally fifty miles from his door."

Schmidt announced closer ties to the state that Reagan referred to as the "Evil Empire" and joked about bombing ("We begin bombing in five minutes.") Sure enough, Helmut Schmidt's political career did end a couple of months later. Perhaps not by accident, his successor Helmut Kohl, a man called by both Bush senior and Bill Clinton as the "the greatest European leader of the second half of the 20th century," was also a guest at the Grove, and no friend of the Soviets.

Mike Hanson, the most current scholar on Bohemianism, listed talks between 1980 and 2003 in his *Bohemian Grove: Cult of Conspiracy*.

Note for the following sampling: except for surprise speakers, the Grove only posted the name and his subject, and because recording of any kind is absolutely prohibited in the property, the minutes are obviously not available.

- Edward Teller: *Nuclear Energy* (1980)
- George Lenczowski: *The Persian Gulf Crisis*
- Casper Weinberger: *Rearming America* (1981)
- A.W. Clausen (CEO of Bank of America, President of World Bank): *The Global Economy— Time to Get Out of The Woods* (1983)
- Dick Cheney: *Major Defense Problems of the 21st Century* (1991)
- Elliot Richardson (Sec. Defense/Attorney Gen. under Nixon): *Defining a New World Order*
- Nixon: Topic Unknown (1992)
- Casper Weinberger: *The World and Mr. Clinton* (1993)
- Newt Gingrich: Topic Unknown (1995)
- Alex J. Mandl (Executive VP and AT&T): *Communications and Weaving Spiders-the Complex Web*

of Futuristic Communications

- James Baker: *The Imperative of American Leadership* (1998)
- David Broder (syndicated columnist): *Direct Democracy—Curse or Blessing?* (1999)
- Kissinger: *Do We Need a Foreign Policy?* (2000)
- Chris Matthews (Liberal MSNBC Talking Head): *American Exceptionalism* (2003)

No matter which came first—the weapon or its user?—it should be wondered why, if formal agreements are forbidden in this place, are they listening about potential accommodations required by an industry (petroleum; offensive armaments) or venture (men on campaigns who promise the money and favors) where they might have a financial interest.

This is the subtle, first-glance conflict that occasionally arises from casual conversation: *these spiders are weaving!* Even Club historian Starr stated in 1977:

> *This club is vulnerable to criticism when its members outrageously violate [the] motto, when they use the club, not as an escape from the market place, but as a device of the market place.*

As Domhoff pointed out, however, the contradiction might not be as first perceived. "After all," he observed, "a Lakeside chat is merely an informal chat by a friend of the family." Like sitting around the dinner table, topics about what's going on in the world are welcomed. Asking for money from a relative across from you is rude, especially as the distance becomes greater in-between.

Next question: How then, is someone initiated into this "family?" Although the membership process is tedious and thorough, the real answer harkens back to a more juvenile period in their lives when some of these near-senior citizens were still in college—deferred from service in Vietnam—and conducting their first shady business deals.

According to published reportage, the liberation to relieve oneself whenever, wherever, is tantamount to saving the whales. A reporter named Phillip Weiss snuck into the Grove seven times for his 1989 *Spy Magazine* article, "Masters of the Universe Go to Camp." "You know your inside the Bohemian Grove," he wrote, "when you come down a trail in the woods and hear piano music from amid a group of tents and then round a bend to see a man with a beer in one hand and his penis in the other, urinating into the bushes." Commentators have speculated this as a celebration of the dominate man's triumph over earth. Others have seen it only as their desire to relive past years. And some have even sensed a tinge of homo-eroticism.

Inebriation, the perfect complement to public (private!) exposure, undoubtedly foreshadows this excitement, and it is even said to be the "unwritten rule."

As such, alcohol is abundant and available all hours of the day and night.

There is also an issue of cross-dressing, as some of the plays require an elitist to be dressed in drag, but this appears to happen only during certain plays and the list of enthusiastic participants not forthcoming.

Let it then be noted: all men who feel free enough to get drunk with, urinate amongst, and cross-dress in front of, can be expected to gain a friendship that borders on family, and there is plenty of all this going on inside the Grove.

As John D. Ehrlichman, Nixon's aid and fellow Bohemian said:

> Once you've spent three days with someone in an informal situation, you have a relationship—a relationship that opens doors and makes it easier to pick up the phone.

Conspiracy, Back to the Basics

Surely, results of this cohesion have varied from the mundane to the considerable. Bragged about in the official annals is the Manhattan Project, perhaps the most illustrious and ambitious undertaking thus far. Here in 1937, USC President Robert Sproul introduced Professor Ernest O. Lawrence, the Berkley physicist who developed the cyclotron so important in the early phases of atomic and nuclear research, to John Neylan and William Crocker. Neylan made himself chairman of the special regents subcommittee to look after the needs of Lawrence's radiation laboratory while Crocker gave Lawrence $75,000 for a bigger building to house more cyclotron. The nuclear device that leveled Hiroshima and Nagasaki was then conceived here in September (after the festivities) of 1942 with Edward Teller, "Father of the H-Bomb."

Journalist Keith Richardson has since compiled a list of Bohemians involved in profiting from apocalyptic weaponry. Harold Brown, Secretary of Defense under President Carter, was a former Director of the Lawrence Livermore nuclear weapons laboratory. Charles Duncan, former head of the Department of Energy, the branch that makes 'nukes, was listed as a member in 1980. Bechtel, Rockwell International, Westinghouse Electric Corp, United Technologies Corp.—all nuclear mainstays—have dignitaries at the Grove. Other "Merchants of Death" (as they were called during World War One) having a good time include people from Boeing, General Electric, and General Dynamic. I'm sure Ms. Moore was thrilled to realize she lived in the perfect spot to do battle with her enemies.

Also a documented reoccurrence at the Grove is the next step in American warmongering: agreements between men who for a couple of weeks have traded in their expensive dark suits for more comfortable attire. In his memoirs, Hoover recalled that within an hour after President Taft had announced he would not seek a second term, "a hundred men—publishers, editors, public officials, and others from all over the country who were at the Grove—came to my camp demanding that I announce my candidacy."

Twenty-some years later the GOP tapped Eisenhower for the nod, and less than twenty after that came the Nixon-Reagan deal of 1968, when then-California governor Reagan agreed to enter the race only if Nixon faltered in the polls. This was confirmed soon after Reagan had left the White House by investigative reporter Weiss, who walked into his busy "Owl's Nest" camp and asked the celebrity president himself. "Yes-yes, that's true," the Gipper said, nodding his head in confirmation.

Another "selection" came in 2000 with Richard Cheney tapped as Bush Junior's running mate. According to Hanson, *CNN* reported in July that 'lil Bush had consulted with his diabolical father at the Grove. Three years later, a July 23rd *San Francisco Chronicle* report stated:

> ...the state Republican hierarchy—especially those close to former [California] Gov. Pete Wilson—would favor [Arnold] Schwarzenegger. At least that's the word that came out of the Bohemian Grove this past weekend, where a number of state and national GOPers, including presidential adviser Karl Rove, happened to have gathered at a club getaway.

Notice the informality of this process. It's not an "up or down" vote for a particular politician, rather a recognition that one would follow the plan better than another.

To correlate my thesis with campaign money, 142 Bohemians gave an average of $1,600 to Bush Sr.'s reelection bid while only eleven of them gave an average of almost $9,000 for Bill Clinton's run. Like a puppeteer sitting above the stage deciding which will best entertain, the One Percent differ on political puppetry even from the altitude of their social statuses.

The Bohemian Grove serves as a place where many of these industrial elitists can come together with their ideological counterparts in the State to *informally* discuss what should be done as the New World Order enters its final stages—at least according to the right-fisted, neo-conservative wing of global government.

Moreover, while protesting the Grove in 2012, Mary Moore told me that the "Democrats have their own places." An environment that sees wealthy "Merchants of Death" together with their ReBlooDlican (Jesse Ventura's new terminology for our "elected" national gangs) friends, very casually discussing the next target and preferred triggerman, at first shows the ripple of this undemocratic cohesion.

The consequential outcomes—some of which are documented—would challenge perspectives shared by those like the late Jack Anderson, British reporter Jon Ronson, and even Domhoff, who have repeatedly suggested that the Grove is only a place of recreation; that the attendees are "too drunk to remember details" and that it's not a place for "consensus building." Professional inquirers apparently never discuss important topics over drinks.

Peter Phillips, who has studied the Grove extensively, and was even invited there twice for his research, answers this question in his coffin-nailing 1993 study, *A Relative Advantage*:

> *Yes. There is a policy setting that occurs at the Bohemian Grove, but it is not a sit down, negotiation type, behind-the-scenes, deal-making process. Rather it is reflected in a mutually-shared conscious knowing of the way things ought to be.*

More specifically, Phillips reported overhearing many conversations about business and politics, and remembered a man who carried a stack of white cards used for note-taking.

On the other hand, he also recalled a conversation in which a group of Bohemians rustled another man awake one night and evicted him from the premises, the reason being that he had asked for a loan. It might be concluded from this that "official" deal-making (i.e: asking for money or soliciting a vote) either happens with good friends in private camps, or after the party is over and everyone has gone home.

Conjecture can, has, and will continue to run rampant under this nothing-is-impossible scenario. For instance, Clint Eastwood is a longtime member of the Grove, and I can only wonder if he's ever had a conversation with a chair made from redwood.

The Murder of Guilt

More than any reason, infamy surrounding the Grove is attributed to their opening ceremony, the Cremation of Care. Alex Jones' 2000 footage caused a shockwave of media attention after going viral online.

What are those people doing!?

The details are true. Every summer for the past 130 years at the Grove, these same powerful people garb themselves in long, colorful robes (yes, do think of the Klu Klux Klan) and gather around a small, manmade lake. Perched across from them on an island is a gigantic 40-foot high stone owl (some estimates are at 50 feet, others say 'concrete'), which is covered in a thick, dark-green moss. This is the Owl of Bohemia, the member's honorable friend. Dusk begins to envelop the forest as they wait for a truly bizarre ritual to begin.

As Beethoven's 7th hums in the background, a procession of seven torch-bearers begin taking their place around the sagacious bird. Attention is now drawn to something wicked. Closer inspection of a large wooden box that has been set in the water reveals a very human-shaped effigy. This is a representation of

"Dull Care," despised enemy of the Bohemian Grove.

The congregation settles, and the High Priest speaks to this "enemy of beauty": "Not for thee...forgiveness, or the restful grave. Fire shall have its' will of Thee!"—condemning Care to oblivion.

The torchbearers light the effigy on fire and send it off into the lake. Suddenly, Care is startled awake. Coming from the stars, seemingly, the mirthful voice ridicules them: "Fools! Fools! Fools! When will ye learn that me ye cannot slay? Year after year...lifting your puny shouts of triumph to the stars!"

Care reminds them all of their inevitable return to the marketplace, to which the Bohemians reply: "We shall meet Thee and fight Thee as of old!"

Dull Care then spits on the flame, signified with an extinguisher and a firework. It is at this point that the members plead to the Owl of Bohemia for some enlightened assistance. With the help of speakers, the Bird (once played by global government enthusiast Walter Cronkite) comes to life and narrates an upliftingly evil song (abridged):

> No fire...No fire...
> Unless it be kindled in the world where Care is
> Nourished on the hates of me...
> And drive him from this Grove.

The Owl tells them that the only flame that can destroy Care has to be lit by the nearby "Lamp of Fellowship," that which "never extinguishes" (it doesn't burn year-around). The High Priest thanks "the great owl" for "thy adjuration." The torch is lit, the effigy set ablaze once more, and then Care suffers its annual doom. Beer and gin-fizzes are dispersed as party music is now amplified.

The Cremation has taken place since at least 1880, and made the inaugurating event sometime around 1910. Many commentators, including myself, opine that "Care" is some representation of a collectivized conscience. For men who make war and profit from it, the banishment of any guilt makes the scene that much more menacing.

Who is Care?

The outline of the ceremony supposedly comes from an old English song with the verses: "Too much care will make a young man turn grey and an old man to clay." Another clue is derived from a cartoon drawn by British satirist James Gillray in 1801. Here, a caricatured wealthy fat man sits drinking brandy and smoking tobacco. Sitting opposite of him is a very grimy man, who appears hopelessly disheveled. Again, "Dull Care" is not welcomed. From this it can be deduced who Care really is: anybody and everybody not associated with the "Higher Circles." (Domhoff's phraseology) Christian conservatives? So much for the Bible's warnings against idolatry and eschewing those less fortunate.

On the other hand, if the scene were viewed as some sort of "dark religion," (my words) as Jones, Mark Dice and many others have often espoused (much to Moore's annoyance), it would certainly take fascism to a whole other dimension.

Even More Sinister Allegations

Unless an abandoned wife at home is taken into account, the purchasing of sex would not necessarily be considered "sinister." The Bohemians call this pastime "jumping the river," which means traveling to either of the two nearby towns for some extramarital attention: Monte Rio—just outside the property—or Guerneville, four miles South on the 116 highway. Domhoff softens the numbers and estimates that less than ten percent take the chance. The story goes that it became more difficult after 1971, when a new sheriff was determined to stomp out prostitution in the county. A criminal indictment for solicitation was brought against the owners of the Gas House Tavern in Guerneville. Naming several Club members—none of whom were in government—it was eventually tossed out of court when it was discovered that their informant was a previously convicted prostitute.

Regardless of the circumstances, many people I know don't consider sex between two consenting adults an act of licentiousness. However, the story of Paul Bonacci, if true, would change the dynamic of this nemesis: from routine para-politicking to the absolute definition of Evil. Bonacci's testimony is the most well-known of the many pedophilia allegations made against up-and-coming Republican heavyweight Lawrence King, who was director of the Franklin Community Federal Credit Union, in Omaha, Nebraska. Senator John DeCamp investigated the charges of King's pedophile network when they were first brought up in 1988. Afraid he was getting too close to the perpetrators, he chronicled the events and published them in his blockbuster *The Franklin Cover-Up*.

Young Paul Bonacci had a habit of recording every minute detail of his life in a personal diary. Quoting directly from this throughout his book, DeCamp describes unimaginable brutality involving pedophilia orgies and worse at the hands of King and others. King did receive a grand jury indictment of 40 counts, but a judge eventually threw them out while dismissing it all as "a carefully crafted hoax," even though several people did endure perjury charges.

However, it wasn't until after its publication when it was revealed that DeCamp had omitted several portions of the diary. In one of these entries, Bonacci claims that his captors flew him to Northern California and then drove to a misty dark forest. While there, he is forced at gunpoint to participate in a pedophilic snuff film which ends with another little boy being decapitated via shotgun blast. Left alive and covered in blood and semen, Bonacci wrote that it all took place under the looming presence of a monolithic owl. (The details could not be republished in even the most macabre of horror magazines.)

Is this confirmation that the One Percent is more evil than the Legion of Doom? While his many statements twenty years later appear consistent, Bonacci is a clinical schizophrenic who spent time in prison after a judge found him guilty of perjury (this was overturned soon afterwards). Then again, he did eventually win a $1 million lawsuit against King after the accused had failed to appear in court. Plus, aside from the tale at the Grove, the many stories that came out of Omaha are repeated time and time again by children with no apparent connection to one another, validating his diary's testimony. DeCamp has since stated that the handwriting is confirmed to belong to a 10-year old Bonacci.

During an interview with Alex Jones, he explained that he "didn't know there was a place called the Bohemian Grove," and didn't include this part because he couldn't collaborate it.

Did Bonacci simply fabricate a nightmare involving demonic owls?

Was it all an elaborate hoax?

Or do blood sacrifices actually take place below the towering redwoods?

The Savage Santa Anas

NOTHING COULD HAVE topped the excitement of that week. At least I didn't think so. Twelve hundred police officers, most dressed like storm troopers, marauding through the Occupy Los Angeles encampment. After seeing them barge through the makeshift barriers, tear the place up, make some 300 arrests, and myself eventually jumping a large steel fence to get away, I didn't think my adrenaline would be raised like that for at least a few more days.

Then, on Thursday at midnight, the first day in the last month of 2011, and 24 hours subsequent of the raid, my brother called me from the bowling alley he manages in Arcadia: "Hey. It's crazy over here! The Winds are insane. I've never seen anything like this in my life," he exclaimed. Recalling something about "sudden gust warnings" on one of the local network affiliates, I thought to myself, *How bad could this really be?*—a preemptive assessment that was slightly incorrect.

There were only three problems hindering my departure: a gas tank low on fuel, a stomach full of beer, and a highly-contentious DUI I was arrested for some months back. How can a driver's license be suspended without a court date that was never announced? It had been hours since my last bottle, and I had eaten plenty of chicken sandwiches in-between. (Chronicling that sentiment as a deflection now—here, in this article—seems wrong, but it allows a certain justification two weeks later.

There's no need to linger on the issue of loathsome alcoholism any longer, except to say that I am sorry.)

The gas tank would make it seven miles. Maybe ten. But no more than fifteen. She always has a little bit left in her. San Dimas is about nine miles from my destination, and the weather here was relatively calm, aside from some gusts that were nothing to write home about.

With each intersection I passed on the way over it seemed more likely that my brother had fallen foul to a slight hint of exaggeration. Pets and neighborhood animals would not be swooped up into any wind tornados tonight, I thought. As I got closer to Peck Road, however, my attitude changed, and I began to notice what he was reporting on: Those savage Santa Anas were destroying the city one tree at a time!

These fearsome winds have long been the subject of folklore and mythology. The novelist Raymond Chandler called them sinister, hot, dry winds that "curl your hair and make your nerves jump and your skin itch," adding that, "On nights like these, meek little wives feel the edge of the carving knife and study their husbands' necks." On the beginning of this day, earliest of the morning, the ravaging Santa Anas affirmed their rightful place in the realm of theater.

When I arrived in Arcadia, paper and trash were being hurled across the darkened sidewalks at lightning pace; shrubs were being uprooted right out of the ground; and even the palm trees—resilient as they are—were tonight engaged in a fierce battle with these cruel Chinooks. My brother picked me up at a nearby Jack-in-the-Box. "This ain't shit," he said as I got into his vehicle, leaving mine there. We drove to Santa Anita Westfield Mall on Baldwin Ave, touring what came to look like an upper-class section of Hell.

Dodging fallen trees strewn across the streets, we followed other cars along the pathway, those pathways now premeditated so very unruly by Mother Nature. One of the many active ambulances drove into the darkness with flashing red lights descending into the fog until they could no longer be seen. Transformers on telephone poles began blowing out all over the city, making the horizon radiate with a brief, faint reminder to one of the drawbacks of our modern technological society.

We stopped on one of the side-streets. Like popcorn, sparks crackled from behind some poor guy's garage. "It's okay," the homeowner told us. "We got everything under control." Blue explosions continued to light up the suburbs. We went to a gas station to regroup. "It was everything you said it was," I told my brother. He put $15 in my tank. "Are you going home?" he asked while pumping. "Yeah," I lied. "Are you?" "No." "Then no more gas." Make that $14.25. My brother occasionally punishes me with sanctions, booze or otherwise.

"Be careful," he said back to me.

I drove off. The savage winds seemed to have grown stronger now. They must have been angry that I didn't flee back home, responding by pitching two furry kittens across a lonely street. It wasn't just the felines who were in danger: outdoor furniture, trashcans, awnings, and trees. Lots of trees.

Getting out of the car to survey the chaos on foot, I discovered that many of the trees had been completely uprooted from the ground, taking large chunks of the sidewalk with them. One was laid out directly across Huntington Drive, compelling me to jump a small center divider and go around it. A proper simile would have God passing wind on the inhabitants of Southern California. We couldn't be mad at Him for doing so, and I'm sure He'd believe the analogy as being proper-enough here.

I made two rounds through Arcadia and Temple City before going home. The destruction was not commonplace. The winds were recorded at 80 MPH. 100 MPH is said to be a mild hurricane. For almost a week, thousands—some 230,000 it was said—were left without power. Light signals, heating, television:

gone. It turned 5 'o clock rush-hour into an all-night event resembling an old horror movie.

Hundreds of trees would now have to be replaced. Schools were closed in Pasadena, Arcadia, Monrovia, Sierra Madre, Altadena, Duarte, Azusa, and, somehow, Glendora—which declared a state of emergency after the power went out at City Hall and the police station.

Nobody else in our area suffered such a fate.

But then again, that's the State, and when they lose power, we all lose power.

K. M. Patten

A Handshake from the Ruling Class: An American Oligarchy Winning the 2012 Election

IT'S SAID IN gambling circles that the house never loses. When I think of that as a political metaphor, the house becomes the State, the owners of which are the banking class, and the game played just recently called the "United States Presidency."

Spectators: you and me.

The chips? All of the unborn.

The stage was so transparent it disputed Ron Paul's statement that the election was merely a continuation of "the status quo." To me, and if nothing else, the 2012 parody seemed to offer a final handshake from our once-again victorious masters. And as MSNBC host Chris Mathew confirmed when discussing those who voted for Gary Johnson and Jill Stein, "People who vote for these numbskulls—*like they don't know the system!*—you have two choices!"

Yet even then Mathews lied a bit

Deviating from its original purpose as a vigilant witness to the State's movement, the "fourth branch" of government—a sovereign, scrupulous, and un-monopolized free press—has dissolved into less-than-a handful of mega-Networks. Throughout the election cycle, the robotic "news" anchors brazenly omitted critical issues while offering insurmountable distortions. With reportage like this, the media institutions always said by Hitchens to seek and maintain the "political consensus" had exerted themselves with superior shamelessness, bringing previously-unseen elevations to the word "circus" and vindicating Jon Stewart's coverage as the only "real" news on TV.

This, however, did result in one thing we can all be thankful for: it made the absence of choice perfectly clear.

Without any "classical-liberal" positing from anyone other than Ron Paul and Gary Johnson, the dominant corporate rulers only had to nudge the two parties into taking the natural next step: amalgamate the two candidates so that no space could ever be seen between them.

Fortunately our friends over at the Center for Money in Politics had charted a river of campaign numbers that always flowed from the same dark mountain. Not surprisingly, quote:

> Broken down by sector, the Finance, Insurance and Real Estate sector once again dominates the world of political contributions with a total of $348.5 million thus far, including contributions from individuals and PACs to candidates, parties and outside groups as well as corporate contributions to outside groups. Within that sector, the securities and investment industry, or Wall Street, has given $144.2 million. In both cases, 63 percent of the funds to candidates and party committees went to Republicans.

The incumbent puppet, Obama, once again received funds from the "blue corner." In spite of the oft-stated prerequisite of "being an American," the exotic and dubious background of President Obama has allowed members of his regime to talk openly about this new age of government without anyone noticing the puppeteers. For example, as a means of measuring the credibility of a candidate or commentator, Chris Matthews would often ask:

"Do you believe in that Birther stuff?"

Maybe, some of us thought, but since this is a man who continues to allow a private (I mean "independent"!) bank to run our country, he's a phony with or without the birth certificate.

"Challenging" the president from the "red corner" was former Massachusetts Governor Mitt Romney. Differences? No pretension was ever seriously attempted. It was painful watching the Networks interpret rhetoric that was indistinguishable line-from-line. And as some were forced to admit, Romney never got the support of the billowing Paulite-libertarians. It's no wonder.

Maybe it was his drafting and implementing "ObamaCare" in Massachusetts; or his statement that the President can overrule Article 1, Section 8 and go to war without Congress; his assurance that he would have signed the National Defense Authorization Act just like Obama did; or perhaps the very hypocritical ten-million-dollar bailout while head of Bain Capital. It went on and on and then on from there.

But who owns the house that sits on the top of that Dark Mountain, pulling the levers and pushing the buttons while out of sight? The One Percent. The Masters, Owners, Planners. *The Elite*. In reality, these respectively labeled power-brokers are the latest incarnation of those fabled "money changers"—that ancient nemesis that destroys wealth. On Election Day, one such tentacle was seen in the form of an appropriate meme that circulated on social media. A picture of Mr. "One World Government" himself, David Rockefeller, "says" he is about to win another election.

There's truth to be found here.

Updating the status of the ownership class, veteran researcher Dean Henderson writes that, "J. W. McCallister, an oil industry insider with House of Saud connections, wrote in *The Grim Reaper* that information he acquired from Saudi bankers cited 80% ownership of the New York Federal Reserve Bank—by far the most powerful Fed branch—by just eight families, four of which reside in the U.S. They are the Goldman Sachs, Lehmans and

Kuhn Loebs of New York; the Rothschilds of Paris and London; the Warburgs of Hamburg; the Lazards of Paris; the Israel Moses Seifs of Rome"—and, of course, the Rockefellers, as far as I can tell the only dynasty originating right here in America. Likely because of Obama's somewhat harsh criticism of Wall Street policies, he fell out of favor with the Owners, who decided to throw their weight behind Romney.

America, like many other Western states, should be known as "fiat empires," based on the "theory" that all card castles topple eventually. In 2012, the Bankster Establishment that this dynasty is part of made it crystal clear that they will continue incubating the very worst of these global institutions while also destroying the best of the local ones. Since our government has blatantly violated every known concept of Constitutional law, these corrupt enterprises are now allowed to make short-term percentages at the expense of unknown deaths and incomprehensible deficits. Under this presumed contract with unborn generations, a debt that "reads" around seventeen trillion dollars is our constant reminder of this evil.

As it goes: in is out, up is down, and black is white—now with concurrence and self-awareness.

Though the contract with our new globalist rulers has not been signed by all, it has been heard by all, which could be considered a genuine verbal agreement. Through default, corporatized global government—otherwise known as the New World Order—has been virtually accepted. Tragically, this vile oligarchy has succeeded in dulling our collective spirit of liberty to the point that we shrug after they admit to conquering us. Omission and nonchalance rendered our beloved Bill of Rights as ineffectual, outdated, and thus void. In his farewell speech to Congress, Paul even admitted that our "Constitution has failed at attempting to restrain power."

As with all legislation, numerous codes and ordinances have blotted-out every last libertarian ideal enshrined in this impossibly perfected document, bringing forth the partnership between central banking and statism that embodies the core of neo-fascism.

Ironically, or perhaps expectedly, the Framer's effort to restrain power with a piece of paper has ended the way it began— by negating the principle of non-aggression. "Happily, there's an answer for these dangerous trends," Paul said in closing. "What a wonderful world it would be if everyone accepted the simple moral premise of rejecting all acts of aggression."

Was he being overly-utopian?

Attempting this would terminate the employment of everyone from George Bush to Barack Obama to Mitt Romney, to even the more respectable puppets like Ben Bernanke and Chris Mathews—finally leading to an indictment of all the many Rockefellers' in the world.

Presumably, the survivors of this current fire will continue forth, procreate, and bear that next generation.

They should be hopeful that we had rejected their handshake and done just that.

Immediate Thoughts and Lingering Questions about the Dorner Manhunt

REAL THINGS WERE happening on the planet while Obama got ready for his State of the Union address. It was even reported that the showdown taking place in the snowcapped mountains of Big Bear had almost interrupted the president's little ensemble. When it was over, the charred body of former Los Angeles police officer and accused murderer Christopher Dorner was deceased, and the San Bernardino PD were packing up and going home.

Living in between the cities of Los Angeles and Riverside, and being part of the Occupy LA crowd for some time, I had an opportunity to witness the event, along with its reactions, as another hand was almost needed to finish counting the dead. Although questions remain, reflections can still be made.

The timeline (now part of officialdom thanks to Wikipedia) starts on the evening of February 3rd, when Monica Quan and her fiancé Keith Lawrence were gunned down in the city of Irvine. Details of the suspect were reported within days: a not so recently terminated thirty-three-year-old black man, built like a tank, who had just been discharged from the Navy.

Two more officers lost their lives during the ensuing nine-day manhunt. Within that first nail-biting week, in which a million dollars was offered as a reward and fifty or more people were put on a protection detail, two versions of Dorner's "manifesto" had been widely circulated online.

In this, he at first defines the purpose of a name, and seems hopeful that he'll be able to "clear" his own. The grievance starts with an Officer Teresa Evans, who he alleges kicked the head of a mentally handicapped man, one Christopher Gettler, in August of 2007. A videotaped statement from Gettler, along with Evan's own lawyer, supposedly confirms these charges. Despite this, the Board of Officers determined that his tattling had no merit, and terminated his employment. "This department has not changed from the Daryl Gates and Mark Fuhrman days...I will correct this error," he writes chillingly. "I have nothing to lose. My personal casualty means nothing."

Ignoring both the Law and the requests of people like Mike Ruppert, who demanded a trial in which Dorner might look into the eyes of his victims, and where the public might hear his allegations, the San Bernardino PD obliged the seemingly mutual 'not-coming-out-alive' agreement. An audio recorded by local news outlets captured several unnamed officers repeatedly shouting to "get the gas" and "burn the motherfucker down"— referring to the cabin off of highway 38 that Dorner, the "walking exigent circumstance," had trapped himself in. "It was not intentional," San Bernardino Sheriff McMahon said with relief. Whew!

The doctored account of these action-packed events were projected by CNN's Wolf Blitzer, who was ordered to cut his live transmission during the standoff. This mainstream perspective is intensified with the recent narrative delivered by Sean Hannity, FOX's "extreme" talking head, who, along with his assistant bimbos (the colloquial term), insisted that "the left" was supportive of this man, chasing conspiracies about his demise instead of grasping the fact that he was a killer who had no rights.

Contrary to the Network whitewash, details about the manhunt—said to be one of the largest ever on this side of the world—have yet to be answered. Included in these are the editorship of the manifesto; the number of wallets discovered; the indiscriminate shooting on of civilians; and the use of what McMahon himself called "pyrotechnic devices"—the gas canisters which ignited the deadly fire.

On February 18th, myself and about fifty other activists and citizen reporters gathered to protest and interrogate the police in downtown LA, just outside their glass headquarters. While at least one man here held a sign saying exactly, "We Support Dorner," others had general derogatory statements about the department itself. The best of these reading simply: "RIP Due Process," the sentiment held by most. From the glossary of network reploids (I mean reporters!), Jim Nash of Channel 5 was the most condemned for biased coverage.

Nobody who stayed around long that day had praised Christopher Dorner or his actions, and I remember this clearly because I hadn't argued the point with anyone. What Nash didn't report were the naming of all those lives lost during the manhunt. As citizen journalist Patti Beer's footage clearly shows, we were here to challenge the authority of the police, not to encourage anyone to murder their enemies. "It is not," Sergeant Baker told the afternoon crowd, when I asked him if burning suspects alive was proper protocol. The innocent bystanders? "Every time an officer opens fire there's an investigation." No comment was made about the audio recording.

During my curiosity in following the news, a trend had developed. Declaredly, in taking revenge for police brutality and injustice, a terminated officer went on a shooting spree. During the manhunt, police open fire on several incorrectly suspected vehicles (miraculously not killing two paper-delivery women). The standoff ends when unnamed police officers call repeatedly for some sort of incineration, setting a fire that forces the suspect to commit suicide and perish inside of somebody else's property. The head honcho of these police officers then tells a ridiculous lie to the questioning public. This offers, in my opinion, a panoramic view of the behavior of law enforcement personnel.

From one side of the spectrum to the other.

Legality to illegality.

Justice to vengeance.

Dorner would then at first appear to be a legitimate whistleblower only seeking to clear his name (as he said very specifically) and expose the evils of an obviously unjust system. And, just by opening up an opportunity for the police to display their atrocities, time might actually see him become an accidental martyr. Strangely though, he did the one thing that would immediately cost him sympathy: he went after the families. "I never had the opportunity to have a family of my own, I'm terminating yours...Look your wives/husbands and surviving children directly in the face and tell them the truth as to why your children are dead."

With this is TMZ's gained footage of Dorner buying scuba equipment just days before the first murders. He couldn't get over the border, couldn't steal a boat (didn't have one), and eventually stranded himself in the frosty mountains. This hasty lack of preparedness shows a lower degree of motivation; completely discrediting his desire to be a genuine Rambo and instead making himself look like he's suffering a violent temper tantrum.

Of course it's still very possible this was only a human being compelled early on to do right, and that experiencing an environment he hoped would be radically different had indeed driven him over the edge.

Yet his allegations seem to be relatively mild in comparison to other reports in the area. I'll leave it to reader to decide whether a heroically-charged young black man joining a flagrantly racist and corrupt police department is only an attempt to light one's own fuse, or whether one should just go along to get along, as something people like friendly Sergeant Baker (a sixty year old black man with some-forty years on the force) have no doubt had to do. Or, if being an officer of the State is kosher at all.

Ultimately, the statistics of racial discrepancy when it comes to police brutality matters very little to someone like me, who's skull, like Gettler's, has also felt random physical blows from an officer of the law.

This man in question was Hispanic.

The greater Los Angeles area is comprised of various racial backgrounds, allowing conjecture to make the mind travel with many different scenarios. Which, it is now asked daily, colored officer assaulted which colored civilian?

It matters little to those of us who have actually felt their boots.

The Zimmerman Spectacle

NOW THAT THE inevitable and unsurprising acquittal of George Zimmerman has been handed down, scores of angry citizens will ask: *What's next?*

At some point, it should cross the minds of those rioting in Oakland and others currently "taking the freeway" in Los Angeles—the same activists who are all about "horizontal" structuring and community organizing—that Zimmerman was a man who indeed did take charge in defending his own neighborhood, one that had recently come under siege by a rash of burglaries.

They'll just have to deal with that truth as it is, and come to grips that the 29-year old, overzealous that he was, did not leave his wife and kids at home one night only to travel five or ten miles out of their little suburb hoping to find trouble, as one might expect a racist killer to do. He was only three houses away, doing something I believe *he believed* was moral and just.

But that isn't the point of the Zimmerman spectacle. It wasn't about "Stand Your Ground." Not about self-defense. Neither was it about a fair trial. Nor is it even community organizing. To them, it's much more simplistic and easier to digest: a bloodthirsty racist stalked a black teenager in the middle of a rainy night and found a way to kill him.

Case closed, it seems.

Frank Taffe, a neighbor of Zimmerman's, disagrees with that

narrative, stating:

> *We had eight burglaries in our neighborhood all perpetrated by young black males in the 15 months prior to Trayvon being shot. It would have been nine—there would have been nine, but George Zimmerman through his efforts of being a neighborhood watch captain helped stop one in progress, documented in the 911 calls February 2. My house was being robbed, and George on his nightly rounds watched this burglary in progress, called Sanford P.D., waited for them, and helped ensure that nothing bad happened to my house. And it's documented the 911 call for February 2. That was my residence that George Zimmerman helped stop.*

Again, facts are facts, and they're not intended to make the race-whores of the liberalized population foam at the mouth, nor to get myself called a "racist" for the ten-thousandth time. (You can't really be a white person in America and not be accused of racism.)

Should it be a question only of race when a quiet Florida community comes under attack by burglars who all happened to be dark-skinned? Zimmerman shouldn't be blamed for categorizing his suspicion any more than all those street activists who now believe "white America" is disregarding the emotions involved only to quietly extol the tragic death of a young person of color. We should be offended at the suggestion that those who thought justice was delivered are now jubilating in the pubs, waiting for the next black person to be killed so we can once again dance the night away and laugh in their faces.

Despite overwhelming evidence to the contrary, including that Zimmerman had tutored young blacks, had led an investigation into the beating of a black homeless man, that he was given the house keys of his black neighbor who had recently been a burglary victim—*that he wasn't even white but of Peruvian descent!*—racialism happened to be the primary factor.

The dominating narrative was given far and wide by people like Al Sharpton and Nancy Grace, and no liberal could escape the vortex of this perception. This does not illustrate a "supremacist" system (obviously extended to that system's main outlet, the Networks) that concerns itself with excusing "whiteness," but more determined to excite emotional biases, and one that can effortlessly conflate situations like this into disproportionate levels of attention that distract from other—in my opinion far worse— abuses by the State.

Example: where were all these crusaders when Marissa Alexander of Jacksonville was recently sentenced to 20 years for firing a warning shot at her abusive husband, who continued to approach her inside of their home? Let down by the "Stand Your Ground" legislation, she was also let down by these same others who were far too busy equating a complicated murder trial with the epitome of racial oppression. Since that involved a black residence, it's apparently not important enough to discuss, and can and will be used to call me and others "racist" simply for reporting on that most unfortunate verdict. It's horrible that those of us who do suffer from a slight twinge of "white guilt" can't ever speak of the problems involved in black communities, because somehow if we do, it's only because we want to be looked at as heroes or to feel jaded or "anti-racist" or something else. Fine. No changing that today.

Yet at some point, as everyone knows, lead prosecutor Bernie de la Rionda would had to have asked State Attorney Angela Corey: "Can we convict him of second degree murder?" Of course not. What magic could? The chances were never seriously believed by anyone, and while there aren't any laws against community watchmen following residents on their tax-paid-for city streets, there are laws against battery and attempted murder.

The real question then has always been who instigated the fight, knowing full and well that the complexities and lack of evidence would mean more division from people who search endlessly for reasons to revolt against a corrupt "system"—having no clue how to define its anatomy, or remedy a solution other than kicking over trashcans, breaking some windows, and blocking a few cars.

That's going to solve a whole lot, I'm sure.

Had there actually been a video of Trayvon assaulting Zimmerman first, nobody would be offering an opinion on this case, unless they are to suggest that city organizers have no right to do their job, and that it's totally acceptable for people to assault others for perceiving them to be a threat. Suppose then it would have been alright to confront those in the Occupy Camps who had a task of following around the numerous "infiltrators"—and thereby attack them on the basis of "what the hell is your problem?"

Of course the President had to weigh in also. Soon after the fateful night, on March 23rd, Obama precariously stated that a hypothetical son would have assuredly looked like the dead 17-year-old.

Really?

All black people look the same? Who can't immediately notice the hook in the water, fishing for those who will—for the sake of some kind of perceived justice—not heed it and extrapolate the racial sentiment to its furthest limit, especially now that his Justice Department ponders federal charges?

Balkanization in the past meant that two opposing and completely incompatible groups were separated by region. Neo-Balkanization today means that despite the many similarities that could be shared between white and black America (in fact all people), it will separate itself with piety, misconceptions, hate—and all while Obama and the New World Order snidely carry out their murderous war on the black population of Libya and other ethnicities the planet over.

The conversation about the trial should never have focused on "race vs. race"; instead, on the role of the community—so precious to these fools causing a mild ruckus—and the exchange of their authority over that of the police, so hated by them as well.

As YouTube commentator "PainLessRisen," a black man who also supported Zimmerman solely on the grounds of self-defense, recently said to all those in the streets: "You need to grow up," urging that if they do tear up their neighborhoods, "do not help them rebuild."

Perhaps if Trayvon Martin had been in charge of watching the neighborhood, the deceased might've had a different pigmentation.

Ah, but then nobody would have heard about it, and no trashcan tonight would feel the lynch mob's wrath.

To Those Watching Piers Morgan

> *The same persons who tell us one breath, that the power of*
> *the federal government will be despotic and unlimited,*
> *inform us in the next, that it has not authority sufficient*
> *even to call out the POSSE COMITATUS. The latter,*
> *unfortunately, is as much short of the truth as the former*
> *exceeds it.*
> —Alexander Hamilton, *The Federalist #29*

THE MASSACRES IN Tucson, Aurora, and Sandy Hook left lingering feelings and perilous thoughts in the hearts and minds of many. Anger makes a few of them vibrate with rage. At someone? Hardly. *Some-thing!* And since it's too difficult for people blinded by the loss of a loved one to understand "the bigger picture," the question of *what* dominates over the *who's* and *why's* and then becomes a blind crusade for justice.

Others, mainly in government, an opportunity for political— and yes, perhaps even genocidal—objectives to be fulfilled.

With zeal, the Network talking heads reminded the sheeple of this collective anger, steering it directly towards an agenda of disarmament. Of all the propagandists, CNN's "centrist" and English-raised commentator, Piers Morgan, has been the most virulent of the bunch, demanding that the president and those in Congress begin extracting "military-style machines" from the homes of the American people. (If I attempted to make this essay melancholy, I would only have to estimate how many of Morgan's 2,000 or so viewers were actually giving him due credence.)

Those marching in DC to Morgan's drumbeat incorrectly identified this issue as an emotional response rather than its correct designation as a moral dilemma left unanswered.

Exactly: *Who, or what, begets violence?*

For many of us looking with an anarchistic perspective (whatever your variety), it would be our nemesis in the State. Those analyzing a bit more might consider that everyone is susceptible to their own internal struggle between Yin & Yang, endlessly toiling with what is right and what is good as many of them navigate a monotonous routine of serving someone else.

A statement made by California Police Captain James touched upon other fundamentals: "A gun is not a defensive weapon. That is a myth...a gun is an offensive weapon, used to intimidate and to show power." The captain does seem to be right! Guns do have a purpose of weaponry. Now then, I beseech every officer, ask yourself: am I someone who, upon witnessing another obliged by the same Oath, who is sure that that person violated the Oath by trampling on the rights of a citizen, not also violating at least the essence of that vow when refusing to denounce their odious behavior or even admit it in front of an audience?

I've recently become fascinated by the weekly compilations of this new, but familiar, totalitarian society, in which sworn officers, often embarrassingly, imitate the actions of school children by randomly tussling with people on the street. One should inquire of the class of citizens most frequently initiating the use of violence and how they're able to do it with near, if not total, immunity. More so, it's likely that witnessing government abuses on a daily basis influences the human mind to accepting trivial acts of rebellion as a practical norm, however more or less violent, that would naturally fuel a very costly class war which is hard to define with simple words and statistics.

Captain James mentioned 55 fallen officers as of last year. A word came to mind. Paltry. The shame? Rudolph Rummel attempted to count the number of lives given over to what he called "Democide"—estimating to a total of some 262 million in the last hundred or so years killed by government, inside and outside of the U.S. What is today banally referred to as "police brutality" is often seen as the precursor to this 20th Century phenomenon.

Therefore, with the small correction I take time to make (and expect you to pay attention to), I remind all sworn to uphold the Constitution and particularly the sacrament of the Second Amendment, needful of capital letters and not to be used as an item bouncing back and forth between the walls of our fully-infected Congress and their lapdogs on CNN, MSNBC, and elsewhere.

Morgan, a seemingly more level-headed poodle, laid out his "national gun policy" in full on Twitter: "Absolutely" no more sales of assault weapons for civilians, period; mandatory safety and training courses for everyone, complete with references and 6-8 week verification; a complete ban for all convicted criminals and anyone with a "mental health disorder"; a hopeful ban on anyone under 25; and, most Orwellian of all, an extensive social media check so he can "know who they are." Then he would introduce a huge buy-back program—because nobody needs more than one gun to protect their house (unless the enemies are either psychopathic goon squads or machine gun-toting robot.)

Like most other neoliberal commentators—and even some neoconservative ones—Morgan's observable framework for this entire debate lies on the use of mind control devices concealed inside of inanimate objects: motionless on a shelf or driveway somewhere, they secretly transmit violent images into the nearest person's brain, compelling them to do horrible things with it. This parody advanced by Morgan stains again his already tarnished career, and is not a circular depiction of the issue.

Yes, the power immediately wielded by firearms and vehicles

has made more than just a few people fantasize about the possibilities of turning a key or pulling a trigger. Though unlike the person who wittingly consumed an exotic cocktail of alcohol and pharmaceuticals, guns and cars are not capable of movement on their own. Why in the first place has the seat been occupied or the weapon now prepared must be addressed before taking advice from some empty suit, void of integrity and who makes his living by insulting the intelligence of a population by refusing to discuss seriously the underlying reasons.

"What other purpose," Morgan retorts about these assault weapons, "do they have other than mass slaughter?" Concededly, vehicles have a different purpose than firearms, and are essential in the everyday modern world. Their "targets" are your workplace, school, home, park—and the everyday commuter usually has no other objective than to "hit them" without casualty.

But is he really to ignore the hundreds of thousands, if not millions of people who get behind the wheel every single day with a different destination in mind? Many of them under distress, high from perfectly legal pills, and some with very delusory— potentially suicidal—senses? In a vertiginously ironic interview with Dan Rather, Morgan said his main problem was that "too many Americans are crazy." This statement should be contrasted with absent reportage of what Alex Jones exclaimed were "mass murder pills"—the subsidized toxins long known to have rotted the brains of these many deranged killers.

With guns, the targets are honest and definitive for individuals without nefarious intent: persons and groups who use weapons in an offensive manner (or animals, but we'll save that for another time). Both Jesse Ventura and Larry Pratt explained these potentials to Morgan in plain English, but despite their efforts, the original intention of the Second Amendment remains ignored: that as a counterbalance to the violent monopoly of the State's power, the monarchistic variety resolutely disdained by all the founders. (Perhaps with Hamilton as the exception)

English royalty could command the populace to comply and assist with enforcement of their declarations, whatever they might have been, and, along with the 3rd Amendment, the framer's idea was to prevent a federalized government from ever raising a permanent "standing army" out of the citizenry.

Since family, community, and personal property were paramount, and guns were and have remained culturally prominent (and irritatingly loud), transparency of these freedom-loving syndicates were thought to be democratic, and a "well-regulated" localized militia that practiced and learnt respect for firearms would prevent a tyrannical State from ever having this exclusive power. This is especially important when considering that despite all efforts against the people, they themselves—primarily the executive branch's domestic terrorist unit, Homeland Security—have been stockpiling massive amounts of ammunition for some time.

The late Christopher Hitchens also journalized these same principles. The polemicist extraordinaire had commented in his 1994 column for *The Nation* that, "A favorite liberal sneer at the opponents of gun control is the suggestion that those who favor self-defense are fixated on the Old West," adding that, "The time might come when the people might have to muster against the state."

The insisted thesis shared by these advocates—the one adopted even by the Dali Lama—that a defensive weapon is the only option when confronted with an offensive weapon, has received rebuttals from Morgan suggesting that the final scene would be another "Shootout at the OK Corral," and then by a useless character named Jim Carrey, spitting on the grave of an activist he can't measure up to; both of whom must now endure Hitchens' realizations almost twenty years on.

His piece reported:

In cases where armed and experienced civilians have

> *intervened to challenge armed criminals, the likelihood of*
> *bystanders being hit has been several times less than in*
> *similar interventions by police."*

Updated studies came in recently by way of Obama's accidental pen stroke, with Mac Salvo reporting:

> *National survey estimates indicate that defensive gun uses*
> *by victims are at least as common as offensive uses by*
> *criminals, with estimates of annual uses ranging from*
> *about 500,000 to more than 3 million per year....*

Are there practical solutions to end gun violence immediately? Of course. As Lew Rockwell suggested with a cool sense of obviousness, start by removing your own children from those unfortunate others.

Meanwhile, let the unscrupulous "educators" and asinine parents who spoon feed them psychotropic drugs know exactly why. Even still, if the aforementioned studies are to be given any merit, having your own weapon might also be a good idea when gallivanting around the various sectors where many of these pharmaceutical zombies reside.

We arrive at last to the edge of a fairly large picture.

Guns, unlike cars, are made with an intention of violence. Suppose then that the purpose of using them against the "elected" (yes, it requires quotations) government is insane and terroristic and warranting of further restrictive provisions.

The old idea of the patriots having a right to water trees of liberty (future generations?) with the blood of tyrants might well have expired. Why then, as many have said, do we have to be continually lectured by—*hypocrites!*—taking residency in the White House, their clownish prolocutors on network television, and threateningly so by the commissars who teach in mainstream academia?

President Obama must have used the word "change" a dozen times when addressing Newtown. "We can't allow this to be a routine," Obama said in a condescending, parental tone. "We must"—he said for a nauseatingly umpteenth time—*change*.

Translation: Tolerate the executive orders he planned on signing in the coming months, as Mr. Soetoro repeatedly makes very clear to the American people, both with signatures and with threats of them.

As everyone knows, regulations do not apply to the State. Prohibitions of any degree would thereby only affect citizens who haven't committed any crimes, and not to those who with mafia-style precision can orchestrate them while eating breakfast.

Ice T sums up the matter, stating that guns should be given up when *everybody* gives them up.

Since local and federalized governments are always the ones with the guns pointed, they should be the ones to begin lowering them.

This would obviously first include the immediate resignation of our royal leaders, most of whom profit handsomely from a vastly overstretched Corporate-, Military-, Intelligence-, Media-, Pharmaceutical-, Prison-Empire, not also to forget their bodyguards, who with mere presence remind them daily of why the Amendment is there in the first place.

K. M. Patten

An Urgent Plea to Cliven Bundy

Mr. Bundy,

You have given the country a rare opportunity, sir. Until very recently, the issue that drew both the ire of statists and the camaraderie of American patriots was your land dispute with the federal government. They were central questions that were asked at the dawn of our Republic, and needed a much-deserved reminder: How much power does the government have? And: What exactly constitutes a property-holder? For 20 years, you have bravely answered this, defying the Bureau of Land Management and telling them that the land belongs to the People, specifically those who toil and live on it. As a note on my own stance, I believe it to be indefectibly American anytime one single person can upset everybody on the political spectrum—from the predictably hysterical liberal Talking Heads on MSNBC and CNN, to Fox's lineup of Neoconservatives, including Bill Kristol, Tucker Carlson, and Glenn Beck. You know as well as I that those on the "Establishment Right" care as much about your plight as the average Democrip (Jesse Ventura's new terminology for our "elected" officials) operative. It's a damn fine thing to witness them all shriek in unity. Well done!

Liberal Logic 101 says this: That "Welfare Kings"

entail those who work the land without submitting to the theft of federal taxation, and are moochers simply because everyone else is federally taxed; therefore, it is not really argued, the land is the federal government's—"theirs"—and therefore you have no right to be a greedy corporatist who doesn't pay what he is supposed to. Even if this reasoning were granted, the statistics cannot bear themselves out, as only 50% of people in this country actually pay those federal taxes, none of whom have given an opinion on the matter. Those who don't submit to federal theft are likely to be international corporations, or those who work and live here without documentation. So, whenever somebody says, "Well, everyone else pays federal taxes," tell them: "That's not true, but if they did, that's their problem." (I understand the issue is "grazing fees" and not taxation; but let us not split too many hairs.) And personally, as a lifelong carnivore who has no doubt consumed the equivalent of at least a dozen of your cows, I cannot find a justification for others, with a meaty diet like mine, to expect more from you other than beef and iconoclasm, especially since many of us have never actually visited that region.

But this issue evolved, on April 19th, when you brought up a rather unpleasant comparison between the Welfare State and the dark history of institutionalized chattel slavery. I'm sorry to say that I depart ways with your analogy, and don't think it a fair comparison whatsoever. A much more reliable set-up would be in the early 20th Century, when, economically speaking, Black America was almost on par with their white counterparts, in spite of the massive discrimination of the day. For a black middle class was rising rapidly in the '20s, '30s, '40s and '50s, with child illegitimacy at about 10 percent, compared to the 75 percent we witness now. No *thanks to LBJ's "Great Society"—in which he dubiously said he'll have "those niggers voting Democratic for the next 200 years"—segments of the black population have been stuck, as you pointed out crassly, in a perpetual state of dependency. It should be noted, however, that blacks are not the only beneficiaries of welfarism: one analysis says that 5.13% of whites are recipients, while 28.75% of blacks are—themselves being only 12% of the population. Nevertheless, we must all give sympathy to the liberal who suggests that you owe them more, while those who pay nothing, or those who take more than they pay in, are somehow free from the suggestion; for their mental faculties have been wounded from years of consuming, not cow meat, but cow defecation (that is, bullshit).*

Aside from the grave numbers, it upsets me to no end that these government boot-lickers have urged on the BLM goons, and have suggested the most evil, sadistic, un-American of remedies—up to and including using drone strikes on you and your family. This vitriol was seen prior to the commentary you gave about "the Negro" (an antiquated term that truly shows the time capsule you've been living in); the forum that allowed these demonic people to express their Statism could be found on Facebook, at the "BundyFest!" page. Fortunately, the creators and maintainers of the event, Sean Shealy and Gavin Hadaller, are not of that breed: they are two very friendly "progressive" activists who insist there is no right side here; that you are a resident in America who must pay like everyone else, but also infer that the BLM are violent enforcers of an illegitimate government. And while Shealy tells me he doesn't believe the Federal Government to be as much, he does write about how the Constitution only allows gold and silver as legal tender, which of course has been ignored for more than a hundred years. What could be more illegitimate than an illegal central bank that gives trillions out to foreign banks?

As you might have heard by now, the event has gone mainstream. Scheduled to kick off on September 5th, and run into October, Shealy promises that it's going to be anarchic—"TOTAL FREEDOM," as the headline of the page reads—with live music playing all day and night, lots of nudity, beer, weed, and perhaps even a few guns. As Mr. Hadaller told me, if it "takes something like 'BundyFest!' to trick people into talking with each other and maybe within all that crap, threats, name-calling, etc., maybe there will be two people from different political views who find out that they have a few things in common." He also makes an interesting point in saying that the land that you own is not the land in which you graze your cattle on. And yet, he would love to see the day that all property tax is abolished. Just like that, two people with vastly different perspectives can seemingly agree to disagree for yet another time and place. "The idea is to be inclusive, not exclusive," as he says. Good. Yet I have my doubts that any of the tough guys on their thread will actually be there in person, and then would not be concerned for the safety of your family. After all, voting once or twice a year in your own neighborhood is much easier than actually having to travel somewhere in order to make a dispute directly; why steal from someone when you can vote for a politician who will do it for you?

This is where you and your supporters come in. You have given press conference after press conference, interview after interview, attempting to clarify your thoughts and to speak to the American people. You even went so far as to call this a "movement." What terminology! Surely that remark has perked more ears *than just mine. Shall we be more direct than this? Can you come to embrace a new Woodstock right in your backyard? Shealy has said that he will respect your property boundaries. Can we all, then, just get along? Maybe figure out this little bit about taxation and property rights and who constitutes an actual welfare moocher? Perhaps eat some steak, drink some beer, and fight the Feds together? It would be wonderful.*

I hope you consider, and I hope to meet you come September.

A Pleasantly Filled Dungeon in My Backyard

This ain't no place for no hero.
This ain't no place for no better man.
This ain't no place for no hero
To call "home."
—The Heavy, *Short Change Hero*

AT THIS WRITING, I've enjoyed more than five years of freedom; and eight years since I first experienced the Los Angeles county jail. My "short" weeklong location would be in a permanent cell; mouse-ineering made a little easier this time around. In here, a 24 hour lockdown, quadruplet of bodies, sucky food, a three minute shower every other day, "entertainment" requiring quotations, and…well, that's about it.

However, all the jail cells had a phone inside, making family conversations for once, and again, the best thing ever. For more specifics: each row of cells is known as an "A"—"B"—"C" or "D" sector. I was in the last, what was called "the basement," where *I think* three tiers were above me.

It was said that this floor also served as a "transport zone," where a recently convicted man would wait to "catch the chain" (go to one of the state's 33 prisons). The first fortunate thing to note is this: no one is housed across from you, and aside from the six or so porters who randomly roam about, the only real company are your cellmates and the doomed anonymous voices that surround. Guards occasionally do counts and walkthroughs; nurses, two or three times daily—if you're lucky.

Has anything changed since I was gone? The answer to this is both yes and no, with a pressure that is more condensed on the latter. What's actually happening is a rearranging of, not deckchairs on the Titanic, but of steely-cold bunk beds and the guards who watch submerged as their own ship slowly sinks.

The prison overcrowding issue is big deal in the Golden State. From the *Los Angeles Times'* recent polemic against Governor Jerry Brown's brilliant idea, they write:

> *Brown's realignment solution when he took office in 2011 required creating a new category of criminal—the 'non-serious, non-violent, non-sex-offender felon.' The 'triple-nons' already in prison would head to county probation when they got out. Instead of three years, they could finish supervision in as little as six months. Those committing new crimes would serve their entire sentences in jail rather than state prison. Parole violators would also go to county jails.*

The paper also notes:

> *The prison population fell sharply at first, dropping from 162,400 to 133,000, but it is rising again. There now are 135,400 inmates in state custody, a number expected to grow to 147,000 in 2019...*

...which of course requires more money. Those Prison-Industrial-Overlords (the California Correctional Peace Officers Association) have prayed that this effort can accommodate for the full implementation of Assembly Bill 109, said by Brown to be the "boldest move in criminal justice in decades."

But Brown—who until 1999 was an official enemy of the C.C.P.O.A., but who has been brown-nosing in his political twilight—is dead wrong.

Some things *never* change.

And those are the secret politics that exist behind those walls, and which lie at the heart of this overcrowding problem. Now, shows like *Lock-Up* do give a good display of gang politicians in action. To a varying extent than the Golden State, these policies run throughout American prison systems. How does this basically work? It works by enforcing a strict regimen of morning wake up calls, of "good-nights," of introducing oneself to the tier, and of work outs. A "shotcaller" keeps the pace of this internalized police system. This floor was inundated by the SouthSiders, the Southern Mexican gangs.

And so how does one enforce when you can't even reach your underlings? Indeed, nobody usually has to, because most people of tabulated colorization readily adhere to these jailhouse rules (a topic that deserves far more attention than I can give in this report), and realize that moments do regularly come when one is outside and amongst the pack (there are plenty of dormitories, as well as church services, showers, doctor's appointments, etc.).

Any departure from this train of thought can, given room and manpower, be very hazardous to one's health. In here, it is not possible to make distance from those who you have nothing in common with.

Fortunately for me, I had all but one cellmate who was either dismissive of these policies, or overtly critical of them. Thirty-two year old "Weto"—the most bland and repetitious of Southsider names—was entirely done with "mandatory" work-outs and having to be awake with shoes on "just in case something cracks off." "Fucking stupid ass shit," he said in several variables. Weto always ignored the "mandate" to be up, which oddly never warranted the cry of insubordination. Does he ever regret joining a gang when he was twelve? "I never would have joined. For what?" Another of them, "Fast" (name-change), also in his gangster denouement, went on about how badly he wanted to get this absconding parole violation done with and to go back to his girlfriend and kids, safely waiting for him some miles up a hill from where his 'hood was. Those scarcely heard stories are always encouraging: inmates who want to leave the gang-life behind and become better fathers, sons, and people.

Many will never think about life beyond the dungeons. For a majority, this is their home. Their cave. Their lair. Their frightening Cerberus is the cordial "dep" (as in deputy) down the way, whom, sometimes on their passing by, stops to humor a half thought-out complaint. "Chico" (change) was the Southsider "shotcaller." "Alright homies, its program time! Program time! Time to get up, brush your grill, roll up your mattress, and put your shoes on!"—followed with loud, incomprehensible, ape-like chants, and ending with several "Uno-Tres!" (Thirteenth letter is "M"—Mexican).

Every. Single. Morning.

And night.

These countless ethnic gang politicians would complete my metaphor, giving Cerberus his additionally needed heads. Meeting "Chico" only once—during that single time we went to "yard," on top of the roof—he was short, bulky, probably around 40 years of age, and friendly to us three white guys. Who could possibly guess how many times this seemingly good-natured man has ordered other Hispanics to be beaten up for choosing to be *individuals?*

Another of this mentality, the single cellmate who couldn't seem to recognize his absolute failing as a carbon-based life form, was "Blaster" (some of my name-changes are admittedly stupid, and unfamiliar to Southsider gangs. I've even forgotten some of the handles since I've been out): 35, seven kids, and a total of two years on the street. He also had a tattoo of a group of demons "raping" (his word) an angel, which might have went along with his sexual preference of strangulating women. "…longest I've ever been out at one time," he said, referring to the nine months of freedom.

Built like a tank, he was polite, almost like a pet gorilla. He often made fun of the only "30-day stress-box" in here, me. What would *you* say to a grown man who is so ecstatic about seeing one of his prison-buddies that, as soon as he greets him, and through the metal bars, gives him a big, wet, sloppy kiss on the cheek?

I asked him the question I'd asked so many during my three years of incarceration: isn't *institutionalism* a very real thing? Possessing a meth'ed-out cranium that was usually bobbling and jiving all over the place, this time it signified a depressing affirmative answer.

Yes, said-narcotic was snorted several times by "Blaster" and Weto. As anarchically retorted, how can the American state stop drug use when it can't even keep them out of the place where it puts the users? Hint: nobody profiting from the black market—on either side of the legalities—would ever want to do a thing like that. I was offered a line, but then, eight years having not done the shit, coupled with five years of high blood pressure, made an easy and definitive no. Although, I did take several hits of a banana cigarette, made and sold by Weto.

The good-night part of the program was the same for the blacks, and the same-but-worse for whites on the other side of the floor that, unlike the former, but like the occupied gang down here, "required" workouts and shoes-on.

"My" shotcaller, "Cowboy" (a true, typical, white man name), in the immediate cell on the floor above me, was friendly, Christian even. There was no real mandatory nothing for "us"— except maybe showers.

Thank God!

"Where you from?" he asked obligatorily during our initial greeting. "San Gabriel Valley," I answered. "Some of your homeboys are on the other side," he said. And then I muttered a barely audible "Oh, alright," leaving the most uninterested response I could to linger on the tier.

It's not something to be overly worried about in cell-living, but he kindly never mentioned anybody again. Both of the other two light-skinned creatures in this section were minor offenders, heroin or theft or something like that; neither cared for the politics. Yes, one had a swastika.

A note of thought for the reader: think how silly it would look for four grown men to be stuck inside of a cell the size of a bathroom, shoes on, sitting upright on their rolled-up mattresses, and doing nothing else except yell and holler and sometimes read whatever books they could find. All day. With some men damned for decades.

As I wrote in 2009:

> The first thing that is imperative to understand is the general mentality of the prison population. The public has a widespread illusion that because it is prison, it must be a place no one would want to go. This is a mistake. The truth is, behind those gates there is an entire community of very comfortable inmates. Indeed they are quite happy being the statistics that you read about in all the reports.

Going on to add:

> From there, one can constantly be told to 'follow the program,' which essentially means do what you're told— by either an officer or another inmate. The Wardens and all the other 'higher-ups' are aware that as long as the inmates are busy fighting each other, they won't be giving them much trouble. So they enforce the racial hatred to keep the population preoccupied.

Sadly, I can *still* report that no effort is made to curtail these resentful jailhouse politics. That is why *this* libertarian, seeing imprisonment as a necessity for certain NAP offenders, can even go so far as to argue for solitary confinement; because 24 hours a day alone is the only form of voluntarism—as well as hope for rehabilitation—behind such walls.

A surefire proof of how this system encourages the internal police system is by demonstrating how the inmates have to rely on one another. For best example, sandals must be worn to the shower; but since none are given out, where are they to be found? Answer: obvious. This means every other day "Cowboy" would have to toss down his pair, and I would have to do my best Michael Jordan impersonation by getting them back up; furthermore having to throw between the metal railings, and doing this before the returning inmates flooded the small four-foot hallway.

Extrapolate that now to the "canteen's" food, clothing, and hygiene products, the "fishing lines" that makes the jailhouse economy that much more convenient, and naturally the debts that can and will accrue from this, and you are left with a simmering cesspool of violence.

"See that guy over there," said "Fast" with a lamenting tone. "He's going to be in here for the next twenty years." It was a porter, a large Native American man, and a victim of AB: 109; of *malum prohibitum*.

What did he do?

"He must have been caught with a grip of cocaine or dope," my cellmate speculated. More violently, the Southsider in the cell next to us, "Sniper" (change), was "offered" a mere 395 years, insisting with a strained nonchalance that he was only sitting in that vehicle while his "homies" performed the armed robbery. Details left unknown, the gentlemanly gangster had proven incorrect the last prison guard he had seen: "Sniper" would not be on the streets for a whole two months; he would bear witness to freedom for a mere fifty-one days.

What does one say to a man who, after five years in prison, almost immediately decides to jump in a car full of armed criminals—and cannot testify against them for fear of retribution?

On the other end, how does one respond to a judge that routinely sends drug-offenders off for decades, and is so far detached from reality that he offers a prison sentence so ridiculous that, even if "Sins of the Father" were applied, could not be completed even by one's great grandchildren? The closest utterance should fall along the lines of mutual acceptance for the perpetual debt; also the erroneous, unconstitutional, and immoral laws; as well as the unquestioned subservience to a State that creates and watches over it all.

Anyway, congruously, these type of "higher risk" inmates have very little to lose, and will probably not for long tolerate the petty crassness of any recently-hired county official. "See how much more legit they act nowadays?" observed several veterans of the system. It was explained to me how, just a few years prior, the guards would never, in the hallways, allow "us" to look at "them." I also recall similar abusive experiences way back when, in Wayside—that deplorable addition to the LA county system. Apparently, this place still made men shudder with annoyance, with many reiterating the "fact" that none were absolutely obligated to attend and could refuse if only at the expense of a visit to the "hole".

With less forewarning were those moments outside of one's set location: during the Twin Towers' maze-like commute, I could faintly hear several commands not to break eye contact with the red, blue, and yellow lines that directed one to his awaiting pit. When disobeyed, usually the threat of one's "time" came up for stake.

Suppose it's thought that the tilt of a man's head could signify a level of his authority, something not intended for consideration while walking down the corridors, but very much encouraged while inside and adjacent to those other cells. Many have felt discomfort as a result of refusing to obey the order for appropriated vision, as confirmed by another Southsider cellmate who spoke of an Asian guard singlehandedly hoisting his 200-pound frame up by the bunch of his shirt (no collars on jailhouse blues) and dragging it down the hall; feet, a convict's word testified, imperceptibly grazing the floor.

In response to these brutalities, the ACLU—already having a field day with lawsuits in the Golden State—has been granted a literal success in transparency: a number of cameras that are being installed to help invigilate the influx of offenders, personally observed on a particularly grim morning with the sound of a noisy drill.

What were the odds that these cameras would be installed on this jailhouse floor the week of me being here?

This inmate population was also speckled with rumors of federal agents, said to be armed with "micro-cameras"—where? I don't know—and who are then "implanted" inside the jails, this so as to bear witness and document firsthand the abuse of inmates from the discretion of the guards, a phenomenon always given much testimony by these numerous veterans.

A quick side note: One afternoon, the jail hosted a "walk-through" with the kids of P.R.I.D.E., a "scared-straight" program. (I believe it was this name—can't find a link.) A line of twenty or so youngsters—all white and Hispanic, no blacks—were put inside of our floor.

Expectedly, the inmates saw a grand opportunity for entertainment. "That one, him right there," said many, doing their best intimidation bit. But how, I had first thought back in Folsom, observing another "divergence" program, could these inmates be such hypocrites? Sure, try to scare the kids at that age from doing whatever you think they're doing, and while not in their criminal prime, but what if they do end up becoming a cellmate? Does that "man" now become a possible subject for eternal inmate-to-inmate obedience? Is the entrance to this dungeon indeed the Rubicon? No going back then, right? No condolences or support whatsoever at that point, *oi?*

It's fantastically ironic considering that many of these men were "jumped" into a gang at that young age. Why not just tell them: "If you ever come inside here, I'll make you my bitch"? Suppose one could look at it the other way, and see them doing nothing more than being honest; but I have never been able to.

One of these kids would not be intimidated. On his way out, he stopped at the bars of a cell down the way, and stared blankly back at the caged specimens. "Props" were given by some; chagrin by others.

For me, it was a fear that he might not have a great family life, and might one day want to find out if he can show his worth in a place like this. And for those questioning the writer's exalted prose, let this irony be known: one of my cellmates actually was named "Caveman." Yes, he was a very darkly skinned black man. And yes, he was one of them trying to intimidate the kids. "I'm not sure what their background is," I explained to Caveman, who was otherwise polite, and who once proudly told an exhilarating story about the white girl he slept with. "They might have it rough. And if smoking some weed is all they're doing, this is really overblown for 'punishment.' Don't you think?" Not completely bright, Caveman never gave a definitive answer, but amused himself nonetheless during those hours.

Moving on.

There is another explanation for the institutionally manifested paranoia. Almost tortuously, the inmate processing through Los Angeles County can take up to several days, going from cell to holding tank and back again without receiving either mat or blanket (hence, mouse-ineering). That is, unless one has an urgent medical need. "What was it?" I asked the nurse about my blood pressure. "One-hundred and seventy four over a hundred and ten," she said. Not a lie. And not a panic. "This happens," I told her calmly. "...very jumpy nervous system...I get really...offended... whenever I become a walking-talking piece of merchandise." All the same to them, several hours later—only—and even after an eventual drop in numbers, I was placed ahead of those before me and quickly housed in the medical dorm. Here I would see the doctor and request any prescriptions that I might need, one of which I do.

Two days passed. No doctor was seen.

After some fuss, I finally saw her, putting me on my 20 milligram Lisinopril and also putting me down for some "vitamins," which seemed to have changed shape and color upon every visit by the nurse—who we immediately get to.

Again: rare is the Golden State inmate who is unfamiliar with someone—indeed many times themselves—who has succumbed to an injury, a stroke, a seizure, a heart attack, and is left thereafter for many hours, either screaming for help or waiting critically for it. One morning, an encouraging announcement was made: "Meditation services. Let's go." The bars cracked and I leapt through them before they could even finish opening, still putting my shirt on.

After one flight of escalators, the group of about thirty of us found ourselves in the jailhouse chapel. A 30-something black gentleman sat in the center. He was the instructor. Not to be overly sentimental, but the sound of someone calmly and quietly explaining the helpful benefits of meditation was a much needed change from the normal hoot and hollering downstairs. After two breathing sessions, 45 minutes onward, the gentleman explained how he was a former inmate here, and how he wanted to give something back after he changed his ways. "Ever notice that?" he asked. ". . . how we think we can affect something that we have no control over?"

He gave a very concise and basic instruction of the—should I say it?—*magical experience* that is a deep session of concentrating on one's breath. We soon got up to go back to our pits. I shook his hand firmly before leaving, just like many in-house chaplains and imams before.

When I got back inside the pit, I realized something: I had missed the nurse! I can go two days without a pill, but it's better not to. I would have to wait until this evening, and hope that the next lady would be kind enough to go back to her station and retrieve my pills—which doesn't always happen.

What good luck though!

The morning nurse came back! She was a black, aging, obnoxious, cantankerous woman. I had already scolded her incompetence earlier for not knowing what pills were what— seeing as I had rejected the "vitamins" and only wanted my B-P medicine. She never came back that day. Now I looked right at her, gleaming face: "Ma'am, I went to meditation and forgot about my pill, do you think I could get it?" She glared at me with a deadpan and croaked with the whiniest, pissiest, most annoyed sound of a voice: "You don't get nothin!"

Then hurried off.

Others were also rebuffed. "Can I get a 'fuck that bitch!?'" one of the inmates said. "Fuck that bitch!" But then that was it. Nothing else would be done. The one other thing in here that helped calm my blood pressure down was in fact the ultimate price I paid—except of course for all the other inconveniences that come with being a *slave*.

I had entered this jail on a Saturday morning. I wrongly believed that I would be out in 72 hours. With every day that passed, I became more and more distraught, stressed, and restless. Yours truly is just not made for incarceration. Mr. Patten is too energetic. Too mobile. Too isolationist. Too free. Lying on a bunk all day, with no choice of food, drink, company, scenery, books; it reminded me how great freedom really is.

Three years of this "life," with varying degrees of liberty inside the prison programs, admittedly made me a little more unhinged than I already was. The Police State, with all its dimensions of routine violence, still occasionally gives me nightmares, even years after my first post-prison panic attack.

Incomprehensibly, many inmates love being in there, and despise those who do not. As a seemingly civilized and "enlightened" society, we somehow allow "civil servants" to exploit this underworld, shred our recognized rights, and perpetuate a fatalistic criminality.

My uncle finally got a competent guard on the phone. She informed him that I would be coming home on Sunday—a full week after I first got here. My uncle was right: I should have just stuck with the goddamn "community service." It was around 4 AM on that morning. I was asleep. A faint noise startled me. Was it my name? I should get up just in case. Two minutes later, the loudspeaker again: "Patten, you coming?" *Crack.* "Yes!" I yelled, jumping up and putting my shirt on, with a mattress that was quickly scooped. The guard was a young blond haired girl, the friendliest around here. Officer…what was her name? "Don't come back," she said. I wasn't really in the mood for conversation, but I think I said: "I didn't plan to the last time I left." And you know what? Eight years is a long time. Hopefully it'll be another eight before I find myself back inside of a hellhole like that.

I left the jail around seven. It was clear and cool outside; the dirty, musky smell of downtown Los Angeles was for once refreshing. Coffee and eggs and bacon and biscuits and gravy: they're great on any other day, but after a week of jail food, they're indescribably great.

The biggest heart-shocker actually came after the release, an "event" that happened during the incarceration, something I would not find out about until my first post-jail Google search. It was the news that after 21 years "undefeated" at WrestleMania, The Undertaker gave up his winning "streak" to Brock Lesnar. "The Deadman" almost looked as much.

Tired.

Hurt.

Old.

A slew of serious injuries had bothered him since the mid-'90s, but like the masterful stuntman he is, he powered through the ensuing years of self-inflicted pain, fatigue, and blood.

At only forty-nine, the professional performer named Mark Calaway must have realized something real-life authoritarians like Raul and Bratsworth and "Chico" had yet to, and seen only then by my luckily inherited cellmates, whilst discovered suddenly by those at the Superdome, noticed instinctively by that teenager, and perhaps, one day, only near death, glimpsed at by all those other ridiculous "Pac-Man" names: no matter how convincing the moniker, no matter how commanding the posture, no matter how much torture has been endured, no matter how many years you've dominated the industry, that sooner—rather than much later—a great many more just stop taking your actions seriously.